THE SLAVES' GAMBLE

THE SLAVES' GAMBLE

CHOOSING SIDES IN THE WAR OF 1812

GENE ALLEN SMITH

palgrave
macmillan

THE SLAVES' GAMBLE
Copyright © Gene Allen Smith, 2013.

First published in 2013 by PALGRAVE MACMILLAN® in the U.S.—
a division of St. Martin's Press LLC, 175 Fifth Avenue, New York, NY
10010.

Where this book is distributed in the UK, Europe, and the rest of the
world, this is by Palgrave Macmillan, a division of Macmillan Publishers
Limited, registered in England, company number 785998, of Houndmills,
Basingstoke, Hampshire RG21 6XS.

Palgrave Macmillan is the global academic imprint of the above
companies and has companies and representatives throughout the world.

Palgrave® and Macmillan® are registered trademarks in the United
States, the United Kingdom, Europe, and other countries.

ISBN: 978-0-230-34208-8

Library of Congress Cataloging-in-Publication Data is available from the
Library of Congress.

A catalogue record of the book is available from the British Library.

Design by Letra Libre, Inc.

First edition: January 2013

10 9 8 7 6 5 4 3 2 1

Printed in the United States of America.

To my wife, Tracy, and son, Banning,
who always keep me grounded!
And to the memory of Mable Ann Jones,
a mother whose firm guidance kept me out of trouble.

CONTENTS

ILLUSTRATIONS

ACKNOWLEDGMENTS

No project is ever ours alone. From the time an author conceptualizes a project until he sees it in print, others help carry the burden. We talk with colleagues about our research; we engage students to undertake topics that often dovetail our own; we ask others to read research proposals, conference presentations, and journal articles; we talk with friends about the book that is almost finished; and we assure family members that we are still working on our project, and they always ask when it will be done. And throughout we think about and look for elusive resources that will provide the evidence or smoking gun to our project. Too many times, we sit alone in a library or an archive, poring through another dusty manuscript collection or staring blurry-eyed at another microfilm machine. In the end, we pursue our topics because we are fascinated by a question that we could not initially answer. My question was a simple one: why did some free blacks and slaves side with the United States during the War of 1812, and why did others join the British, the Spanish, the Native American tribes, or the maroon communities? Though a simple question, it proved to have a complicated answer.

As you read this book, you will encounter individuals who challenged me to find their stories—the people who made hard choices that affected the remainder of their lives. As you do so, you will ultimately learn why I followed this path and why they and others made the choices they did. As you unravel their stories, you will understand why they did what they did and the consequences of their choices. Had I known the answers some fifteen years ago, I might have followed a different path. Fortunately, I did not know the answer, and I have learned much from their journeys!

Because this project took some fifteen years to complete, I will forget to mention some people. If I do forget someone, please forgive me. My graduate mentor Frank L. Owsley, Jr., or Larry, shared this topic with me when I was looking for a new research topic. He graciously offered a few rough chapters that pointed me in the direction of this much-different project. I am extremely thankful for his generosity, patience, and guidance. My history department colleagues, especially Ken Stevens, Steve Woodworth, Jeff Roet, and Don Coerver, have shared their time and knowledge, and I am grateful. My graduate students over the years—Claire Phelan, Joe Stoltz, Brook Poston, Sam Negus, Andrew Jackson Forney, Gary Ohls, Ed Townes, Larry Bartlett, Brenda Fields Davis, Dan Vogel, Amber Surmiller, Amanda Milian, Chris Dennis, and David Greer—have cheerfully endured my passion with the War of 1812, and sometimes it has helped them, too. I have also profited handsomely from the friendship, professional advice, and reading done by Don Hickey, Alan Taylor, Dan Preston, Sam Watson, and Nathaniel Millett, and their own scholarship has helped improve this project in immeasurable ways. The SHEAR poker players—Jim Broussard, Richard John, Dan Preston, John Ifkovic, John Van Atta, Sam Watson, and John Belohlavek—have rejuvenated my interest in history year after year without asking when the project would be done.

Many public and private institutions have been gracious in allowing me to use their records and affording me welcomed assistance. Staffs outside the United States that were particularly helpful include the National Maritime Museum of Greenwich; the Public Records Office in Kew (now the National Archives); the British Library in London; the Royal Engineers Museum in Chatham; the Royal Artillery Museum in Woolwich; the National Army Museum in London; the Royal Marines Museum in Southsea, Portsmouth; the Brymor Jones Library, University of Hull; the Southampton City Archives; the Public Records Office of Northern Ireland in Belfast; the Ulster American Folk Park in Omagh, Northern Ireland; and the National Archives of Scotland and the National Library of Scotland, both in Edinburgh. Alan Giddings, formerly of the National Maritime Museum in Greenwich, shared his expertise and resources—his help was critical in locating the much-needed manuscripts of British naval officers. I wish to offer considerable thanks to the staff members at the National Archives, the Navy Department Library, and the Manuscript Division of the Library of Congress, all in Washington, DC.

Many departments of archives and history on the state level also offered invaluable assistance: Alabama, Georgia, Mississippi, Wisconsin, Louisiana, Maryland, Virginia, Tennessee, and Ohio, in particular. I am also in the debt of those staff members at the university libraries at

Wisconsin, Indiana, Louisiana State, Florida, Texas Christian, Virginia, and the University of New Orleans. The Houghton Library at Harvard, the Howard Tilton Memorial Library at Tulane, the Louisiana State Museum, the Virginia Historical Society, the New York Public Library, the New York Historical Society, the State Historical Society of Wisconsin, and the Detroit Public Library deserve special thanks. The Henry E. Huntington Library in San Marino, California; the Virginia Historical Society in Richmond; and the Naval History and Heritage Command provided fellowship support that permitted me valuable time to work at their facilities, and I am truly grateful for their generosity. The Ohio Historical Society, the Lilly Library of the University of Indiana, The Historic New Orleans Collection, the Maryland Historical Society, the American Antiquarian Society, the British National Army Museum in London, and the National Library of Scotland in Edinburgh have graciously allowed me to use illustrative materials. Cartographic illustrator Tracy Ellen Smith produced the outstanding maps.

Former dean Mary L. Volcansek of AddRan College has steadfastly encouraged my scholarship, rewarded me for my accomplishments, and also offered a much-needed sabbatical. My colleagues—Lacie, Renee, Tiffany, and Gloria—at the Fort Worth Museum of Science and History have constantly prodded me in ways that expand my understanding of the past; my former boss Charlie Walter understood my need for time to write books and exhibits. Warren Reiss, Linda Healy, Randy Lackovic, and the staff at the Darling Marine Center of the University of Maine have given me cool weather and the quiet time needed to finish the last assignments of this book.

I would also like to thank senior editor Luba Ostashevsky and her staff at Palgrave Macmillan who willingly took a chance on a War of 1812 book. Though the bicentennial is not as big as the one that celebrated the Declaration of Independence, this book does share another freedom story. Finally, my agent Mike Hamilburg has showed persistence and dogged determination finding a home for this project, and that is what an author needs.

My wife Tracy and our son Banning are part of every project that I undertake, and for that reason I dedicate this book to them. Banning has heard of the War of 1812 his entire life—in fact, he may know more about the war than any other elementary student—and though this book ends one chapter in our lives, its ending also permits a new chapter to begin. This new chapter will undoubtedly have a War of 1812 focus, too.

INTRODUCTION

On a bright sunny Monday morning, June 22, 1807, the frigate U.S.S. *Chesapeake,* under the command of Capt. James Barron, departed Hampton Roads, Virginia, on a shakedown cruise for the Mediterranean. The decks stood cluttered with supplies, civilian baggage, casks, cables, and ropes, while the ship's guns had been secured for heavy weather. Gun implements had been stored below decks, and the passages to the ship's magazine were blocked with all types of items. The vessel resembled a floating store ship rather than a warship as she passed the Virginia Capes. During the early afternoon, Capt. Salusbury Price Humphreys of the H.M.S. *Leopard* hailed the U.S. frigate and demanded that Barron surrender four seamen who had allegedly deserted from the British fleet. After a lengthy discussion, Barron politely but firmly refused, unwilling even to muster his men so identification could take place. Within ten minutes the frigate began maneuvering alongside *Chesapeake* with gun ports open. Then suddenly, without warning, the *Leopard* fired a shot across the *Chesapeake*'s bow, a signal for the American ship to halt. When Barron disregarded Humphreys's signal, the British ship then fired a devastating broadside directly into the *Chesapeake.* Wooden splinters flew in every direction as smoke and screams of pain enveloped the American ship. A few minutes later, a second broadside belched from the *Leopard,* causing further damage. Amid the chaos, American sailors tried to load, ready, and fire their cannon, yet to no avail. Before Barron's sailors could surrender and haul down the American flag, a third British broadside ripped through the *Chesapeake,* inflicting even more damage.[1]

For fifteen minutes Barron had screamed orders to defend the ship, but none of the American shots struck the British vessel. Seeing no other choice, Barron ultimately ordered his colors struck and then offered his ship to Humphreys as a prize of war. While Captain Humphreys refused to accept the ship as a prize, within fifteen minutes British officers had boarded the *Chesapeake,* requested the ship's log book and muster roll, and assembled the American crew on deck. Examining each man, the British identified four sailors—Jenkins Ratford, William Ware, Daniel Martin, and John Strachan—as deserters and took them forcibly back to the *Leopard.* Afterward, the British ship quietly slipped away for its anchorage at Lynnhaven Bay, while the *Chesapeake,* with twenty-two holes in its hull, limped back to Norfolk with three dead and eighteen wounded; a fourth man died days later.[2]

The *Chesapeake-Leopard* Affair represents one of the most dramatic and demeaning episodes in the early history of the United States. It is one of the events that caused the second war between the two countries, and the issue remained unsettled until the mid-nineteenth century. Yet unacknowledged in this affair is that three of the four sailors—Daniel Martin, John Strachan, and William Ware—were black men. Additionally, all three claimed to be Americans. Martin and Ware even maintained that they had protection papers—identification documents that verified nationality—and Strachan swore he left his papers aboard the British ship he had previously fled. Jenkins Ratford, the lone white, did not claim to be a U.S. citizen, and as a result British officials sentenced him to death for desertion, mutiny, and contempt, carrying out the execution on August 31, 1807. Despite their status, all four of these men had believed themselves safe from harm aboard the American frigate.[3]

Most Americans responded to the affair with demands for war. It violated American honor and sovereignty. Federalists and Republicans alike discarded their ideological differences, publicly deploring the British atrocity and demanding that justice be served. Town meetings across the country condemned the act of aggression and drew up petitions urging retaliation. Citizens of Charleston and Norfolk even wore black crepe bands to honor those killed in action. Americans everywhere toasted their sailors, condemned the British, and strongly embraced a renewed patriotism. And while race did not figure into the national dialogue of the *Chesapeake* Affair, it nonetheless remains central to the episode and to the history of the subsequent War of 1812 between the two countries.[4]

Black sailors and soldiers saw the War of 1812 with Britain as a means to advance their own agenda. For free blacks, the war provided them the chance to enhance their individual and collective status within society. Slaves believed it would provide an avenue to freedom, as had happened during previous wars. Moreover, the multinational aspects of the war—fought across the North American continent and on the seas, among Britons, Americans, Spaniards, and Native Americans—created many opportunities for blacks as they tried to achieve their goals. In the end, the war provided an unparalleled chance for slaves and free blacks to join the side that promised freedom or advancement, and they ultimately played the competing powers against one another in the attempt to secure this promise.

All sides tried to mobilize the free black and slave populations in the hopes of defeating the other. While the overwhelming majority of American blacks were slaves, several thousand of them, along with a handful of free blacks, joined the U.S. Navy and Army. Other slaves joined with the Spanish and the British military. Regardless of which side they supported, slaves and free blacks hoped to better their material conditions or to fight for causes they believed would empower them in the future. Many runaway slaves and some free blacks joined borderland mulatto and Indian communities outside U.S. authority in the attempt to maintain their freedom against aggressive American frontiersmen and southern slaveholders. Yet winning their freedom remained a difficult task.

This book examines African American combatants during the War of 1812 as a way to understand the evolution of American racial relations during the early nineteenth century. In many instances black participants—slaves and freemen—chose sides, and these choices ultimately defined their future. The War of 1812 represented a major dividing line in the history of American race relations, one that is often obscured by the Civil War. By the early nineteenth century it appeared that while the number of slaves increased, slavery as an institution was fragile; northern states had abolished slavery or instituted provisions for gradual emancipation. Even some southern states had loosened the bonds of slavery, providing for individual cases of emancipation.

The War of 1812 halted all progress. Many slaves used the presence of British troops and the militia's absence as an opportunity to flee to British freedom, convincing southern slaveowners of the need to tighten their bonds of control. Then, when fleeing slaves returned as British soldiers, carrying weapons and leading redcoats into the heart of American slave communities, it proved conclusively that slaves could not be trusted and that arming slaves did not offer a military solution for white manpower problems.

Ultimately, black participation in the war shaped the history of the United States in the nineteenth century. It bolstered the southern plantation system. It changed the United States' policy on militia enrollment.

When African American participation finally again became an issue of contention during the American Civil War, blacks enlisted in segregated companies commanded by white officers just as had been the case during the War of 1812. Finally, the war opened new lands across the Gulf South that permitted the growth and expansion of the plantation agricultural system, and the cotton-producing Deep South was born. Yet black participation also had another Atlantic World dimension in that it represented the greatest nineteenth-century diaspora of blacks from the United States. And as they relocated to the British colonies of Bermuda, Canada, or Trinidad, they took their American identity with them while consciously modifying it to suit their destination.

A MAJOR CHALLENGE OF THIS PROJECT has been to provide a face or an identity to an often nameless and unidentified group. In too many instances the participants remain but vague references without description. Even so, this project tries to reconstruct some individual participation as a way to provide a name and a face that illustrates the larger collective struggle encountered by African Americans during this tumultuous period. Hopefully readers will acknowledge and understand the individual contribution as told in the stories of Peter Denison, Prince Witten, Charles Ball, Ned Simmons, Jordan B. Noble, and George Roberts, and also realize how their efforts contributed to collective black action during this conflict. All of these men wanted freedom, and the different choices they made to secure it reveal much about the times in which they lived.

CHAPTER 1

BLACK SOLDIERS IN NORTH AMERICA

"Never of any use after they have carried arms"

In his study of Indian-white relations from the mid-seventeenth to the early nineteenth century, historian Richard White keenly described a middle ground where the white man and red man created a common world, adapted to changing lifestyles, and learned to accommodate cultural differences. His middle ground, located around the Great Lakes region, described "the place in between: in between cultures, peoples, and in between empires and the nonstate world of villages. It is the place where many of the North American subjects and allies of empire lived." Although White's book depicted only the relationship between Indians and whites, the basic thesis also applies to the world of African Americans during the same period because they too often occupied a middle ground between whites and Indians, between English and Spanish, and between the status of citizen and slave.[1]

Europeans, mainly the English and Spanish, brought African Americans to the New World in bondage, forcing them to perform the arduous and demanding tasks that whites felt were beneath them. Because of this expectation, from the beginning, Europeans constructed a two-tiered social system based on race. Whites were expected to fulfill their obligations as subjects of their respective empire, while blacks spent their days toiling for their white masters. Spaniards and English alike were expected to use all available resources to expand their respective nation's empire in the New World, and settling slaves became one means of strengthening their hold over indigenous lands. Yet solidifying imperial claims by utilizing a system of slavery was only part of the process and did not take into consideration external factors such as the vastness and danger of the land itself, disease, and hostile Native Americans. These extenuating circumstances strained white resources, ultimately forcing Europeans to compromise on what they expected from both citizens and slaves.

By the beginning of the eighteenth century most of the European imperial boundaries in the New World had been defined, and this created an intense competition for any remaining land. Spain had consolidated its control over Central and South America and the Caribbean. France had expanded its holdings down the St. Lawrence and Mississippi River basins. Meanwhile Britain had secured a foothold along the Atlantic coast of North America. Each European power had carved out western empires, but their claims often overlapped and were sometimes tenuous at best. This resulted in a series of wars (1689–1763) fought in Europe as well as North America, which had a devastating effect on the colonies: they depleted the white manpower supply and ultimately forced colonial leaders to turn to free blacks and slaves to supplement their military forces. For more than a century this necessity afforded blacks who were willing to take up arms more opportunities, even though prejudice and old values prevented them from securing any degree of equality.

The many conflicts prior to the War of 1812 reveal the conditions under which the British, Americans, Spanish, and Native American/ maroon (fugitive runaway blacks who settled away from whites) communities relied on blacks as combatants. By the beginning of the nineteenth century black soldiers had clearly demonstrated their value in the military, serving in a variety of offensive, defensive, and supporting roles. They had also won a variety of concessions—depending on for whom they fought—showing that military service offered an avenue for converting those hard-earned concessions to freedom. It was no surprise that these same groups turned to African Americans and that they willfully served during the War of 1812; black soldiers had proven themselves to be effective troops, and their desire to improve their well-being materially provided strong motivation for taking up arms.

"LEST OUR SLAVES WHEN ARM'D MIGHT BECOME OUR MASTERS": BRITISH COLONIAL AMERICA AND EARLY UNITED STATES

The use of African Americans as soldiers in the United States evolved over a long period of time. Even so, the shortage of white soldiers in the North American colonies combined with a Native American and foreign threat compelled colonials to use any fighting men, black or white, in their struggle for survival in a hostile, untamed land. Not surprisingly, life or death was determined by a combination of persistence and luck, not by skin color.

The ever-present threat of warfare against Native Americans became a common life-shaping feature of colonial existence during the seventeenth century, which ultimately forced each colony to devise a means of defending itself. For example, Virginia, which initially had a limited white population, expanding boundaries, and problems with Indians, armed blacks until their Native American difficulties abated during the late 1630s. By that time Virginia's white population had grown by an estimated five thousand, creating a mistaken belief that the Indians had been overwhelmed by force of numbers and thereafter would not offer further resistance. Such confidence in January 1639 prompted the colonial assembly to declare that "all persons except Negroes" had to secure arms and ammunition for defending the colony.

This legislation soon became problematic. During the spring of 1644 the aging Powhatan chief Opechancanough attacked the Virginia settlements, slaughtering more than three hundred. The Virginia assembly, despite the renewed violence, excluded blacks from military service, and by doing so the colonial government drew a distinction between the servants of the colony and the slaves, who were obligated to masters who served the colony. That presumption was further confirmed at the beginning of the eighteenth century when a special act prohibited blacks from holding "any office, ecclesiastical, civil, or military." Any black carrying a "gun, sword, club, staff, or other weapon" would be punished. One exception did permit blacks living on the frontier to possess weapons for their safety and defense, but only if they had white supervision. Virginia had passed laws proscribing blacks from carrying weapons or serving in the militia, but amended those laws when necessary.[2]

Other southern colonies experienced comparable threats and dealt with them in a similar fashion. Near the end of the First Anglo-Dutch

War in 1654, the General Assembly of Maryland required that "all persons from sixteen years of age to sixty," including free blacks and slaves, be provided with weapons to serve the commonwealth. In 1715, during the peaceful aftermath of some two decades of warfare, the Maryland assembly reversed its previous policy and precluded "all Negroes and Slaves" from military service. Likewise, the South Carolina assembly used slaves in 1671 to build fortifications around the ill-defended city of Charleston. During Queen Anne's War, the assembly further required that "trusty slaves" be armed with a "serviceable lance, hatchet, or gun" to protect the colony from a Spanish attack. Should those armed blacks capture or kill an enemy—and such a deed would have to be verified by a white witness—the slave would be granted freedom. If a slave was wounded in battle or taken prisoner and then escaped, he too would be emancipated. Apparently these conditions worked so well for South Carolina that in April 1708 the assembly renewed the provisions, employing blacks as full-fledged members of the militia.[3]

Northern colonies with smaller slave and free black populations faced similar difficulties. The Dutch colony of New Netherland in 1641, experiencing increased problems with the Algonquian tribes along the lower Hudson River, required that slaves be armed with a "tomyhawk and a half pick." Recurring Native American troubles, combined with constant encroachments by the surrounding English colonies, also forced the Dutch to arm blacks as a defensive supplement. During the most destructive conflict in New England, King Philip's War in 1676, Rhode Island required its surprisingly large slave population to muster in the militia and perform the same training as white Englishmen.[4]

By the end of the seventeenth century the English North American colonies had defined their black-white military relationship. Slaves and free blacks served as soldiers during a crisis, but once the trouble had passed both groups were relegated to their former subservient positions. The eighteenth century brought far more crises and more opportunities for African Americans to demonstrate their value as soldiers and citizens, but did not further clarify the already existing black-white relationship.[5]

The troubling Yamasee War, beginning during the spring of 1715 because of white encroachment on Yamasee land and debt owed by the tribe to British traders, brought new opportunities for blacks, as it threatened not only the South Carolina frontier but also red-white relations throughout each of the English North American colonies. Success against the colonists could provide confidence for other Native American tribes and spur bloody conflicts all along the western frontier. Such a possibility demanded concerted action by the colonies. South Carolina's governor Charles Craven desperately asked Britain, New England, Virginia, and North Carolina for help, but he was forced by the need for men to hire a thousand soldiers (half of whom were African Americans) to meet the Indian threat. Fearing a growing Indian uprising and a possible slave insurrection, North Carolina leaders warned caution "lest our slaves when arm'd might become our masters." Not surprisingly, that fear resonated strongly throughout all the slaveholding colonies and emphasized how careful whites would be when arming blacks to counter Native American threats. During 1719 South Carolinians, foreseeing the fears that North Carolina leaders had warned against, revised the state's militia laws, giving slaves cash rewards rather than freedom for capturing or killing one of the enemy.[6]

Although white Carolinians had used blacks to defeat Native Americans in the past, thereafter the Carolina assembly provided Indians with guns, ammunition, and supplies to capture escaped slaves. They relocated Indians to areas with high concentrations of slaves so they would "be an awe to the negroes." According to one Carolinian, it made "the Indians & Negro's checque upon each other . . . [or] we should be crushed by one or the other." Later eighteenth-century wars demonstrated precisely how white southerners hung between the horrors of slave insurrections and the atrocities of an Indian uprising.[7]

The War of Jenkins' Ear (1739) (Jenkins's ear was cut off by a Spanish Coast Guard official off Cuba), which evolved into the larger and more important King George's War in North America (beginning in 1744) and was also part of the general European War of Austrian Succession (1740–48), exacerbated an already tenuous situation. British and Spanish frontier fighting along the Georgia-Florida border, which had been ongoing for years, offered slaves and free blacks renewed opportunities for freedom. During January 1739 Gen. James Oglethorpe, founder of the Georgia colony, led an unsuccessful eighteen-month assault-turned-siege against Spanish St. Augustine. Although the assault—executed by regular redcoat soldiers, white militiamen, Indian allies, royal naval forces, and about eight hundred slaves—and subsequent attacks during 1742 and 1743 failed to dislodge the Spanish from Florida, according to one colonial they temporarily "spoil'd [Spain's] usual Methods of decoying our Negroes from Carolina, and elsewhere." The attacks also accentuated a growing American problem. The Spanish government and military warmly received runaway slaves and free blacks as a means of bolstering isolated segments of their far-flung empire, and the shortage of white troops forced Spain to rely on black soldiers as a means of ensuring the defense of Florida.[8]

By 1744 diplomatic relations between Britain and France had deteriorated, and the two countries declared war on each other, joining the War of Austrian Succession. France enlisted the support of her Native American allies, setting the northern frontier ablaze in violence. Although the New England colonies, which bore the brunt of this war, had forbidden blacks from bearing arms and mustering with the militia, this immediate crisis and the shortage of white soldiers again forced New Englanders to accept blacks within their ranks. When Massachusetts governor William Shirley recruited soldiers to meet the French threat, blacks from Massachusetts, New Hampshire, Connecticut, and Rhode Island volunteered, often identified as "Nero," "Cuffee Negro," "Adam a Negro," or a similarly descriptive name.[9]

African Americans played important, although often overlooked roles in the military operations that made Britain the greatest imperial power of the late eighteenth century. Regardless, defining the motivation that prompted these men to bear arms proves far more difficult than chronicling their activities. One slave, Toney, a cook who served aboard several Boston privateers, did so because his master Samuel Lyndes enrolled him in the service; generally, slaves surrendered to their masters half of any wages or prize money earned, which meant that military service could be profitable, provided the slave survived the experience. Even so, some colonies such as New Jersey refused to arm blacks. In other instances slaves attended their masters who were fighting in the conflict and became unwilling participants in a struggle in which they had no interest.[10]

Many free blacks, such as George Gire, saw the military as a means of advancement. After the French and Indian War, Gire petitioned the Massachusetts legislature and received, because of his "hard service," a pension of forty shillings per year. Forty shillings was not a great fortune, but the money demonstrated nonetheless that the legislature acknowledged and appreciated his sacrifice. Some may have chosen to bear arms because they believed it their duty as freemen, while others joined the conflict only because they had been forced to do so. In fact, some communities tried to use war service as a means to purge all criminals, paupers, and free blacks from their neighborhoods. Despite the reasons for their service, it cannot be denied that free blacks and slaves had found a place for themselves in the eighteenth-century military.[11]

A single theme regarding blacks and the military had emerged during the seventeenth and eighteenth centuries. Colonial law and social pressure forbade free blacks and slaves from bearing arms, but the defenselessness of the colonies, the constant Indian and foreign threat, and a limited white population willing to muster in the military revealed an immediate need to enlist the services of black soldiers. By the 1770s that pattern had been well established, and it remained in place during the first months of the American War for Independence.[12]

Blacks had played prominent roles in the events leading to the war. The "first martyr" of the struggle was the runaway slave Crispus Attucks from Framingham, Massachusetts, who died during the March 1770 Boston Massacre. A Rhode Island mulatto named Aaron helped torch the infamous British revenue cutter *Gaspee* off the coast of Providence in June 1772, while black militiamen Prince Easterbrook of Lexington, Pompey of Braintree, and Sam Croft of Newton all fought against the British on April 19, 1775, at the Battles of Lexington and Concord. At the June 1775 Battle of Bunker Hill black and white militiamen again confronted the British. One black soldier, Salem Poor, fought so bravely during the battle that fourteen white officers recommended him to the Massachusetts General Court for commendation; this "brave and gallant soldier" later suffered alongside his white compatriots at White Plains and Valley Forge.[13]

After Bunker Hill, British forces withdrew to the safe confines of the Boston peninsula while colonial militiamen swarmed the outskirts of the city, making sure that redcoats did not venture into the countryside again. Included among the units that surrounded the city was Col. John Nixon's New Hampshire regiment with three slaves, another New Hampshire regiment with two black militiamen, as well as regiments from Massachusetts, Connecticut, and Rhode Island, all with black soldiers. In fact, Gen. John Thomas, commanding one of the American brigades outside Boston, acknowledged the presence of black troops, remarking that they were "equally serviceable with other men, for fatigue [duties] and in action." Despite their bravery and the praise of white officers, Thomas reported a growing prejudice against black soldiers. He noted that southern militiamen did not tolerate black troops, but, then again, southerners held prejudices against any soldier who resided north of the Potomac River.[14]

During the spring of 1775 the Continental Congress meeting in Philadelphia created the Continental Army and appointed Gen. George

Washington as the commander-in-chief. Upon assuming command at Boston in early July, he found too few troops to continue an effective siege of the city. In previous instances, such a shortage of fighting men would have guaranteed black participation, but in this case it did not. The Massachusetts legislature had previously decided against using slaves, even though the legislators had deemed free blacks acceptable. Even so, Army adjutant general Horatio Gates warned his recruiting officers against enlisting any "stroller, negro, or vagabond." During September 1775 southern congressman Edward Rutledge, fearing the repercussions of arming slaves, pleaded unsuccessfully for his fellow delegates to ban free blacks and slaves from the military altogether. The Continental Congress did not take such action, but a month later a military council including Washington and seven other generals, meeting at Cambridge, Massachusetts, agreed to exclude free blacks and ban slaves from the army.[15]

The conflict took an unexpected turn on November 7, 1775, when royal Virginia governor John Murray, Earl of Dunmore, issued a proclamation that offered freedom to any slave who would join the English cause. This introduced a racial dimension to the struggle as well as indicated the extent to which Britain would resort to maintain her empire. The Continental Congress agreed, on the heels of Dunmore's announcement, to allow Washington to re-enlist free blacks who had already served, but no other new black volunteers would be accepted. Most of the New England assemblies and many mid-Atlantic colonies agreed to accept blacks only as re-enlistments, refusing to enlist any other willing slave or black soldier. The colonies south of the Potomac, however, refused to address the issue at all. For the most part, southern colonies held fast to the presumption that military duty was a white occupation. These decisions during the fall of 1775 and spring of 1776 effectively eliminated fifty to sixty thousand possible soldiers from the American cause and much-needed manpower. As the Patriot war effort stumbled during the summer and fall of 1776, white Patriot leaders would have to reevaluate the decisions to exclude blacks as soldiers.[16]

Even though northerners and southerners willingly prohibited blacks from serving in the military, both groups wanted them to work on military fortifications or in other defense-related occupations. During early 1776 William Alexander, the American commander at New York, ordered that all male slaves had to work every day with picks and shovels until the city's fortifications had been completed; free blacks had to work every other day at the same jobs. Similarly, the South Carolina assembly leased slaves to work on the defenses of Charleston. When the British Navy appeared off that city during the summer of 1776, press gangs rounded up every available black man to work on an additional battery, which helped repel the enemy. Before the end of the war Virginia bought slaves to work in lead mines, tanneries, iron mills, and armories, and as blacksmiths, sawyers, and laborers. The state of Maryland hired slaves to work in the Antietam cannon foundry while North Carolina employed slaves as carpenters, sawyers, firemen, stockgetters, and hostlers.[17]

During the fall of 1776 the war worsened for the Patriots, making it more difficult for the colonies to recruit white soldiers. Washington's army, which at one time had numbered some twenty thousand on paper, had only three thousand troops by the end of 1776, of which 1,400 were effective fighting men. Washington had lost New York City, British forces had seized Newport, Rhode Island, and the colonial army had been forced to cower west of the Delaware River. Washington's surprise attacks at Trenton and Princeton during late December 1775 and early January 1776 barely prevented the further disintegration of the Patriot force.

Because of these setbacks the colonists finally turned to black combatants. By early 1777 the lower house of the Connecticut legislature recommended that slaves be hired from their masters, sworn into the Continental Army, and declared "de facto free." Although the upper house did not concur, hundreds of free blacks and slaves joined nonetheless; Cuff Wells, slave of a Colchester, Connecticut, apothecary, enlisted and became a surgeon's assistant and later "received his freedom because of his service in the Army." Unable to fill its conscriptions quotas with white troops, Rhode Island also turned to slaves—who were to be purchased and then given freedom, bounties, and pay for their service—and General Washington thankfully welcomed them. In fact, recruitment for the Rhode Island battalion proceeded so quickly that the legislature discontinued the program after only four months. New Jersey agreed to enlist "all effective men between fifteen and fifty," initially allowing slaves but later permitting only free blacks to enlist. Some colonies, such as Virginia and Maryland, did not modify their restrictions at all but instead turned a blind eye to the law. In several instances wealthy slaveowners enlisted their bondsmen so that they or a family member could escape the dangers of war. Not surprisingly, these same families were often the ones who extolled their patriotism the loudest.[18]

Black soldiers fought in virtually every engagement during the pro-longed contest. Prince Whipple, a free-born African who served as Gen. Abraham Whipple's bodyguard, crossed the Delaware with George Washington in December 1776 and fought at Trenton and Princeton. Likewise, black soldiers participated in Horatio Gates's celebrated vic-tory at Saratoga and suffered with Washington at the frozen canton-ment at Valley Forge. During the 1778 attack against Newport, Rhode Island, a Hessian officer noted, "No [American] regiment is to be seen in which there are not Negroes in abundance; and among them are able-bodied, strong and brave fellows." Col. Christopher Greene's all-black Rhode Island regiment, of which the Hessian officer had commented, bravely repelled three British assaults, "distinguish[ing] itself by deeds of desparate valor." Among the soldiers fighting was Henri Christophe, who later ruled over an independent Haiti.[19]

It has been estimated that by the end of the war somewhere be-tween eight and ten thousand blacks had fought for the Patriot cause. Of course, no one will ever know the exact number because their names are interspersed with those of white soldiers on muster rolls, regimental pay-rolls, and morning reports, often listed merely as Caesar; John, Negro; Peter, Negro; Cato; or some other nondescriptive surname. Sometimes they were not identified at all.

Despite their presence in virtually every colonial company, only a few blacks ever achieved distinction or the rank of sergeant—Paul Bar-ney, James Baylen, Samuel Blanchard, and Samuel Middleton, who commanded the Massachusetts all-black militia regiment "Bucks of America"—and only Colonel Louis, who fought with the Continentals during the American Revolution, achieved an officer's commission. Col-onel Louis, the son of a black father and an Abenaki mother who had grown up among the Indians and became a chief, won a lieutenant-col-onel's commission during June 1779. Although some gained notoriety for their daring deeds or bravery on the battlefield, thousands of other black soldiers did their duty and simply faded into the haze of history.[20]

The war certainly provided opportunities for blacks, but primarily in the North. Almost all of the northern states had begun emancipating blacks by the time of the Constitutional Convention of 1787—Vermont (1777), Pennsylvania (1780), Massachusetts (1783), and Rhode Island and Connecticut (1784). By the beginning of the nineteenth century all of the northern states had abolished slavery, but the southern states did not follow suit. During the Revolution, South Carolina and Georgia had stubbornly refused, even in the face of British invasions, to enlist black soldiers, much less offer them freedom. This recalcitrance prompted thousands of southern slaves to use the turmoil of war to disguise their escape to the frontier, to the British, or to Spanish Florida.[21]

Historian Benjamin Quarles succinctly described the plight of blacks during and after the Revolutionary War, proclaiming "that in President Washington's America, the Negro would meet with discriminations contrary to the ideals proclaimed in the America of General Washington." During the Revolutionary struggle America had offered a promise of hope for blacks, yet that vision would not be as optimistic nor would it progress as quickly as initially anticipated. Following the conflict many slaves gained their freedom: some were emancipated because of their military service, some earned enough money in the struggle to purchase their freedom, some won freedom when the northern states abolished slavery, and some fled to the frontier, to the British, or to Florida to find their freedom.[22]

Once the United States no longer faced a crisis that threatened its survival, the government no longer needed to arm blacks. In fact, almost as soon as the war had ended, Secretary of War Henry Knox recommended that only "able bodied white male citizens" enlist in the militia. This eventually resulted in the first federal Militia Act of May 1792, which, while not barring blacks from mustering, did limit militia membership to citizens, of whom few were black. While the federal government had given states the authority to determine membership within the militia, the vagueness of the 1792 act enabled states to interpret the law as they chose. For example, North Carolina allowed free blacks to bear arms and muster alongside whites. South Carolina and Georgia meanwhile permitted free blacks to serve as musicians or laborers; the U.S. Marine Corps also used blacks as drummers and fifers to assist in recruiting. The U.S. Navy initially banned "Negroes or Mulatoes," but that decision was later modified because of the shortage of white seamen available for shipboard duty.[23]

By the beginning of the nineteenth century African Americans had won concessions partly because of the ideological dimension of the revolutionary struggle and partly because of their devotion to that cause. Not surprisingly, these concessions worried whites committed to slavery, and they worked to keep slaves and free blacks from using the military and state militias as avenues of advancement. Federal law publicly proclaimed that the martial branches were white occupations, and many states supported that legislation. Regardless, free blacks often found their way into the army and militias as laborers, servants, musicians, and soldiers. These institutions gave free blacks a means to demonstrate publicly their resistance to second-class treatment; if slaves could win acceptance into the military, perhaps in time they could win freedom. Furthermore, both slaves and free blacks could construe military duty as the patriotic responsibility of a free citizen, which elevated the status of both groups and moved them closer to par with white citizens. As relations between the United States and Britain deteriorated during the early nineteenth century, blacks would again be called on, and again they would help determine the outcome of the dispute.

THEY "KEEP IN AWE THE NEGROES WHO MULTIPLY AMAZINGLY": HOW THE BRITISH USED BLACK TROOPS

In 1776 Thomas Paine wrote in his passionate treatise *Common Sense* that "there is something very absurd, in supposing a continent to be perpetually governed by an island." He also indicated that the relationship between the two "reverse[d] the common order of nature," especially given the resources and relative size of Britain and North America. Such a forthright observation appears to the modern reader to be undeniable, yet Paine's statements belied more serious strategic and political problems facing the British government by the late eighteenth century. How could the manpower reserves of a small island nation provide the necessary military population to garrison an empire that after 1763 stretched around the globe? Britain's population could not provide the necessary men in peacetime, much less during times of war.[24]

When in November 1775 the Earl of Dunmore offered freedom to slaves who would join the British, he quickly recruited some 800, greatly supplementing his meager military force. But more importantly, Dunmore's armed black troops threatened the southern colonies with the possibility of a bloody and violent slave insurrection with all its destructive consequences. Dunmore's actions resonated strongly with a Virginia population surrounded by slaves who were eager to throw off their shackles and secure their freedom. Fortunately, the full-scale slave insurrection that Virginians feared never materialized. On December 9, 1775, the governor, anticipating a Patriot attack on Norfolk, rushed his small force south of the city to Great Bridge, a fortified span that dominated the land approach to the city. Within twenty-five minutes Dunmore's army had been routed by a superior colonial contingent. Feeling that he could no longer hold the city, Dunmore believed he had no alternative other than to retreat to British ships in the harbor. Then smallpox swept through the black army packed aboard his ships, ending his plans to invade the Virginia heartland. Dunmore responded by using his water-borne force to raid the Chesapeake coast.[25]

Pennsylvania Loyalist slaveowner Joseph Galloway, writing in 1778 to the Earl of Dartmouth, offered a poignant observation about the use of blacks during the American War for Independence: "that in the class of fighting men among the Negroes, there are no men of Property, none whose attachments would render them averse to the bearing of Arms against the Rebellion." Not surprisingly, Galloway's statement offers a simple explanation for the black exodus to British authorities: slaves could gain their freedom and maybe property by fighting for King George III, while their only prospect under the Patriots appeared to be continued servitude. When Dunmore offered his proclamation, he held out the reality of freedom to those blacks willing to sacrifice, and this promise made a tremendous impact on the slave population of North America as well as on the course of the war. Slaves escaping to the protection of the British flag contended that they, just like their colonial masters, were fighting for life, liberty, and the pursuit of happiness.[26]

Dunmore's Chesapeake slaves had not represented the first or only black fighting force recruited by the British. As early as 1662 Charles II had presented three hundred slaves to officers stationed in Jamaica. The grant provided the soldiers with tangible property, connected them intricately to the land, and, more importantly, bolstered the small military force on the island. The lack of white troops in the Caribbean made this experiment so successful that the government provided other slaves to officers some years later. The European wars and the colonial struggles of the eighteenth century hastened the use of free blacks and slaves so much that by the middle of the century, the practice had been almost universally adopted throughout the Caribbean. It was no surprise that during the War for American Independence, the British, desperately needing men, recruited black troops for the campaigns in the North American colonies.[27]

Loyalist leaders from across British North America saw the value in using black combatants, and they offered a variety of recommendations for enlisting them. During the fall of 1775 Loyalist Anglican minister Jonathan Boucher suggested to George Germain that the government arm both slaves and Indians in the Chesapeake region, which would force colonials to remain vigilant in fear "either by apprehension of having their slaves armed against them, or their savage Neighbours let loose on their frontiers." Later that same year East Florida governor Patrick Tonyn encountered a deluge of runaway slaves descending into his colony. The unexpected arrival of so many slaves forced him to organize them into militia companies just to maintain order. Much to his surprise, he contended that his militia would hold any Patriot force at bay and "keep in awe the Negroes who multiply amazingly." During the British attack on Savannah in December 1778, Gen. Augustine Prevost permitted some two hundred slaves to be armed, and they later participated in several engagements contributing to the conquest of the city. The garrison of Savannah still had some 150 armed black troops—or more than 10 percent of the total force—during the spring of 1782 when the British finally evacuated.[28]

There were several noteworthy episodes of slaves and free blacks serving as British laborers, pilots, scouts, guides, skirmishers, and even spies in every theater of operation during the war. Yet of all the units organized in North America, Charleston's Carolina Black Corps represented the most effective fighting force recruited by the British during the conflict. This contingent—a prototype black regiment that later became part of the British West Indian establishment—gained a much-deserved reputation as a disciplined and effective fighting unit during the Charleston campaign and the subsequent garrisoning of that city. In fact, British general Alexander Leslie had so much confidence in these men that he authorized the purchase of all those slaves who had previously been promised their freedom. When the British army evacuated Charleston in December 1782 some three hundred ex-slaves departed for St. Lucia, where they served together as a unit until the end of the war. In 1798 the British War Office incorporated the remaining ex-slaves into the 1st West India Regiment.[29]

The American War for Independence taught British commanders valuable lessons about the military prowess, reliability, and value of black soldiers. Slaves and free blacks served with distinction against the Patriots in North America; they also fought valiantly against the French invasion of Tobago in 1781 and St. Kitts in 1782; free black militia units in Barbados and Jamaica gained reputations as outstanding soldiers, equaled only by British redcoat regulars; and plantation owners in the Caribbean willingly raised armed contingents of slaves during the war. The conflict also convinced British policy makers that black troops could play important roles in defending the empire as they fought not only against the Patriots and the French enemy, but also against slave insurrections.[30]

During the decade following the Revolutionary War the racial composition of the British Caribbean changed noticeably. The white population of the islands continued to dwindle in both numbers and proportion. The resulting shift permitted increased mobility for free blacks and slaves. The new social paradigm also forced Britain to rely more heavily on slaves as domestic servants, tradesmen, and military supplements, with blacks serving in the army as soldiers and laborers. In fact, the British government quickly found that black troops could perform the exhausting manual labor associated with fatigue work, which in turn relieved white troops from the arduous tasks that weakened their immune systems and made them susceptible to debilitating diseases. Black soldiers could also be reconstituted into pioneer (or settlement) units, whose mere presence combined with their work potential strengthened the British position in the islands.[31]

Neither the British ministry, colonial governors, nor colonial assemblies were eager to count on black soldiers as the main defensive force. There were too many instances in which they had "manifested such a mutinous and disorderly disposition as to be more dangerous than . . . serviceable." This "disorderly disposition" created anxiety within the white colonial population, who saw armed blacks as providing a dangerous example to slaves and runaways who undoubtedly wanted their freedom as well. Nonetheless, the escalating European war with France after 1791 and the defenselessness of the Caribbean provided the British with only one alternative if the empire was to survive—Britain had to arm its own slaves and incorporate them into its own military establishment. By April 1795 Henry Dundas, Secretary of State for War and Colonies, authorized two regiments of black troops, thereby Africanizing the British military in the West Indies.[32]

While the government in London gladly used black troops to fulfill the empire's manpower needs, West Indian merchants, planters, and assemblymen adamantly feared that arming and training black soldiers would undermine the traditional right of planters to arm their slaves as they saw fit; this was a basic attack on the foundation of British slavery in the West Indies because individual owners believed only they could make decisions that impacted their own slaves. As such, colonials refused to recruit blacks or assist military officers in organizing black regiments. Without local support, the British Ministry had no choice but to order military commanders in the colonies to purchase slaves newly imported from Africa. This arrangement provided undeniable advantages, such as decreasing the possibility of securing blacks influenced by radical French revolutionary ideas, and also reducing the price that had to be paid, as ship slaves were far less expensive than those who had already been seasoned and trained. During the period from 1795 to 1808 the British government purchased an estimated 13,400 slaves, costing about £925,000 (average cost of £69 each). Apparently the slave trade afforded a discreet and easy opportunity for recruiting men into the West India regiments, even though it directly involved the government in the controversial traffic in human beings. Unknown to the British public at the time, the government bought more slaves than any other single entity, thus becoming one of the largest slaveholders in the world.[33]

During the period 1793–1815 the British raised no less than seventeen temporary slave/free black units in the Caribbean, nine of which were subsequently incorporated into the twelve West India regiments. These units initially bore the names of their commanding officers or the title "Corps" or "Regiments of People of Colour and Negroes." Every regiment had a white officer corps and regimental staff, although some did eventually have black sergeants; no black soldier became an officer until well into the twentieth century, as they supposedly did not possess the necessary prerequisites. Most white Englishmen believed that blacks lacked the manners, education, and demeanor that British officers were expected to possess. Moreover, few slaves and free blacks could afford to buy an officer commission, the cheapest of which in 1776 cost some £400. These limitations relegated black troops to rank and file appointments with no possibility of promotion to officer. Even so, several thousand joined, which, combined with the more than thirteen thousand purchased slaves, provided the British with the men needed to defend the Caribbean effectively.[34]

By 1798 the conflict in the Caribbean had begun to turn in favor of Britain. The slave regiments organized in the West Indies without question allowed Britain to maintain her profitable colonies. Those soldiers also increased Britain's control over the entire region, which simultaneously stripped France of any financial benefits that might have been derived from her colonies. But as Britain tightened its hold over the West Indies, the need for additional black troops—recruited and purchased via the slave trade—declined. Britain no longer needed to rely completely on imported slave soldiers, and this provided a strong incentive to abolish completely the international slave trade by March 1807. Although Britain outlawed the slave trade, an Order in Council on March 16, 1808, ordered all illegal slaves seized by the navy to be enlisted into Britain's land and sea forces. While the government had declared the slave trade illegal, the fruits of that illicit traffic continued to supplement the British military establishment.[35]

Once the French threat in the Caribbean had been eliminated and the need for black troops diminished, colonials reasserted their position within the islands, restricted the liberties of slave soldiers, and worked to disband the black regiments. Under local jurisdictions black soldiers remained slaves first, meaning that they had to abide by the restrictive slave laws of the islands, and soldiers second. This dichotomy perplexed military officers, who acknowledged that black soldiers would be unable to carry out their duties if they had to remain subservient to civil authorities. Moreover, one judge could order the public whipping of a black trooper, while it took only two to condemn the same soldier to death. This encroachment threatened the security of the Caribbean and the effectiveness of the West India regiments. Yet colonials did not understand the larger imperial picture, only the local fear that slave soldiers had bold ideas of equality after they had "carried arms." This apprehension forced colonials to try to restrict black troops while in uniform, so that those same restrictions would not seem unusual once the military emergency had ended and their regiments had been disbanded.[36]

While local authorities believed that the black soldiers were subject to slave laws, the soldiers considered themselves to be free, having the same rights as white soldiers; they jealously guarded their rights and prerogatives. White officers had implanted this belief and a sense of pride in the blacks because it boosted their confidence and made them better soldiers. Additionally, the colorful yet inappropriate uniforms—most were wool-based, long sleeved, and had multiple layers, which proved too warm for a Caribbean climate—distributed to each soldier served to reinforce that confidence. The British government had also bolstered the soldiers' feeling of equality by ordering officers to show the West India regiments equal "attention and favor." Yet the colonial assemblies continued legal and prejudicial attacks against the black regiments throughout the 1790s and early 1800s until the civilian-military controversy was finally settled once and for all. The Mutiny Act of March 1807 proclaimed that black slaves purchased by the government and then serving in the King's forces were thereafter free. Not surprisingly, this brief proclamation had a momentous impact on Caribbean society, because it instantly liberated an estimated ten thousand slaves then serving under the King's colors. It also made a notable impact on the forthcoming war with the United States; slaves liberated by the British during the conflict would be considered free and either enlisted in the military or resettled rather than being reenslaved.[37]

"BLACK FUGITIVES CONVERT THE PROVINCE INTO A THEATER OF HORRORS": SPAIN'S BLACK AUXILIARIES

Spanish Florida had long been intricately linked to the English colonies to its north. When the Spanish landed on the peninsula during the sixteenth century, it had little to offer to the conquistadors, as there was no gold or silver, nor was there a proverbial fountain of youth. But as the Spanish Empire expanded throughout the Caribbean and Central and South America during the 1500s, Florida came to represent an important outpost that guarded the northern rim of the western empire. More importantly, St. Augustine (founded in 1565) served as a defensive base for protecting the Florida Channel, the transatlantic trade route through which the Spanish treasure galleons passed. By the beginning of the seventeenth century Florida and St. Augustine, with its wooden fort, had become the northernmost Spanish military barrier along the Atlantic. Unfortunately, the Spanish Empire had spread beyond its ability to defend itself adequately, and Florida could expect little additional support. Ultimately, the Crown would turn to black alternatives.[38]

The menace that confronted Spanish Florida actually began in April 1670, when English and Barbadian colonists landed about twenty-five miles up the Ashley River and settled Old Charles Town. Although the southernmost English colony until that time had been near the Virginia border on Albemarle Sound, this new settlement was but a few days' journey from St. Augustine. In 1672 the Spanish used black and Indian slave labor to build Castillo de San Marcos, the powerful masonry fort that became their military stronghold in Florida. Likewise, the English responded by moving their Carolina settlement to the confluence of the Ashley and Cooper Rivers, where they constructed New Charles Town— later known as Charleston, South Carolina.[39]

The two neighbors spent the next century living in an uneasy proximity, which was further aggravated by the tumultuous relations between the two conflicting European powers. Spain and Britain were thousands of miles from Florida and South Carolina, yet the problems between the two reverberated distinctly throughout the contested southeastern borderlands, forcing both St. Augustine and Charleston to be ever vigilant against an unprovoked attack.[40]

While the British turned primarily to Indians to strengthen the position in South Carolina, Spain relied on Indians and blacks to protect Florida. During the last two decades of the seventeenth century runaway slaves from South Carolina began appearing in increasing numbers at St. Augustine, strengthening Castillo de San Marcos. This greatly undermined the morale of the English colony to the north while offering Spain a manpower supplement for Florida's defensive needs.

During November 1693 Charles II of Spain issued a royal proclamation freeing all slaves who fled to Florida and accepted conversion and baptism. This official statement, which seemed to deal with a localized problem, actually had greater ramifications, as it helped influence events in Florida for the next century and provided a refuge for runaway slaves and blacks in St. Augustine. The Spanish government, moreover, incorporated these elements into the community, instilling them with the idea of civic pride and obligation. By the beginning of the eighteenth century Spain had effectively incorporated blacks into its colonial defensive framework, including the fifty-seven black militiamen who helped defend Castillo de San Marcos against a force of white Carolinians, Indians, and black slaves in 1702. During this decade-long conflict the Spanish colony suffered greatly as British forces successfully raided outlying settlements and missions, butchered Spain's Indian allies, and reenslaved runaways who they captured. Even so, the British could not capture St. Augustine's fort, and this stronghold remained a defiant symbol of freedom and hope for Carolina slaves.[41]

Carolina slave revolts in 1711 and 1714, combined with the Yamasee War in 1715, heightened tensions and further aggravated relations between Carolina and Florida. These incidents also made the English more vigilant to Spanish enticements to slaves. When Carolinians discovered a slave conspiracy in 1720 whose participants wanted to flee to St. Augustine, it reconfirmed English suspicions. During the next decade slaves fled in increasing numbers to Florida, and despite the Carolinian protest, Spain continued incorporating them into the black militia. During 1726 a group of fourteen slaves who had fought with the Yamasee fled to Florida, joined the militia, and participated in a series of successful raids against their former masters. The following year the Spanish also sponsored other successful raids, prompting the English to retaliate in 1728 by again attacking St. Augustine. During this British siege the black militia once again proved itself one of the city's most effective fighting forces, with the Crown praising them for bravery and in 1733 again offering freedom to runaway Carolina slaves. Royal officials had obviously realized the military potential for black soldiers and used them to keep the borderlands in a constant state of flux.[42]

In February 1739, Florida governor Manuel de Montiano set aside a place for the fugitives near St. Augustine called Gracia Real de Santa Teresa de Mose. This community, soon with its stone and earthen fort, would become the first all-black settlement in North America and an important Spanish outpost in Florida. It served as an advance location that could warn St. Augustine of a British approach. The black freemen who settled at Mose promised to defend Spanish Florida at all costs. Even more importantly, Mose became a prominent and vivid example of black resistance to English slavery and an entrêpot for those slaves willing to risk their lives for freedom. Not surprising, within a few months of the settlement's founding, slaves along the Stono River in South Carolina rose in a bloody and violent revolt, killing any whites they could find. During the September 1739 Stono Rebellion armed slaves burned, killed, and looted as they tried to escape to Spanish Florida. Though white Carolinians brutally suppressed this Spanish-influenced insurrection, Mose and its armed freed black militia remained until 1763 as a defiant symbol, calling for other blacks to take a similar chance for freedom.[43]

During the 1750s Spanish officials tried to strengthen their defenses in Florida, but they lacked resources and materials. The city of St. Augustine became a poor and isolated center of a broken government—a remnant of a once-powerful Spanish Empire. The alluring fort at Mose became little more than a deserted outpost as most of the blacks returned to St. Augustine. After 1763 any possibility for runaway slaves disappeared altogether. In the Peace of Paris ending the Seven Years' War, Spain transferred Florida to England for the return of Cuba, captured by British forces in 1762. With the exchange more than three thousand Spaniards, blacks, and Indians evacuated the colony. The Florida refuge and the example of Mose—an opportunity for blacks to gain freedom, land, distinction, and even income—had disappeared.

Spain regained Florida in 1783, and runaway slaves once again began to trickle into the colony. Slaves from the southern United States arrived via canoes and crude boats, by horseback, and on foot. Bringing their meager possessions, they found their way through the southern pine forests and tangled swamps. They often stumbled across maroon (black runaways or fugitives) settlements or renegade Indian communities in the interior and chose to join these armed and isolated groups. Some continued south to St. Augustine or Pensacola, where they requested, and usually received, asylum from Spanish authorities. But in either scenario, slaves consciously embraced their preferred method for securing and maintaining their freedom—armed defense within an isolated fringe community or immunity within a crumbling Spanish colony.

Americans viewed with trepidation the runaway communities developing in the swamps and forests of Florida. These armed communities afforded slaves the opportunity to own property, including cattle and farms. Also, these settlements generally were not controlled by the Spanish government, and many southerners saw this as a dangerous example that could provoke slave rebellions on nearby American plantations. During the late eighteenth and early nineteenth centuries the mere presence of these settlements prompted repeated American militia and Indian expeditions into the swamps to destroy the maroon communities and round up runaways. Their existence also created a flurry of official American complaints, which ultimately forced Spanish officials in Florida to reconsider their sanctuary policy. Finally, in 1790 Florida governor Juan Nepomuceno de Quesada agreed that runaway slaves thereafter would have no legal protection in Florida.[44]

Spanish officials in Florida had agreed to receive no more runaway slaves, but that compact did not prohibit free blacks from entering the colony. The French Revolution and its Haitian equivalent, which brought tremendous instability to the Caribbean world, dislocated blacks and whites alike, prompting many to seek the stability of an isolated colony that had not been tainted by revolutionary ideology. Florida offered that prospect until January 1796, when Gen. Jorge Biassou, caudillo of Charles IV's Black Auxiliaries in St. Domingue, and twenty-five of his followers relocated to St. Augustine. These men, who revolted against slavery in Haiti before joining with the Spanish, had bravely fought against French planters, British and French soldiers, and other black Haitians. They were also quite familiar with the revolutionary notions of liberty, equality, and fraternity and how these concepts applied to free blacks and slaves.[45]

Although the arrival of Biassou and his black auxiliaries heightened tensions along the Georgia-Florida border, their presence allowed Spain to hold onto the colony during a period of intense chaos. Seminole and Lower Creek Indians, led by William Augustus Bowles as director of their independent Nation of Muskogee, allied with British and American filibusters and formally declared war on Spain, pillaging the north Florida frontier from 1800 to 1802. Florida's new governor, Enrique White, had to turn to Biassou's soldiers and the black militia—to supplement his limited white force—if he intended to keep the colony for Spain. Fortunately, the premature death of Biassou in July 1801 and subsequent peace with the Muskogee Nation in August 1802 brought a momentary calm to the Florida frontier. The presence of black soldiers in Florida, combined with Spain's weak and ineffective control over the colony, provided Americans with the necessary justification for invading the peninsula before, during, and after the War of 1812.[46]

"A PLENTIFUL REFUGE TO THE RUNAWAY NEGRO": INDIANS AND MAROONS

The British and Spanish use of black combatants offered serious reasons for colonial Americans to be concerned. Both European nations instilled a sense of pride and equality in their black troops, armed them with weapons, gave them training, and provided them with the opportunity to exact revenge against their former masters. The use of black soldiers evoked great fear within American communities, especially in the South, where the possibility of a slave insurrection loomed large. The presence of armed maroon communities in the interior, however, appeared even more troublesome: they remained hidden in the swamps and isolated forests, acting as magnets for other runaway slaves and serving as symbols of resistance and defiance.

The frontier represented a mysterious no-man's—or no-*white*-man's—land where runaways were beyond the reach of white authority during time of war. Once slaves reached the frontier, they could, and frequently did, assimilate with the Indians or even segregate themselves into isolated, self-sufficient maroon communities. Both possibilities offered the chance for continued freedom as long as the whites were kept at bay by the fear of Indian uprisings. Yet once that fear had been removed, runaways often found themselves betrayed by the same Indians who swapped peace, slaves, and information for guns, alcohol, and trade goods. As long as a tense three-cornered relationship existed among whites, Indians, and blacks, maroon communities and individual runaways could enjoy both the sanctuary and security of the interior.

Although slaves from both north and south sought an asylum from their plight, the method they employed differed greatly depending on circumstance and location. Many northern urban slaves resisted their predicament by setting fires, stealing, murdering, or even committing suicide. Others found ways to blend into the city's black community: they ran away by disguising themselves and mingling with other free blacks and slaves. Some chose to take to the sea or move to the interior, where they perceived limited white authority. They took any chance to secure their freedom and to injure the white society that had held them in bondage.[47]

In the southern colonies slaves had limited options. They could certainly set fires, steal, murder, or commit suicide, but they had fewer chances to mingle with an established urban black population or to take to the sea. Even so, they found far more opportunities to flee into the interior because of the proximity of open lawless territory. South Carolinians had learned as early as the 1680s that the forested and swampy frontier of the colony, the nearby Spanish Empire, and the presence of numerous black-friendly Indian tribes—such as the Choctaws, Chickasaws, Yamasees, and Lower Creeks—tempted slaves to flee. In fact, more maroon communities reportedly emerged in South Carolina during the seventeenth and eighteenth centuries than in any other North American colony.[48]

In the struggle to define the continent during the colonial period, whites employed both slaves and Native Americans as counterweights. Slaveowners who feared the prospect of an Indian-slave alliance warned their slaves of the dangers associated with Indians. Likewise, white southerners sometimes turned to Indians to help suppress slave insurrections as well as to keep slaves in check. Englishmen offered clothes, guns, ammunition, as well as bounties for the return of runaways, which demonstrated the value of slave property and also fostered greater enmity between the two groups. Yet in some instances runaway slaves and Indians joined together and/or united with other European powers. For example, during the 1720s, fugitive slaves and Native Americans helped the Spanish attack outlying Carolina settlements, prompting imperial concerns about the defense of the profitable South Carolina colony. This development embodied one of the greatest fears that southerners confronted—the possibility of rebellious slaves and hostile, barbaric Indians being supplied and abetted by a foreign power.[49]

The English attempt to keep Indians and slaves separated failed miserably during the eighteenth century as both groups easily intermingled. It is impossible to determine the number of slaves who found sanctuary within Native American communities, but the number must have been substantial considering how often clauses, such as those insisting on the return of runaway slaves, were inserted into Indian treaties. For example, in the early part of the century the Tuscaroras of North Carolina provided protection to a large number of runaways, who in 1711 fought

alongside them against white Englishmen. A runaway named Harry supposedly designed the Indian fortress on the Nuese River. Four years later
the Yamasee and their black allies attacked white South Carolinians.
After 1720 both Cherokees and Creeks harbored runaway slaves, returning them only if it improved their situation. Otherwise, most tribes
ignored previous agreements and permitted blacks to remain in Indian
settlements where they were assimilated into Native American society.[50]

On the eve of the American War for Independence, William Bull,
a native-born member of South Carolina's provincial council and later
lieutenant governor, commented on the possible double-edged threat
facing the colony and the consequences that might result. Carolinians
wanted to eliminate the perceived Indian menace from the interior yet
believed it would create "a plentiful refuge to the runaway Negroes . . .
who might be more . . . difficult to reduce than the Negroes in the moun-
tains of Jamaica." If the Native American threat was not reduced, the
frontier sanctuary would provide a "refuge for all Criminals, Debtors,
and Slaves who would fly thither from Justice of their Masters." Neither
prospect offered any degree of comfort to white Carolinians, as both
underscored great fears.[51]

During the American War for Independence the British convinced
both Native Americans and slaves to take up arms against the rebellious
colonists, and the long-range effect devastated South Carolina and Georgia. Both colonies had sizeable slave populations and a nearby Spanish
presence, and both suffered increased defections and frontier violence
once the British shifted their military operations southward. In mid-
December 1775 British ships stood off Charleston, prompting a number of slaves to flee to Sullivan Island, where they thought they would
be protected. Early in the morning of December 18, white Carolinians
quietly descended on the slaves' camp, killing and capturing runaways
and destroying British supplies. The operation demonstrated how white
Carolinians would deal with the threat they faced. By the time the war
turned with full fury to the south, British agents had enlisted the support
of Creeks and Seminoles, who with their black allies and runaway slaves
escalated the war along the South Carolina and Georgia frontier. This
new tri-cornered racial dimension intensified the war in the south and
thereafter left a legacy of Indian and black defiance to white authority.[52]

Cornwallis's surrender in October 1781 did more than any other single event to create the legacy of Indian-black defiance. British forces had
given both groups a degree of autonomy that they could not suddenly
rescind with a treaty negotiated in the safe confines of Paris. As British

forces evacuated, many slaves chose to leave with them, while others fled to the remote swamps and woodlands of the interior. Runaways from Virginia and North Carolina absconded to the Dismal Swamp, where they built cabins, planted gardens, and raised livestock at least until the 1790s. Armed blacks along the Georgia–South Carolina border began raiding coastal plantations. Based from a swampy site along the Savannah River, they had built homes protected by a wooden palisade and farmed rice paddies that surrounded the camp. By the spring of 1786 the maroons had become more audacious, even attacking Georgia militia units. Their presence now threatened white authority and control throughout the South. That October Georgia and South Carolina militia forces routed the village, burned all the structures, destroyed the food supply and rice still in the fields, and captured and executed one of the leaders of the settlement. Though vividly illustrating the white attitude about maroon communities, the attack did not discourage them. Other black and Indian settlements emerged on the Chattahoochee River in western Georgia, at Miccosukee in northern Florida, and at other remote locations either in Spanish territory or far removed from white settlements in the United States. White authorities had destroyed the largest maroon sanctuaries, but smaller groups of black runaways continued harassing the countryside throughout the late eighteenth and early nineteenth centuries.[53]

Miccosukee was the most influential of the smaller maroon communities. Located near the Georgia-Florida border, east of present-day Tallahassee, the Seminole town and its nearby black settlement became the center of William Augustus Bowles's "Nation of Muskogee." From there Bowles enlisted runaway slaves in his Muskogee army and navy, sought a British protectorate, and raided the Georgia frontier. From 1800 to 1802 the Muskogee force pillaged the Spanish Florida frontier in an unsuccessful attempt to win support from Britain. Yet after Bowles's downfall in 1803, this settlement declined as most of the maroons melted away into the surrounding forests and fled to other isolated communities.[54]

The Revolutionary struggle had unleashed powerful ideological forces that greatly influenced the North American black and Indian populations during the mid-eighteenth century. By the latter part of the century the same ideological movement had embraced the island of St. Domingue, and there it revealed the true fervor of those powerful forces. A slave insurrection beginning during the summer of 1791 swept the island, and soon news of it percolated throughout the Caribbean and North America, inspiring other slaves to seek their freedom as well.

The possibility of a North American slave insurrection was not lost on southerners as rumors of rebellions shortly appeared in Virginia, North Carolina, and Georgia. During the next ten years rumors of other slave rebellions infected the cities of Richmond, Charleston, and Wilmington, as well as Bryan County near Savannah. As details of the black Haitian military successes reached the United States, southerners worked more diligently to isolate their slaves from inflammatory information. They also moved quickly and forcefully against existing maroon communities in an attempt to remove all enticements of insurrection. Finally, they tightened controls over the institution of slavery itself.[55]

The presence of maroon communities in the South and their confrontations with whites revealed that blacks were more than auxiliaries to Indians or any other power. They joined with Native Americans when it benefited them to do so. They also chose to settle in separate maroon communities when that option seemed more appropriate. At one time or another, maroons fought Spaniards, Englishmen, Americans, and Indians. At other times they were allied with each. Although maroon communities provided sanctuary, security, as well as asylum for slaves, these runaways still made preemptive strikes against whites to protect their precariously held freedom. After all, blacks had previously been armed by Spaniards, the British, and American patriots, and their decision to join with other maroons or Indians represented a conscious choice to defend with arms what rights they believed they had won.

AFRICAN AMERICAN COMBATANTS HAD MADE valuable contributions to all sides during the colonial and revolutionary periods. They helped the Spanish and English carve empires out of the forests. They wielded axes to fell trees for homes, fences, and outbuildings; they used hoes to turn the soil and scratch out a living; and, equally important, they carried weapons when called on to confront an approaching enemy despite its ethnicity or nationality. In the beginning both the Spanish and English had armed blacks as auxiliaries and used them to offset the numerical superiority of Native Americans. But as the institution of slavery increased, both groups came to regard blacks as a manpower supplement that could be mobilized in times of emergency; colonial Americans of Spanish or English descent rewarded slaves with freedom for faithful and diligent service. By the beginning of the eighteenth century courageous military service had become a means for slaves to secure their freedom, and the almost continuous warfare of that century afforded ample opportunity for blacks to demonstrate bravery.

One hundred fifty years of North American warfare redefined the black-white relationship in the New World. Spaniards began augmenting their military in the Western Hemisphere with black auxiliaries by the mid-sixteenth century. The English North American colonies began doing the same a century later. By 1800 Spain, Britain, and even the United States had developed a long-standing tradition of turning to slaves and free black soldiers in times of crisis. Moreover, slaves had ably demonstrated time and again that they were as brave and possessed the same abilities as white troops. The only problem with using blacks as soldiers was that it challenged the role that slaves and free blacks were expected to play in society. One British military governor expressed that fear succinctly when he warned, "A Negro is never of any use after they [sic] have carried arms." How could whites expect slaves to return to their servile positions after they had fought to defend liberty or freedom?[56]

CHAPTER 2

FIGHTING IN THE NORTH 1807–13 AND ON THE SEAS

"Absolutely insensible to danger"

Shortly before 1807 Catherine Tucker indentured her Detroit, Michigan, slave Peter Denison to Elijah Brush on a one-year contract. When the indenture matured, Denison, his wife, and their four children were to be granted their freedom. This represented a common practice for slaveowners who did not have work for their human property, yet still had to maintain them. The value of the indenture could offset the costs to maintain the slaves, and, in some cases, the income also proved more important as an infusion of liquid capital than the value of the slaves themselves. This may have influenced Tucker's decision to indenture Denison and agree to his freedom; she could gain cash while also decreasing her expenditures. In any case, Brush agreed to the indenture, paid the labor costs, and prepared to grant Denison his freedom. At the last moment, however, Tucker claimed Brush had taken this action without her knowledge or approval. She demanded Denison's return. Brush filed suit on Denison's behalf, forcing the Michigan territorial government to protect Denison's freedom. Instead, Judge Augustus Woodward upheld property rights, claiming that Denison remained the property of Mrs. Tucker. He also ruled that all bondsmen living in the territory as of

May 31, 1793, and belonging to a slaveholder as of July 11, 1796—the day that Britain turned the territory over to the United States—would remain a slave.[1]

Peter Denison's life story reveals how shrewd blacks were at finding the best opportunities for freedom. After learning in the early fall of 1807 of the *Chesapeake-Leopard* Affair, territorial governor William Hull allowed the slave Peter Denison to form a militia company of free blacks and runaway slaves. During the Tucker-Brush hearing Denison had apparently gained the confidence of Detroit's black population, even though he remained a slave. According to Hull, under Denison's leadership, the troops "frequently appeared under arms" and "made considerable progress in military discipline." The governor even maintained that these men acted in an "orderly manner" and demonstrated an unquestioned "attachment to our government, and a determination to aid in the defense of the country." Yet the *Chesapeake* crisis that had prompted Hull to turn to Denison and the city's black population passed, and the militia was disbanded.[2]

Even so, that did not conclude Denison's story. When news arrived on the northwest frontier during the summer of 1812 that the United States had declared war on Great Britain, Governor Hull commissioned Denison as a captain in the Michigan militia. When the war came to Detroit in August, Hull surrendered the city to British general Isaac Brock. Peter Denison was taken off with other white and black prisoners to Canada before being paroled. By 1816 reports existed of a black Peter Dennison living as a free man in the community of Sandwich who attended St. John's Church of England, just east across the river from Detroit. Perhaps this Denison, now listed as Dennison, spelled his name differently or the secretary at the church spelled it incorrectly. Regardless, Dennison had sent for his wife and four children and leveraged his own military service to relocate to Canada, purportedly as a free man. Peter Denison's story reveals the changing nature of the Michigan–Canada borderlands as well as the changing definition of slavery in this region. Initially Canadian slaves fled south to the freedom of Michigan, yet by the end of the War of 1812 the path to freedom had shifted dramatically, leading north to Canada and propagating the image of the northern-bound Underground Railroad that we celebrate today. Yet for a narrow window of time, Peter Denison experienced how the fluidity of the borderlands greatly altered the slave's path to freedom and our understanding of the North American slave diaspora.[3]

"RENEGADE NEGROES KEPT FOR
DESPERATE SERVICES": PREPARING FOR WAR

Relations between Great Britain and the United States were tense in the years after the Revolutionary War. The British government continued treating the United States as a *de facto* colony, resenting that the new country had risen like a phoenix from the ashes of the once-mighty British Empire. Americans, in contrast, saw every British slight as an insult to their character and country; they cherished the independence that had been bequeathed to them by their founding fathers and took offense to any country or person who threatened their republican experiment. The differences between the two countries and between Americans and Englishmen were far less than either side would admit.[4]

Troubles in the old northwest—Michigan, Illinois, Ohio, Indiana, and Wisconsin—highlighted the difficulties between the two countries. Britain retained Canada as well as military posts in the northwest after the Revolutionary War, and it supported Native Americans, encouraging them to resist continued American expansion. The British government relied on Native Americans to serve as a buffer between the vulnerable Canadian colony to the north and the ever-expansive Americans. The Indian alliance also allowed Britain to allocate fewer regular troops to North America, which permitted the royal government to bolster other areas of the empire. In addition, friendship with Native Americans permitted Britain to retain strategic and economic control over important fur-trading lands to the south and west of the Great Lakes. Ultimately the alliance provided security as well as military and financial benefits to the Crown while simultaneously antagonizing and threatening the United States. This alliance helped provoke a lingering war between the Indians and the United States that was not settled until 1794. Although the Indians were defeated, during the next eighteen years they recovered from their setback and prepared for another possible conflict with the Americans. And, again, they anticipated that their British father, King George III, would support them in their struggle.[5]

After 1805 the threat of a Native American uprising on the northwestern frontier escalated as the tribes began to consolidate their forces, challenging the federal government's policy of expansion and ultimately transforming the northwest frontier into a powder keg on the verge of explosion. Indiana governor William Henry Harrison and Governor Return Jonathan Meigs of Ohio pleaded unsuccessfully to the War

Department for troops that would keep the Indians in check. Yet the War Department did not dispatch any immediate support.[6]

Meanwhile, Michigan governor William Hull encountered his own problems as he tried to protect Detroit from increased Indian raids. Hull, like Harrison, did not have enough troops to garrison Detroit and protect the outlying communities, so he decided to turn to the city's increasing black population. The number of runaway slaves arriving in Detroit and Michigan had been growing since the beginning of the nineteenth century because the Michigan Territory, as well as the other territories of the northwest, did not permit slavery. Proscribed by the U.S. Ordinance of 1787, this meant that the region offered a refuge for slaves fleeing from Upper Canada—the upper St. Lawrence River, or present-day southern Ontario. The institution of slavery had also been prohibited in Canada in 1793, but the provisions did not immediately apply to all of those held in bondage. As such, the Michigan Territory held the prospect of immediate freedom to those slaves in Canada, prompting many to risk their lives crossing the waters of the treacherous Detroit River. If they survived the crossing and walked ashore to freedom in Detroit, the ex-slaves unfortunately found few jobs and limited opportunities, as well as other difficulties.[7]

Hull discovered that of the increasing number of runaways coming to Detroit from Canada, many fled from "the most influential Inhabitants on the British shore." In 1795 slave William Kenny fled from then-British-controlled Detroit to the U.S. Ohio Territory, where he took up residence with one of the territorial judges. Kenny refused to return to Detroit and concluded a letter to his former British master Alexander McKee: "No More at Present But still remains Your Ob't Servant." The law of the Northwest Territory made Kenny a free resident of Ohio, but by 1804 the territorial assembly required that he and all other free blacks register with the government. The Ohio territorial government kept on file certificates of manumission for free blacks, which guaranteed their freedom. In an 1807 case, Canadian John Askin sent his fifteen-year-old slave George to Detroit on an errand, where he saw black men commanded by Peter Denison drilling in the town square. Denison then offered George a musket and the opportunity to join the black regiment; if George had accepted Denison's offer, it would have been a publicly defiant act against slavery in the free Michigan Territory. Ultimately, George refused, choosing to return to his master where in another ten years he was guaranteed his freedom under the gradual emancipation clause of Canadian law. By 1810, some 120 free blacks resided in Detroit, though it is impossible to determine how many had run away from British Canada. Even so, the stories of William Kenny and George reveal how the first Underground Railroad led south from British Canada to free American territories in the northwest United States. Only later in the nineteenth century did the northern-bound trail or Underground Railroad lead to Canada and freedom.[8]

The influx of runaways suppressed wages for unskilled laborers competing for the few jobs available in Detroit and the surrounding area. Rather than having idle indigents loitering about the city, during the fall of 1807 Governor Hull commissioned Peter Denison to enlist the runaways and a select group of local free blacks into an all-black militia company. Hull had learned that Anglo-American relations had hit rock bottom that summer because of the *Chesapeake-Leopard* Affair, giving the appearance of certain war. Acknowledging his lack of defenses, Hull took the only course of action available to him and armed blacks, but he created quite a controversy in doing so. British sympathizer James Askin reported to his brother Charles, a British soldier serving in Canada, that the Americans were preparing for war, that Detroit's defenses had been notably strengthened, and that the city also had "a Company of Negroes mounting guard." Apparently the black militia made an even more vivid impression on Lt. Col. I. Grant, the British commander at nearby Fort Amherstburg, who reported that the Americans had a company of thirty-six "Renegade Negroes kept for such desperate services as may be required at this side, they being well acquainted with it."[9]

The Anglo-American war scare subsided over the next several months, but the controversy that Hull had created with his black militia escalated in intensity on both sides of the Detroit River. Many influential Americans in the territory feared the presence of armed runaway Canadians residing in Michigan. A committee headed by territorial judge Augustus B. Woodward passed resolutions alleging that Hull had overstepped his authority. A petition also submitted to President Madison charged that the governor had taken action that was "extremely dishonourable to the Government on this side of the river; violates the feelings of the opposite side; . . . and eventually injures our own people, by exciting the others to retaliate in the same way." Demanding that Hull provide copies of all the military commissions he had issued, the legislature eventually concluded that "the conduct of the executive availing the country of the services of the black people, was not only proper, but highly commendable; especially as it was at a period when the safety and protection of the territory appeared to require, all the forces, which could be possibly collected."[10]

Although Denison's black company was disbanded after the 1807 crisis had passed, the dispute concerning the militia unit appeared repeatedly before the territorial legislature. During the summer of 1811 the legislature debated "the propriety of organizing a military company comprised of slaves that had run away" from Canada. Judge Woodward, who also served in the legislature, vehemently argued against Hull mustering fugitive slaves into the militia. A year later, when the country was on the verge of war, Hull issued militia commissions to Captain Denison, Lt. Ezra Burgess, and Ensign Bossett—all three black men. After learning of these enlistments, Judge Woodward instantly demanded that Hull address "two inconveniences" regarding slaves and the militia. He wanted to know under what authority Hull had granted the commissions and supplied the black militia with weapons, as well as how the governor could flagrantly encourage slaves from Canada to flee to the Michigan Territory. Hull maintained that once arriving, the runaways became free citizens of the Michigan Territory, and, like white citizens, they could bear arms in times of crisis. They would be needed when the United States declared war on Britain because Detroit would be among the first theater of operations.[11]

Although the causes of the War of 1812 were many, complicated, and debatable, Anglo-American relations had deteriorated progressively since 1783. The hated policy of impressing American sailors into the British navy and the onerous Orders in Council—a series of British decrees between 1783 and 1812 that restricted neutral trade—as well as the British presence in Canada and their support of the Native Americans further soured relations between the two countries. The United States had tried to avoid a war with Britain, and successive administrations had responded with a series of unsuccessful commercial acts—the Embargo, Non-Intercourse, and Non-Importation—that left the nation with only two alternatives: war against or submission to Great Britain. When the United States finally declared war on Britain on June 18, 1812, President James Madison did so with the desire to vindicate American sovereignty on land and sea and to uphold national honor.[12]

THEY "HAD THE GOOD FORTUNE TO BE IN THE BATTLE": FIGHTING IN THE NORTHWEST

African American participation in the war in the northwest was limited. There were no all-black American militia or regular army units in 1812 and 1813, and even individual presence, when noted, was poorly documented; the army had not opened its enlistments to black troops, and the states of Kentucky and Ohio, which provided the overwhelming majority of militia troops for the campaigns in this region, had not permitted blacks to muster. Moreover, the documentary record chronicling their service is fragmentary at best. In some instances a black soldier, slave, or servant made a brave or gallant contribution to the effort, which was then recorded for posterity. In others, casual references in diaries, letters, or reports are all we have. Regardless of the role that blacks played or whatever prominence they achieved, they sacrificed together with whites along the northwestern frontier and helped define the outcome of the struggle in that region.[13]

Governor, and General, Hull soon received orders from the Madison administration that informed him of the declaration of war and also determined his fate. Secretary of War William Eustis instructed Hull to "take possession of [Fort] Malden," which lay on the eastern (Canadian) side of the Detroit River some fifteen miles south of Detroit. Hull gathered his men, cautiously moved across the Detroit River, and prepared for the assault against Malden. He advanced with trepidation and ultimately delayed his attack because he did not have adequate carriages for his 24-pounders—the heavy guns that he thought necessary for a successful siege. Then, on July 28, news arrived in Detroit of the disaster from the north—the American loss at Mackinac. With this information, Hull returned to Detroit, freeing a number of slaves.[14]

Hull had lost the confidence of his men, and even the British began to ridicule his leadership. Gen. Isaac Brock took full advantage of the American general's anxiety and advanced his small British, Canadian, and Indian army toward Detroit. Brock also brazenly offered Hull the opportunity to surrender, playing on Hull's fears by warning the general that should a battle or "war of extermination begin," his Indian allies would "be beyond [his] controul [sic] the moment the contest commences." Although Hull initially refused to surrender, he understood Indian warfare. He also understood that since the Indians had joined in overwhelming numbers (estimates claimed at least two thousand warriors at Malden), they would commit unconscionable outrages against the entirety of the region. On August 16, Hull, believing he could limit future Indian depredations committed in the Michigan Territory, surrendered Fort Detroit and, ostensibly, the entire northwestern army. The British transported Hull, his officers, and the regulars as prisoners to Lower Canada (consisting of the lower St. Lawrence River Valley and the shores of the Gulf of St. Lawrence), while the volunteers and militia, including Peter Denison and his black compatriots, returned to their homes on parole until exchanged.[15]

During the summer of 1812 three of the six most important American forts in the northwest had fallen into British hands. These setbacks demonstrated the impotence of the initial American war effort and forecast greater disasters ahead. After Hull's defeat, command of the northwest fell to Gen. William Henry Harrison, who immediately mobilized troops—from Ohio, Indiana, Kentucky, western Pennsylvania, and Virginia—and prepared to invade Canada. As he awaited his chance to move north, Harrison launched a series of punitive expeditions against the hostile Indians, and he quickly moved to relieve Fort Wayne, which had been surrounded by them.[16]

Twenty-six-year-old African American Joseph Faudril was one of the black soldiers who found an opportunity at Fort Wayne. The five-feet-five-inch Faudril, who in December 1813 enlisted as a wagon maker in the First Infantry regiment, was most likely a free man, given his age and specialized trade. Regardless, he faithfully executed his duties and even undertook additional assignments. It may have been these extra jobs that won Faudril a leave of absence or the opportunity to return to his Kentucky home to retrieve his wife Elizabeth and their children. In any case, Faudril provides an interesting example of how free African Americans could find a place for themselves in a military society that valued contribution more than the color of an individual's skin.[17]

By the fall of 1812 Harrison had learned some disturbing information: runaway slaves were being lured to many of the Indian towns. During a December 17 attack against one such town on the Mississinewa River in northeastern Indiana, Harrison's soldiers killed eight Indians and "one big negroe [sic]" and captured forty or so Miamis, while countless other Indians and runaways fled. They learned that the small village was not a major Indian town, which they had expected, but instead was but one in a string of many small outposts. Black servant "Troy Waugh," who had accompanied Capt. William Garrard, survived the cold campaign against the Mississinewa without injury, only to suffer frostbite during the long, frigid retreat back to Ohio. Sgt. Greenberry Keen found a similar string of Indian villages during his wintry trip from Pittsburgh to Fort Stephenson on the Sandusky River, and he reported a "Negro Town where there are a n[umber] of Indiens [sic] and Negroes [who] all profess to be friendly."[18]

During late January 1813, Col. Henry Procter's large British and Indian contingent swept down on unprepared Americans at Frenchtown,

Michigan Territory. Within minutes the American defenses crumbled. Kentucky militiamen fled in panic, and the Indians followed in hot pursuit, brutally killing the soldiers in a scene of unparalleled carnage. Maj. George Madison surrendered the remnants of the American force, including his slave Peter Williams, who "had the good fortune to be in the battle and . . . [later] claimed all the indulgences due a veteran." Of the thousand-man force, only thirty-five Americans reached the safety of the Maumee Rapids; more than five hundred were taken prisoner, and some 350 were killed during the fight.[19]

Despite the American disaster, the real atrocity happened the following day when Indian guards broke into the town's liquor supply, became drunk, and started killing prisoners. They burned cabins and ruthlessly killed those trying to escape. The twenty to thirty survivors—including the slaves of Col. William Lewis and Capt. Nathaniel Hart, and Col. John Allen's slave Solomon—were either taken to Fort Amherstburg or distributed to various Indian villages. Some of these slaves were held in bondage, traded to other tribes as spoils of war, taken to Canada to be sold for profit, or ransomed from captivity. When the black and white prisoners came through Detroit some weeks later, Black Jim and one of trader John Kinzie's children "redeem[ed] a negro servant . . . with an old white horse," and the grateful slave Solomon "preferred returning to servitude." The slave Peter Williams had luckily survived the battle of Frenchtown and the River Raisin Massacre—an event that grew in infamy as the war progressed.[20]

Slaves experienced the same hardships and discomfort as white soldiers during the northwestern campaigns, and they confronted the same Indian and British enemy. Indians did not discriminate when they took prisoners; they captured black and white Americans alike, depriving the United States of valuable soldiers. The constant raids, the intense butchery, and the possibility of capture and enslavement terrified these American soldiers—even black slaves—who did not understand Indian culture. Throughout the spring and summer Harrison remained entrenched in Fort Meigs, protected from the horrors that many of these soldiers had already experienced at Frenchtown and on the River Raisin. They did not relish another terrifying adventure. Fortunately, by the end of the summer, the Americans had gained an advantage in the northwestern theater that would be further reinforced by Oliver Hazard Perry's September victory on Lake Erie. The war in the northwest, in which both blacks and whites had suffered intensely, was beginning to wind down.[21]

"NEITHER THEIR BLACK NOR RED
ALLIES ARE VERY POTENT NOR BRAVE":
WHITE ILLUSIONS ON THE NIAGARA FRONTIER

Americans along the frontier bounding the Niagara River had also confronted combined British and Indian enemies, fought savage engagements, and suffered serious setbacks in the northwest during late 1812
and early 1813. After quick offensive strikes by the Americans into the
heart of Canada, the conflict quickly bogged down into a war of attri-
tion, with each side trying to exhaust the other. American soldiers could
not seize Canadian territory and then maintain their foothold. Likewise,
British forces could not launch a sustained offensive campaign into the

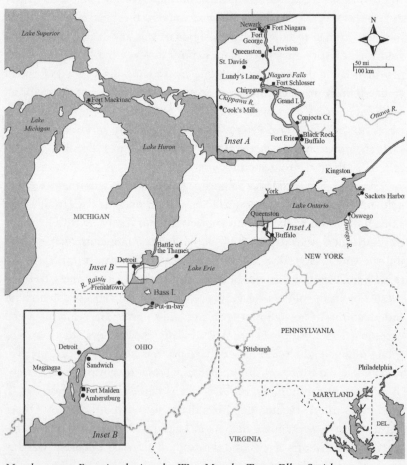

Northwestern Frontier during the War. Map by Tracy Ellen Smith.

United States until near the end of the war, and even then their plans did not proceed as expected. The Niagara campaign—through a narrow strip of land dominated by the turbulent Niagara River, separating Lakes Erie and Ontario and dividing Canada and the United States—stagnated into a nasty, brutal tug-of-war, with each side both winning and losing, but with neither side gaining the decisive advantage.

Gen. Isaac Brock, the victor of Detroit, found that British forces along the Niagara frontier consisted of only some 2,100 men, including regulars, militia, and warriors from the Grand River Iroquois, the Mississaugas, Delawares, and Ojibways. The Canadian legislature, at the request of black veteran Richard Pierpoint, had also created a militia company of black troops who wanted to "defend everything they called precious." Even so, the number of British soldiers paled in comparison to the 6,300 men available to American generals Stephen Van Rensselaer and Alexander Smyth on the opposite side of the Niagara River.[22]

On October 13 Van Rensselaer moved his forces by boat across the Niagara River toward the village of Queenston, which sat on a small plateau rising some 170 feet above the river. The Queenston Heights—a massive ridge where the Niagara River breaks through the Niagara Escarpment—towered over the village, defined the region, and offered Brock's British army numerous defensive options. Brock had also enhanced the natural features of the site by constructing a redan (a V-shaped earthen breastwork) on the upper slopes of the heights and arming it with cannon, which allowed this position to command the river below. Landing on a protected or sheltered beach area directly below the heights, Van Rensselaer's army took an obscured fisherman's path that ran from the beach up to the Heights, ending some ninety feet above the British redan. Within minutes, three companies of American soldiers made the perilous climb and found themselves some thirty yards behind Brock's position. Then suddenly the Americans swarmed down the hill, mortally wounding Brock in the chest as they approached. Then, as Lt. Col. Winfield Scott's Americans entrenched themselves on the heights, British troops evacuated Queenston and reorganized their defenses a mile downstream. Meanwhile, a British relief force from nearby Fort George, which included regulars and militia, Indians, and thirty-eight blacks of Gen. Roger Sheaffe's "Coloured Corps," were making their way toward the Heights.[23]

The Canadian "Coloured Corps," organized and commanded by white captain Robert Runchey, had been recruited from Niagara, York, St. Davids, St. Catherine, and the Bay of Quinte District after the declaration of war. The all-black segregated company also had volunteers from several other militia regiments, including Sgt. William Thompson and thirteen men who chose to transfer from the 3rd Regiment of York Militia. Yet some Americans believed that these "companies of Negroes" were actually "runaways from Kentucky, and other states, who are commanded by white men."

These black soldiers volunteered as provisional or incorporated militia—unlike the normal Canadian sedentary militia units where all adult males were required to serve at all times—and enlisted only for the duration of the war. After the initial crisis at Queenston, the British relegated the Coloured Corps to a labor company, where they received between four and five times as much pay as their regular militia compatriots. By the end of the war they had been attached to the Quartermaster General's Department. Given the salaries, financial incentives, and terms of enlistment, it was not surprising that these blacks willingly enlisted in the Canadian units. Obviously they saw military service as a means to enhance their well-being and as a way to create a better life.[24]

The British uphill counterattack against Scott's partially entrenched American soldiers represented the battle's turning point. Sheaffe sent his regulars against the American left while the militia, Indians, and Coloured Corps moved against Scott's right. The Indians gave war-whoops and screams, which terrified the Americans, while the blacks "advanced in gallant style, delivered a volley, and then charged, driving in the American right at the point of the bayonet." The British attack immediately overwhelmed Scott's command, and the Americans retreated toward the cliffs and river. Some of Scott's soldiers panicked, jumping to their deaths or drowning while trying to cross the river rather than letting themselves be captured by the Indians. Scott, meanwhile, surrendered. The battle of Queenston was over.[25]

Gen. Henry Dearborn, the former secretary of war who subsequently assumed command of the northern theater after the Queenston disaster, wanted to de-emphasize the Niagara region, sever British supply and communication routes further down the St. Lawrence River, and focus Cdre. Isaac Chauncey's operations on Lake Ontario. Chauncey, who had constantly complained to the Navy Department about his shortage of seamen, welcomed the opportunity and gladly accepted any black or white sailor willing to sign aboard his ships. He enlisted a considerable number of African Americans, who he later boasted were "not surpassed by any seamen we have in the fleet." His frigate *General Pike* had "nearly 50 Blacks on board . . . and [Chauncey reported that] many of them are amongst my best men." That number represented about 17 percent of the frigate's crew, excluding marines. Ned Meyers, later made famous by author James Fenimore Cooper, reported that five blacks served with his gun crew aboard the *Scourge,* and that all five, as well as three other African Americans, had drowned when the gunboat capsized in early August 1813. Regardless, Chauncey had obviously come to rely on black sailors, admitting "that the Colour of the skin" did not "affect a man's qualifications or usefulness."[26]

The April 27, 1813, American attack against York had both positive and negative consequences. Chauncey's flotilla transferred Gen. Zebulon Pike's soldiers across the lake and executed a successful joint army-navy amphibious operation against York, the capital of Upper Canada and an important dockyard on the north shore of Lake Ontario. During the landing, Pike's soldiers encountered some opposition from the Glengarry Light Infantry Fencible Regiment, a unit composed of "runaway sailors, English, Irish, Dutch, Americans, Canadians, and a sprinkling of Africans." Even so, Pike's soldiers easily entered the town and raised the Stars and Stripes because the British main force had already evacuated. It was the first significant American victory of the war, but it had been a costly conquest because almost all of the British army escaped capture. Also, more than two hundred Americans had been killed—including General Pike—and wounded when the British detonated their main magazine. In retaliation, gangs of American soldiers, sailors, and sympathizers plundered, looted and burned the town and wreaked havoc on the surrounding countryside, an important omen for the future.[27]

Secretary of War John Armstrong and General Dearborn had believed that a successful attack against York would force the British to send a relief column from Fort George to retake the capital. Chauncey could then transport the men via ship from York to the Niagara Peninsula, where they would join with Dearborn's army to sweep through the region. In fact, after the May 1813 American capture of Fort George, one officer wrote to the editors of the Baltimore *Whig* that "their Indians are not of much use to them. They run as soon as the battle grows hot. I saw but one of their Indians and one negro (with the [distinctive] Glengarry uniform) dead on the field, a proof that neither their black nor red allies are very potent nor brave." While the commentator publicly discredited the British and their allies, many served admirably, including former slave John Baker, who had been brought to Canada after the American Revolution. Baker served with the New Brunswick–raised 104th Foot, was wounded during the fighting at Sackets Harbor, and was later fought at Lundy's Lane, Chippewa, and in Europe at the Battle of Waterloo, dying in January 1871 at the age of ninety-three. Also, the British attached to every infantry battalion a unit of ten men who were usually given all construction-related tasks, and blacks comprised the entire unit of the 104th Foot.[28]

The American invasion of Canada eventually stalled at Fort George. The British army—including Runchey's Coloured Corps—quickly besieged the fort, successfully preventing the Americans from invading deeper into the Niagara Peninsula. Black Canadian troops contributed greatly to these British operations in the Niagara region, serving in virtually every engagement during 1812 and 1813. Along with Native Americans and militia, black soldiers provided the necessary manpower that permitted Britain to withstand repeated American onslaughts and hold on to Canada. Without being able to drive deeper into Canada during 1813, American forces eventually evacuated Fort George, destroying much of the previously captured military material as well as the town of Newark. This indiscriminate destruction of Newark prompted the British to retaliate by cutting a swath of destruction through New York, as British forces burned and pillaged Youngstown, Lewiston, Manchester, and Buffalo. The 1813 war in the Niagara region had ended on a less than satisfactory note for the Americans.[29]

"A MOTLEY SET, BLACKS, SOLDIERS, AND BOYS": LAKE ERIE AND THE WAR IN THE NORTHWEST

When the War of 1812 had begun, Oliver Hazard Perry commanded a small flotilla of gunboats at Newport, Rhode Island, but he desperately wanted a more active station. Unfortunately, a shortage of seagoing ships, an abundance of naval officers, and the British blockade of the American coastline prevented aggressive junior officers such as Perry from serving as they wished. Yet as the tempo of the war increased during the fall of 1812, Perry learned of an opportunity for another assignment. The newly promoted Master Commandant specifically requested a transfer to the Lakes and willingly offered the services of "fifty or sixty men . . . who are remarkably strong and active"; among those Perry volunteered were several black seamen, including Newport Hazard and a freed slave from Newport named Hannibal Collins. Perry and his men arrived on Lake Erie in late March.[30]

The failed military operations during the fall of 1812 had forced the U.S. government to focus new energy on the Lakes, especially Lake Erie, and Perry's appointment indicated the importance of the forthcoming campaign season. He was instructed to oversee ship construction at Erie, Pennsylvania, and to ensure that the vessels, essential for gaining control over the lake, would be ready by the beginning of June 1813 to assist the army with its invasion of Canada. Despite the dreadful hardships associated with carving a fleet out of the remote Pennsylvania wilderness, by mid-July Perry had somehow launched an eleven-ship squadron. Yet he needed men to put the ships in action.[31]

Perry experienced great difficultly securing the men he needed for his ships. Isaac Chauncey had refused to transfer sailors because he wanted first to eliminate the British presence on Lake Ontario before concentrating operations on Erie. Finally, sixty men arrived in mid-July and another fifty-five by the end of the month. Although Perry was happy "to see any thing in the shape of a man," he was frustrated with the perceived quality of sailors Chauncey had sent. They were, he angrily penned, "a motley set, blacks, Soldiers, and boys," and Perry imprudently questioned whether Chauncey had supervised their selection. Already incensed that Perry had gone over his head and corresponded directly with the Navy Department to secure a separate command on Lake Erie, Chauncey curtly informed him that "a part of them are not surpassed by any seamen we have in the fleet." He also retorted that he had "yet to learn that the Colour of the skin, or cut and trimmings of the coat, can affect a man's qualifications or usefullness." Disregarding their race, Chauncey claimed he had fifty blacks aboard his flagship, and that the soldiers had between two and seventeen years of experience at sea. They were "excellent seamen," many of whom Chauncey insisted were "amongst my best men," and Perry would soon find them "as good and useful as any men on board [his] vessel."[32]

Perry was not assuaged by Chauncey's tactful verbiage, but he was calculating enough to understand the diplomatic purpose. Even so, he carefully chose his own words as he asked the secretary of the navy for another duty assignment, and he further criticized Chauncey and the men he had sent. The sailors may "be as good as they are on the other Lake," Perry mocked, "but if so, that squadron must be poorly manned indeed." Chauncey had already admitted that he had fifty fine blacks aboard the *General Pike*. If so, the quandary Perry publicly acknowledged was not a racial one, but rather that Chauncey, whether knowingly or not, had transferred the dregs of his squadron to Lake Erie and kept his best veteran seamen for his own ships. It seemed blatantly obvious to many that Chauncey had ridded himself of his sick, inexperienced, and undisciplined men and forced Perry to deal with them. On Lake Erie, Sailing Master William Taylor observed that many of the men who arrived from Lake Ontario "were barely able to assist themselves," while purser Samuel Hambleton griped that the men sent "consisted principally of the refuse of Commodore Chauncey's fleet."[33]

The turning point in the struggle for Lake Erie occurred during the early fall of 1813. For some three-and-a-half hours on September 10, Perry's nine vessels carrying fifty-four guns confronted and battled Robert Heriott Barclay's British squadron of six ships for control of the lake. The American fleet had superior firepower over the British, including an almost 2–1 advantage in weight of broadside. During the engagement, fought near Put-in-Bay, Ohio, Perry decided to take the initiative and close on the enemy. At a critical stage during the battle when his flagship *Lawrence* appeared to be lost, Perry hauled down the ship's flags, jumped into a small boat—in one of which freeman Hannibal Collins manned an oar—and transferred his command to the sister ship *Niagara*. Shortly

Oliver Hazard Perry's Victory on Lake Erie. "Perry's Victory," painted by William Henry Powell of Cincinnati in 1865, illustrates the American victory over the British fleet in the September 1813 Battle of Lake Erie. Among the sailors rowing Oliver Hazard Perry's boat was Hannibal Collins, a black man depicted in the background with his arm raised near the bow. Courtesy of the Ohio Historical Society.

thereafter the undamaged *Niagara,* with its complement of gunboats, had broken the British line of battle, forced the enemy squadron to surrender, and effectively destroyed the British threat on Lake Erie. The battle for the lake had ended, and the balance of power in the northwest had unquestionably shifted to the United States.[34]

Perry's choice to close on the enemy during the battle resulted in the destruction of his flagship as well as high casualties—80 percent of his crew aboard the flagship *Lawrence* either died or were wounded. Seamen Newport Hazard and Jesse Williams were both wounded while aboard the flagship, and in 1820 the state of Pennsylvania awarded Williams a silver medal for his services during the battle. Fifer Jesse Walls and seaman Isaac Hardy both died during the engagement; Hardy's wife Diane later secured his pension by proving their marriage with a certificate signed by the pastor of the First Presbyterian African Congregation in Philadelphia. Shipboy Jack Russell—who was either a slave, an indentured servant, or an apprentice—served aboard Perry's flagship and later turned over his prize money to his master George Mason. Salem, Massachusetts, native Anthony Williams survived the battle, dying as an old man during the 1830s.[35]

Cyrus Tiffany was one of the most noticeable African American seamen in Perry's crew. "Old Tiffany," as he was affectionately called, was Perry's personal servant as well as an excellent fifer, an instrument that he had reportedly played for George Washington. On the day of the battle Perry armed Tiffany, placed him on the berth deck of the *Lawrence,* and instructed him to force up to the main deck everyone skirting their duty. Perry knew that this assignment would keep his favorite servant out of harm's way and most likely save his life. Even so, during the heat of battle the overzealous Tiffany allowed the berth deck hatchway to become crowded with the wounded he would not permit below, condemning them as skulkers. Tiffany, one of the few aboard the *Lawrence* who did not die or suffer injury during the engagement, remained at his commodore's side until Perry's death in 1819.[36]

There were far more African American sailors among Perry's crew than the few mentioned above—an estimated 10 to 20 percent of his sailors were black. The exact number will probably never be accurately determined, even though historians have carefully scrutinized the returns from the battle, the muster and payrolls, as well as the prize lists for Perry's crew. In 1862 Dr. Usher Parsons, who was one of Perry's surgeons, recalled that in 1814 "about one in ten or twelve of the crews were blacks," which only represented 8 to 10 percent. Perry noted that blacks "formed a considerable part of his crew," and he praised them, claiming that they "seemed to be absolutely insensible to danger." He also recalled that when Captain Barclay came aboard the *Niagara* and saw the "sickly and partly-colored beings around him, an expression of chagrin escaped him at having been conquered by such men." Regardless of how many actually participated in the battle, a sizable number of blacks made valiant contributions to a victory that changed the course of the war in the northwest.[37]

Later on the afternoon of September 10, Perry drafted a short message to General Harrison: "We have met the enemy and they are ours." Those words, which have become some of the most famous in American military history, underlie important consequences for the war in the northwest. Now, with unquestioned control over Lake Erie, Harrison's army was able to retake Detroit without a fight since the British could not keep open communication and supply routes to the west. By September 27, 1813, British regulars and their Indian allies evacuated Detroit and Amherstburg and moved into Upper Canada. Eight days later General Harrison's force caught up with now Gen. Henry Procter's retreating British army—500 Indians and some 450 regulars—about two miles from Moraviantown, on the Thames River fifty miles east of Detroit. Immediately attacking, angry mounted Kentuckians screamed "Remember the Raisin!" while American regulars and militia methodically drove the Indians into the swamp on the left of the battlefield. Within a few minutes the Battle of the Thames was over as the British soldiers surrendered and the Indians melted into the swamp after hearing that their famed leader Tecumseh had been killed.[38]

The combined naval and military campaigns on Lake Erie and along the Thames decided the war in the northwest for the Americans and shattered Tecumseh's fragile Indian confederation, which had been confronting American expansion for some two decades. Nearly all campaigning in the region stopped as many of Harrison's troops were transferred east to assist in the Niagara operations. Also, the redeployment of Harrison's troops forced the army to raise new regiments for the northwest, including the 2nd U.S. Rifle Regiment; in July 1814, black musician Samuel Looks, who enlisted in the regiment at Chillicothe, Ohio, remained with the army for the duration of the war, but he did not see any combat.[39]

Even without capturing Mackinac, the war in the northwest had been a success, and it had highlighted the services of African Americans during the struggle. Perry had complained prior to the Battle of Lake Erie of having "a motley set, blacks, soldiers, and boys," but after his victory he praised these same men, claiming that the blacks "seemed to be absolutely insensible to danger." Perry's attitude concerning his black sailors reflects the opinions of many others concerning African American participation during the struggle; blacks were deemed unacceptable as combatants except during times of crisis. Yet once they demonstrated their bravery, ability, and loyalty, commanders had to acknowledge and reward their services. During the struggle for the northwest the "motley" blacks unquestionably demonstrated their bravery. Unfortunately, their efforts took place along an isolated frontier where few took notice of their participation.[40]

"[U]TTERLY INSENSIBLE TO DANGER": THE MARITIME WORLD IN BLACK AND WHITE

Blacks had been part of both the American and British merchant service and the Royal Navy since the early colonial period. The low pay as well as the harsh and dangerous life of the sea likely did not attract enough people, and shipowners had always recruited all able-bodied men to fill the needs of an extensive maritime establishment. Ships had traditionally recruited from many nations, including Africa, Asia, Europe, and North America. The conditions bound men closely together: although seamen differed not only in race but also in tradition and religion, their shipboard culture was homogenous; the ship represented a kingdom of its own, and the seamen were citizens of their captain-king. There, possibilities were endless on the oceans and seas. Still, significant numbers of seamen were always discharged or deserted in foreign ports, especially in America, where they believed they could find a better life. Since U.S. naval officers recruited most of their sailors from the merchant service, they inevitably enlisted men of all races and nationalities who had served together.[41]

Between 1800 and 1812 American merchantmen carried more than 90 percent of the country's growing imports and exports. Ships flying the Stars and Stripes frequented virtually every harbor in the world, and only Britain could boast more merchant ships than the United States. With only seventeen American seagoing warships, the availability of so many American-flagged merchant vessels provided abundant opportunity for black sailors to function on the fringes of white society and avoid the overt racism and bigotry of the landed world. They seized the opportunity and signed aboard ships in droves. During the period 1800–20, for example, Philadelphia-area blacks held 17 to 22 percent of seafaring jobs, even though they made up only some 5 percent of the region's population. Meanwhile in Providence, Rhode Island, they held some 20 percent of the ships' berths, even though they composed 8.5 percent of the city's population and only 4 percent of the state's population. Likewise in New York, Boston, and Baltimore, black men, and an occasional woman, stepped in to fill the perpetual shortage of needed sailors.[42]

During 1798 both the secretary of the navy and the secretary of war had barred black enlistments in the U.S. Navy and Marine Corps. But once the War of 1812 began and the conflict spread to the northern lakes and the oceans of the world, the U.S. government, privateers (private persons or ships authorized by governments to attack foreign shipping during wartime), and merchantmen all found themselves short of sailors, creating new opportunities for black mariners. The number of black enlistees in the U.S. Navy increased substantially. Despite the need for able-bodied soldiers, in late November 1812 Secretary of the Navy Paul Hamilton instructed commanders to "give the recruiting officer orders to enter none but white able bodied Citizens." A few months later, in March 1813, Congress passed an act prohibiting the employment of any "persons of color" aboard any public ship. Even so, recruiting officers still looked for warm bodies to fill their ships' allotment of crewmen, and blacks peppered the ranks.[43]

Blacks serving aboard U.S. naval vessels and privateers constituted between 10 and 20 percent of the crews of both. American naval officers circumvented regulations and listed men on warships' muster rolls according to their maritime talent, rather than by the color of their skin. While the exact number of black sailors in the navy remains unclear, reportedly the number serving aboard the U.S.S. *Constitution* consisted of 15–20 percent of the crew. After the *Constitution*'s brazen August 1812 victory over H.M.S. *Guerriere,* Capt. Isaac Hull reported in a salty tone that he "never had any better fighters than those niggers, they stripped to the waist and fought like devils, . . . utterly insensible to danger and to be possessed with the determination to outfight the white sailors." When *Constitution* took the British frigate *Java* a few months later, in December 1812, the Americans liberated a black New Yorker named John Freeman; the British had forced Freeman into service in late October 1812, but after the American victory he joined the crew of the *Constitution.* Existing records indicate that blacks comprised some 33 percent of the 1,011 sailors exiting the Royal Navy during the war, and approximately 30 percent of 221 impressed sailors who chose to go to prison rather than serve in the British navy. In effect, the naval and maritime world was in black and white, though few at the time denoted the gradations of color.[44]

On June 1, 1813, Capt. James Lawrence of the U.S.S. *Chesapeake* foolishly engaged the British frigate *Shannon* off Boston. Days before the battle, Lawrence had mustered his crew on deck and had given an impassioned speech, trying to restore the confidence and morale of his multinational force. Using a bugle as a vivid and rousing symbol, he called for a volunteer to blow the instrument in case the British boarded the ship during the battle. Swept up in the emotion of the moment, black seaman William Brown proudly and immediately stepped forward for this important duty. Yet Brown did not know how to blow the bugle, and Lawrence had not verified that he could perform this important act. During the short-lived fifteen-minute engagement British marines quickly swept aboard the *Chesapeake*. Caught up in fighting, Brown failed to blow the bugle. Many of the crew also cowered below decks when the fighting began, providing little resistance to the British boarding party who easily took the ship. Lawrence lost his life in the battle. For his failure, William Brown was later charged with cowardice and neglect of duty. A court-martial ultimately sentenced him to forfeit his pay and receive three hundred lashes with the cat-o-nine-tails. President James Madison later commuted Brown's sentence to only one hundred lashes. Nonetheless, William Brown became a scapegoat for Captain Lawrence's impetuous attack, proving undoubtedly that blame as well as patriotism frequently crossed color lines.[45]

The crews of many merchant and whaling ships also included a surprising number of black seamen. Along the coast of North Carolina during the war, slave Moses Grandy hired himself out on canal boats when the British blockaded the Chesapeake Bay. He provisioned and hired boats and crews and even kept the books, with his master James Grandy receiving an annual fee. Moses did not choose to flee to the British because he had considerable liberty to make choices and earn money, which eventually helped him legally secure his freedom. While transporting goods through the Dismal Swamp Canal, Grandy encountered runaway slaves working beyond the fringes of white society. In Norfolk, he navigated a maritime world where blacks worked in almost every occupation, including as carpenters, blacksmiths, sailmakers, caulkers, and ropemakers. Their labor greased the skids of the Atlantic maritime world, ensuring that ships could go to sea and that whites continued to make a profit. Blacks became so intertwined with this world that they could easily move into multiple maritime professions. A few years after the war, even the Fredericksburg overseer of the poor bound the young black boy "Moses" to a ship so he could learn to be a mariner and have a gainful occupation.[46]

Slaves also served aboard merchant ships, and occasionally they comprised a ship's entire crew, as they were more cost effective to employ than traditional sailors. In December 1813 the all-black crew of the *Patty* successfully navigated increased British presence during a cruise between Philadelphia and Puerto Rico. During the fall of 1814 and the early months of 1815, three ships sailed from New Orleans to Pensacola with all-slave crews, and their capture could have possibly brought freedom or impressment aboard a British ship for the slaves. In fact, slaves shipped out of every American port, although ports further north had fewer slave crew members. The one northern exception was Philadelphia, where more slaves were enlisted because the "City of Brotherly Love" was the nation's most active seaport.[47]

Black sailors had few opportunities to rise through the ranks. They were frequently relegated to working as seamen and cooks and only occasionally as coopers and carpenters. At the same time, an especially fortunate, smart, and hard-working black man might eventually become a ship's captain, as did free blacks Paul Cuffee, Richard Johnson, Pardon Cook, and later William A. Leidesdorff. In fact, sea service became a family tradition for Cuffee and his New Bedford, Massachusetts, dynasty of sons, sons-in-law, grandsons, nephews, and various other relatives. Some of these captains even owned ships and recruited all-black crews themselves.[48]

Although it is difficult to determine the exact numbers of black seamen during the era, a congressional action at the end of the eighteenth century made the process easier for historians. In 1796 Congress passed the "Act for the Relief and Protection of American Seamen" in an effort to protect American mariners against British impressments. Passed after officers of H.M.S. *Regulus* boarded the American merchantman *Lydia* and took five men whom they said were British citizens, the law required all American seamen to carry protection papers (proof of their citizenship). The law also required each district collector of customs to maintain lists of those seamen who presented validated proof of their U.S. citizenship. Granted, not every merchant and whaling captain required their crew members to carry protection papers, but the certificates nonetheless were a godsend to black seamen trying desperately to avoid the institution of slavery.[49]

Blacks who possessed such documentation could also use them as free papers because they had been issued by government officials, and they carried a description of the holder. Frequently they made reference to tattoos, clear evidence that the individual was a seafaring man; rarely did members of the general public adorn themselves with tattoos. When the printed description did not match the individual, American customs officials seized the document. Yet many descriptions were so broad and vague that nearly anyone could use them. Counterfeit papers could also be easily obtained, even though there was no way to determine if these forgeries could pass inspection every time in each port. Unfortunately for black and white sailors alike, protection papers did not offer the perfect method for avoiding impressment.[50]

During the period 1812–15, a group of eight hundred Philadelphia seamen registered for papers, including some 140 blacks, or about 18 percent of the total number. Prior to 1812, black sailors shipping out of Philadelphia represented only about 10 percent of the total crews. During the war, the number of black seamen almost doubled. The average black sailor was twenty-four years old, approximately five feet, seven inches in height, and had few tattoos. They appeared to have about the same literacy rate as their white shipmates, and a large proportion of those who obtained certificates in Philadelphia had been born in Maryland and Delaware, suggesting that many of these men may have been runaway slaves trying to use the certificates as proof of freedom.[51]

The U.S. Navy faced more difficulty recruiting full complements of sailors for their vessels than did privateers or merchantmen. Privateer tours generally lasted two to three months, whereas navy tours were at least twelve and occasionally twenty-four months. Privateers won a portion of the prizes they took, and even after the federal government taxed the captured prizes, sailors received considerably more compensation than was paid to naval seamen. While seamen serving in the navy also shared in prize money from ships they captured, they experienced far fewer of these opportunities. The U.S. Navy also transferred men from duty on the high seas to ships on the harsh, wintry stations of the Great Lakes and Lake Champlain, which resulted in many desertions. Finally, sailors believed privateer service to be less dangerous, even though many still found themselves languishing in British prison camps until well after the end of the war.[52]

Following the February 1813 victory of the American warship *Hornet* against the British sloop-of-war *Peacock* off Guyana, the triumphant crew attended a theater performance in New York City in honor of their bravery in battle. The crew "marched *together* into the pit, and nearly one half of them were negroes." A former runaway slave named Bob, or "Old Peacock," celebrated the occasion despite his legal status and reportedly received a quarter section of land for his service after the war. Whether the black mariners were slaves or free did not matter as long as they had defeated the British, and in that particular engagement and celebration, patriotism trumped color.[53]

In October 1812 Stephen Decatur's frigate *United States* slipped out to sea, and the captain went aboard the privateer *Ariadne* because of rumors of a mutiny. Apparently he took six ringleaders in chains aboard the American frigate. Yet one of the most impertinent of the group had not been removed—the cook, "a stout Negro fellow," had abused the captain and mates and continued to dish out insubordination. When an officer and crew from the privateer *Yankee* later went aboard the *Ariadne,* the cook aggressively chastised them, referring to them as "pirates and villains." Ultimately the black cook was tied to the ship's windlass, and each of the *Yankee*'s boat crew gave him twelve lashes for his impertinence.[54]

During the afternoon of Christmas Day 1812, a squall suddenly struck Cmdr. Nathaniel Shaler's privateer *Gov. Tompkins* from the north. Then a large British frigate began bearing down on the privateer. While trying to get his light canvass up and make sail, he suffered a broadside from the British ship that killed two men and wounded six others. "The name of one of my poor fellows who was killed ought to be registered in the book of fame, and remembered with reverence as long as bravery is considered a virtue. He was a black man, by the name of John Johnson." Shaler described how a 24-pound shot struck Johnson's hip, taking away all the lower part of his body. Even so, the "the poor brave fellow lay on the deck," constantly extolling his shipmates, "*Fire away boys, neber haul de colour down!*" The second casualty, John Davis, was also a black man, and he died in much the same manner. Shaler recalled how Davis fell near him and several times pleaded to be thrown overboard because he was in the way of his fellow sailors. From the gallant service of his two brave tars, Shaler could only conclude, "While America has such sailors, she has little to fear from the tyrants of the ocean."[55]

British privateers also carried black sailors. During early November 1812, a U.S. naval officer reported that an armed British privateer had been cruising between Savannah and Charleston, "mand [sic] Chiefly with Blacks about 70 in number" and causing mischief. A year later, during the fall of 1813, off the coast of North Carolina, the British privateer *Mars* sent small boats inland to pursue two unarmed American coasters near New Inlet. As one of the small boats strayed too close to shore, it unfortunately became stuck on a sandbar, permitting North Carolina militia to wade out and capture the raiding party, which included thirteen black sailors who would be held as British prisoners of war. In July 1813 a black man named George Mitchell went ashore in northern Virginia, claiming to be "a free man from New York" impressed by the British in 1806. Even though he maintained his free status, he learned that going ashore in a slave territory could lead to a more precarious situation. Mitchell would be imprisoned, and the question arose: Would captured blacks be prisoners or prizes of war?[56]

When captured off a southern U.S. port, the question of black seamen's status proved perilous. During the spring of 1814, for example, the American privateer *Midas* captured the British privateer *Dash* and took the vessel into port at Savannah. Among the British crew were nineteen freemen and twenty-two slaves, whom the *Midas*'s crew wanted to claim as spoils of war. The owners of the American ship asserted that the slaves were property that had been seized and not, they argued, prisoners of war who should be exchanged with the British. Despite the owners' position, the slaves were finally handed over to British officials—in some cases more than two years later (late June 1816). The debate over property rights, slave restitution, and spoils of war continued to work its way through Congress and diplomatic channels for years to come.

Conversely, slaves captured near northern free states did not suffer the same trials and tribulations. During May 1813 the American privateer *Holkar* captured a British privateer off New London, with "sixteen negroes" aboard. And although the privateer's owners claimed that they were private property, the American captain took them into port and turned them over as prisoners of war without further discussion. Black British mariners obviously found that their location on the Atlantic greatly determined their future prospects and possibilities of freedom.[57]

Most blacks navigating the maritime world did not lead or participate in a slave insurrection or even use the sea to escape bondage. Virtually all did use service aboard merchant or naval vessels or aboard privateers to broaden their sense of self and further denote the constraints of their status. The War of 1812 hastened opportunities for blacks to solidify their individual status, regardless of whether they remained entrenched in their maritime environment or they embraced opportunities within the broader British Empire.[58]

FEW AFRICAN AMERICANS PARTICIPATED in the northern land war. When they participated, both sides took advantage of their willingness to fight. Prior to the war Michigan territorial governor William Hull offered freedom to runaway Canadian slaves by enlisting them in an all-black militia unit, arming them with weapons, and giving them a reason—their continued freedom—to defend the United States. They remained in the Michigan militia until the fall of Detroit during 1812. Once the war began, both sides found reasons to arm any individual for defense, be he red, black, or white.

Since Canada had only a scant number of regular troops, British commanders relied extensively on their experienced Indian allies, as well as on the few blacks who enlisted within their units. Capt. Robert Runchey's "Coloured Corps," which consisted of blacks from throughout Upper Canada, supported the weakened British units at the Battle of Queenston early in the war, making a notable contribution. Other black soldiers participated with infantry and labor units in the Niagara campaigns of 1813. Even though the U.S. Army did not open its ranks to African Americans until the last full year of the war, black servants, waiters, aides, and sometimes soldiers still participated in all of the land campaigns in the north. African Americans also served aboard the country's naval vessels and gained recognition because, as Perry noted, they were "absolutely insensible to danger."[59]

The presence of blacks in the maritime world, whether serving on privateers on the high seas, enlisting aboard U.S. seagoing ships, or serving with Chauncey or Perry on the Great Lakes, shaped the outcome of the war. The desperate need for men aboard British and American ships and privateers opened doors for blacks to prove their loyalty and bravery while also permitting them to earn a living in a racially bicolored world. As the war continued, it provided African Americans more opportunities to prove their mettle and ability as sailors and soldiers.

CHAPTER 3

THE FLORIDA PATRIOT WAR OF 1812

"For freedom we want and will have"

Prince Witten, born Principe Huiten about 1756 in South Carolina, escaped from Georgia to Spanish St. Augustine sometime around 1786, after several previously failed attempts. The "talkative," six-feet-tall, "strong built and brawny" carpenter brought along his wife Judy Kenty—a "smart, active [house] wench"—and their children, eight-year-old Glasgow—"a well looking boy of an open countenance and obliging disposition"—and six-year-old Polly—who had "lively eyes and pitted with the small pox." Georgia assemblyman Lt. Col. Jacob Weed, who owned Prince, had made arrangements to return the slave's family to their former Loyalist owners, who had relocated to the Bahamas. Weed suggested that Prince had secreted his family away "to Florida to avoid a separation from his family to which he is much attached." Once there, Prince hired himself out to Minorcan Francisco Pellicer and worked as a carpenter for a number of prominent officials.[1]

Working so close to the Georgia border proved dangerous for former slaves. Colonel Weed reportedly learned of Prince's location and promised to cross the border and take him and his family by force if necessary. Such a possibility proved too distinct for the Wittens, and the family moved to St. Augustine. Shortly thereafter Prince signed a new work contract with Jayme McGirtt on his North River plantation, which stipulated that his wife Judy would cook and perform domestic work. Yet when McGirtt sent Judy into the field to work, Prince took him to court for violating their contract. Stating that "he could not permit" Judy to do field labor, Prince requested and was granted his release from the contract, as well as the wages for his thirty-eight weeks of work. Fortunately, skilled carpenters such as Prince were in short supply in St. Augustine, and this meant that he never had trouble securing a job. Additionally, his workmanship permitted Prince to demand reasonably high wages; high enough, in fact, that he invested some of his money, ironically, in slaves.[2]

Living with his family in a rented St. Augustine home in 1795, Prince petitioned Governor Quesada for land north of the city. The entrepreneur wanted to build a house for his family and the city's other free blacks, and to cut timber to construct those structures. Governor Quesada agreed, but the 1795 American invasion forced the Spanish to recall all settlers outside of St. Augustine back into the city. After the crisis had passed, Prince asked the governor for land south of the city that he intended to farm, and again the governor granted his request; Spanish officials understood that free black communities outside of St. Augustine strengthened their control over the area and also vested black homesteaders in maintaining the status quo.[3]

The Spanish also co-opted black males into performing military service for the poorly defended and remote colony. While serving in the free black militia, Prince gained a reputation for outstanding service during an American invasion in 1795, achieving the rank of sergeant, the highest rank allowed for black local militiamen in Florida. Moreover, free blacks further entrenched themselves into the community through church membership, marriage, and godparentage; Prince formally married Judy in the Catholic Church after a twenty-one-year union, taking the name Juan Bautista "Prince" Witten; Judy became María Rafaela, while Glasgow took the name Francisco, and Polly the name Rafaela. In April 1796 young Rafaela married Jorge Jacobo, the military heir and brother-in-law to St. Domingue general Jorge Biassou, thereby linking the most important local military family to the leading family of the Black Auxiliaries of Charles IV.[4]

With General Biassou's death in 1801, Jacobo took command of Florida's black militia, and his father-in-law Prince Witten served as one of his captains. Thereafter, whether fighting against French-inspired

Georgia marauders, William Augustus Bowles's Indian supporters, the "Patriots," or American troops, the native-born Prince distinguished himself, winning accolades from his Spanish rulers and disdain and contempt from his American enemies. Prince commanded the local black militia when they won the most important engagement of the Patriot War in September 1812, and by doing so, he achieved the unique distinction of becoming a black officer. But unfortunately, the local accolades won by Prince could not alter the changing geopolitics of the Gulf Coast.

"NEGROES, WHO ARE THEIR BEST SOLDIERS": FLORIDA'S PATRIOT WAR

In April 1791 American Secretary of State Thomas Jefferson reported to President George Washington that Spanish governor Quesada had invited Americans to settle in East Florida. Quesada apparently wanted to increase settlement in the isolated province, offering land in exchange for oaths of loyalty. These new settlers would protect the Spanish colony from potential violence caused by the anticipated spread of the French Revolution. Spanish royal officials had cautiously warned their Caribbean administrators to inspect everything entering their provinces for fear of incendiary materials or sympathizers to the French Revolutionary cause. Jefferson, believing Quesada's unsolicited offer would provide a blessing for the United States rather than for Spain, wished one hundred thousand Americans would accept this invitation because it would deliver to the United States "peaceably what may otherwise cost us a war." Quesada believed that it would preserve Spanish control over the isolated colony instead.[5]

In 1793 citizen Edmond Charles Genêt landed in Charleston. As a minister of the French Republic, he immediately made plans to import the revolution to North America. He encouraged the Creek Indians to act against Spain on France's behalf, he recruited Americans with promises of land, commissions, and money in Spanish Florida, and he planned an invasion of the Gulf region. Governor Quesada soon learned that many of his new citizens, including American runaway slaves and discontented Spanish slaves, would quickly forsake their Spanish oaths, siding instead with the American invaders. He immediately began arming all of the free blacks and mulattoes of the province and assigned them to protect the approaches on the northern frontier. Quesada insisted that these men would "be loyal and will defend themselves to the death in order not to return to their former slavery." In fact, some fifty free blacks

who elected their own sergeants, one of whom was Prince Witten, effectively patrolled the rivers, while a unit of slaves trained as artillerymen.
Additional black soldiers from Mexico soon arrived under the command
of Col. Sebastián Kindelán y O'Regan. Quesada also required slaves and
free blacks to work on the colony's defenses and to row government supplies via boat to outlying posts.[6]

During the summer of 1795 the American revolutionaries finally
attacked, quickly overrunning two artillery batteries north of St. Augustine. Quesada instructed everyone to evacuate south of the St. Johns
River, and then he burned the lands north of the river. This scorched-
earth policy, combined with Quesada's roving bands of black defenders,
soon dislodged and demoralized the American invaders, who retreated
north to Amelia Island. Afterward Quesada sent out parties of free
blacks, including Prince Witten, to scout the retreating Americans and
to round up rebel property, and they remained in service until the end
of the year.[7]

When Quesada assumed control of the colony he found that his
troops lacked discipline and were so poorly trained and supplied that
they could not maintain order. He had pleaded with his superiors in
Cuba for reinforcements, supplies, equipment, and money, but his requests always fell on deaf ears. In combination with the tenuous Florida
border relations, Quesada was left in a precarious situation, chronically
short of what he needed to defend the colony. By supplementing his few
white troops with free blacks and slaves, Quesada cobbled together a
formidable fighting force of *de facto* black citizen-soldiers in Spanish
Florida that held back the tide of American expansion. Future Spanish
officials also subscribed to this model, as they too lacked the money,
men, and resources to adequately defend their isolated outposts. In this
regard, "the excellent company of free blacks" had faithfully served the
Spanish Crown, but not for reasons of loyalty. Instead, they had much to
lose should an American invasion succeed because they could very well
find themselves back in the plantation slavery system. Free blacks and
slaves brokered their participation to secure a tenuous feeling of freedom
that remained intact as long as Spain retained control over Florida.[8]

In January 1796 Quesada finally received reinforcements in the
form of the disbanded Black Auxiliaries of Charles IV, commanded by
Gen. Jorge Biassou. Five years earlier these black troops had fought in
the slave revolt that erupted on Saint Domingue, and under the former
slave Biassou, self-titled the "Viceroy of the Conquered Territories,"
had gained a much-deserved reputation as fierce fighters. Courted by

France's enemies Spain and England as a way to undermine French control on the island of Hispaniola, during the spring of 1793 Biassou and fellow black revolutionary leaders Jean-François Papillon and Toussaint L'Ouverture all agreed to ally with the Spanish. Their rebellious slave army received the prestigious moniker Black Auxiliaries of Charles IV, and the three leaders received gold medals and documents expressing the gratitude of the Spanish king. Afterward the Auxiliaries won several bloody battles against French troops before the French Assembly abolished slavery in May 1794. Thereafter the tide of the struggle changed. Toussaint soon offered his services to France while Papillon and Biassou remained loyal to Spain. These divisions within the black army intensified the island struggle, and in July 1794 the Black Auxiliaries massacred more than one thousand French men, women, and children at Bayajá. Other atrocities by both sides soon followed. Eventually France and Spain were forced to divide the island, and Spain disbanded the Black Auxiliaries.

Jorge Biassou. Jorge Biassou commanded the Black Auxiliaries of Spanish King Charles IV on Hispaniola during the racial violence of the early 1790s, gaining a reputation as a skilled leader. Relocating to St. Augustine, Florida, in 1796, he commanded the colony's free black militia until his death in 1801. Image taken from Juan López Cancelada, Vida de J.J. Dessalines, Gefe de los negroes de Santo Domingo *(Mexico: En la Oficina de D. Mariano de Súñiga y Ontiveros, 1806).*

After evacuating Bayajá, Biassou departed for St. Augustine. The party, which consisted of Biassou's immediate family and some twenty-five followers, had been given little time or choice in their evacuation. The French had made it clear that because these black soldiers were unpredictable, their leaders had to leave, although they permitted common soldiers to remain on the island. Spanish officials, who had previously extolled the virtues and bravery of the black army, now refused them permission to migrate as units or en masse or to choose their destination. Cuba's governor, Captain Gen. Luis de Las Casas, uneasy with news that the disbanded black slave soldiers were on their way to Havana, quickly dispersed them throughout the Spanish Empire, including to Florida. Quesada's warning to Cuba that Biassou's presence at St. Augustine troubled Florida slaveowners who "fear he will set a bad example for the rest of his class" mirrored the reports of other Spanish governors confronted with the presence of these troublesome soldiers. Yet in Florida, Quesada's problem appeared even more acute.[9]

Biassou, often referred to as the Black Caudillo (political-military leader) in Spanish records, quickly extended his influence throughout the Florida colony. Three months after his arrival, his brother-in-law and military heir, Sgt. Juan Jorge Jacobo, married Rafaela Witten, Prince's daughter, and this immediately strengthened Biassou's influence throughout the local community while raising the stature of Florida blacks and the Witten family. Other marriages between the two groups, along with the births and baptisms that followed, created a kinship network that further intertwined and strengthened the black community. In 1799 Biassou requested permission to organize two separate companies of *pardo* (mulatto) and *moreno* (black) militias to be placed under his command, and for them to have equal status to Florida's white militia units. This racially divisive request, separating black skin and tan from white, would give Biassou's extended family the chance for further advancement, as well as assisting his own social and financial position.[10]

While Spanish officials did not immediately grant Biassou's request, the caudillo soon had the chance to lead an army for his Spanish king. In 1800 the Seminole and Lower Creek tribes, led by the self-proclaimed "director general" of the "State of Muskogee" William Augustus Bowles, declared war on Spain. Bowles's army of Indians, free blacks and slaves, and land-hungry Anglos began raiding throughout the colony. The *Nassau Gazette* reported that "the Muskogee Army has marched to plunder, pillage & lay waste [to St.] Augustine, from whence they have already brought a number of Prime Slaves & some considerable share of very valuable property." East Florida governor Enrique White dispatched his local free black militia to protect St. Augustine's western frontier. Meanwhile Biassou and the remaining free blacks defended the city's southern frontier. Throughout the winter of 1800 and the spring of 1801 Florida's free black militia conducted several expeditions against the marauding Seminoles, and they excelled in the bush fighting necessary to defeat them. By early July 1801, Biassou had become sick, and he suddenly died at his home in mid-July; Spanish officials accorded Biassou the procession due a military hero. With Biassou's death, command of the free black militia descended to his brother-in-law Juan Jorge Jacobo and his captains Benjamín Seguí and Prince Witten.[11]

The black militia fighting Bowles's confederation encompassed Biassou's former dependents, Florida's free blacks, and fugitive slaves from the United States. They had experience fighting against the Indians and Americans even though they were but "artisans and field hands"; the group also included farmers, carpenters, hostlers, a butcher, and cowboys, as well as several guides and mariners. Always posted to the most dangerous and exposed locations, including positions on Amelia Island and the St. Johns River, they conducted daily land and river patrols and convoyed people and supplies to and from St. Augustine. During June 1802 Prince Witten led two successful expeditions against the Muskogee, reportedly killing many and destroying their encampments. Two months later Witten's militia rescued a besieged detachment of white dragoons at an isolated outpost, saving their lives. Sporadic fighting continued until Bowles's capture in the spring of 1803 and his premature death during December 1805 in a Havana prison. With peace in Florida, the black militia could return to their normal lives. Spain's black soldiers had preserved royal control over the colony again and in doing their hazardous duty at low pay and in desolate, dangerous, and sickly locations had reaffirmed their status and position within the Florida community. Fighting for freedom meant their continued freedom as granted by the Spanish king. It also meant keeping Florida free from the Americans and the plantation system.[12]

American immigration into Spanish Florida since the early 1790s renewed the fear of plantation expansion and slavery. Yet during the same period, the number of slaves absconding to freedom across the Georgia–Spanish Florida border had also increased. By 1804 the area around St. Augustine and the St. Johns River could boast some 2,300 slaves and innumerable free blacks and runaways. Once the U.S. Congress prohibited the international slave trade into American territory, effective January 1, 1808, Amelia Island in Spanish Florida became a haven for smuggling human cargo into southern Georgia. Thereafter North Florida resembled a strange amalgamation of relationships, with free blacks residing in Spanish settlements, slaves working on nearby Anglo American plantations, and runaway slaves allied with and living near Seminole settlements. Always short of soldiers, the Spanish required all adult males including free blacks to serve in the militia, a situation that offered additional incentive and opportunities for black advancement, which enticed American slaves to flee to Spanish Florida.[13]

The presence of armed free blacks, armed fugitives among the Seminoles, and potentially armed slaves scared American planters in the South who saw the possibility of a slave rebellion washing across the Spain-U.S. border. During March 1810, the rumor of an insurrection filtered through Georgia, prompting state and Spanish Florida officials to take immediate action. A Georgia slave, stressing that his fellow conspirators should remain secretive, had written to a North Carolina slave that the revolt would begin on April 22 with slaves killing their masters and seizing weapons, "and that will strengthen us more in armes—for freedom we want and will have, for we have served this cruel land long enuff." The Spanish sent the militia throughout the Florida colony to ferret out insurrectionists and even confiscated slave weapons used for hunting, helping to ease American fears. Nonetheless, the rumors of insurrection spread to North Carolina, Tennessee, and Virginia, and before the end of the year, they had reached as far north as Kentucky.[14]

If insurrection spreading throughout North America and the Caribbean were not enough, news soon percolated from the borderlands that "the inhabitants on the frontier are considerably alarmed" because Indians and their black allies within Spanish territory had been committing "crimes of a serious nature." These outrages unquestionably threatened locals on both sides of the border. Meanwhile, British-flagged merchant ships anchored in Fernandina harbor—a Spanish port exempt from American embargo and slave trade laws—loaded with American produce, which undermined U.S. state and national laws. State and federal officials railed against the British presence that had quickly emerged—Georgia congressman George Troup counted twenty British vessels anchored in the St. Mary's River in February 1809. Since both the Spanish and the Seminoles had reportedly allied with the British to limit American expansion, Troup saw no alternative than for the United States to take immediate possession of Florida, "to prevent the British having a footing there." American occupation presumably would also solve the problems with runaway slaves, armed free blacks, and hostile Indians and maroons.[15]

Spain's inability to maintain order and stability in Florida contributed to the September 1810 West Florida Rebellion, in which American settlers stormed and captured the dilapidated Spanish fort at Baton Rouge, present-day Louisiana. The West Florida revolutionaries quickly drafted a Declaration of Independence and requested annexation into the United States. Rumors of the impending arrival of Spanish black troops from Cuba or Veracruz, combined with fabricated accounts of a British landing at Pensacola and stories of American adventurers seizing additional Spanish territory, encouraged President James Madison to take quick action. A month later, acknowledging that Britain had a "propensity to fish in troubled waters," Madison issued a proclamation on October 27, 1810, instructing American officials to take possession of West Florida based on the Louisiana Purchase of 1803. Spanish West Florida governor Vicente Folch, realizing that the Baton Rouge revolt could spread east to Mobile, Pensacola, and perhaps on to East Florida and St. Augustine, boldly initiated negotiations to "deliver [the entire] province to the United States under an equitable capitulation."[16]

During late January 1811, Madison instructed Gen. George Mathews, former governor of Georgia, and Choctaw Indian agent John McKee to arrange secretly the surrender of the Floridas. Madison also gave Mathews the authority to negotiate with any Florida official and permission to withdraw funds from banks in New Orleans and Savannah to pay for the Spanish garrison's evacuation from the colony. Yet soon after appointing Mathews, Madison learned that Folch had withdrawn his offer to negotiate; black reinforcements from Jamaica reportedly would be landed in the province soon to bolster the colonies' defenses. Nonetheless, Mathews still traveled to St. Mary's, Georgia—hoping to negotiate with acting East Florida governor Juan José Estrada—where he soon gained firsthand information of the unsettling turmoil affecting the region.[17]

The presence of "several hundred fugitive [sic] slaves from the Carolinas and Georgia," in addition to black troops, British agents, and Spanish operatives in East Florida, convinced Mathews to use military forces to seize the colony for the United States. He had authority to negotiate with the Spanish, and he also claimed to have secret orders from the president and the secretary of state that allowed him to invade and capture East Florida. Although uncertainty still remains about the content of Mathews's secret orders, it is probable that he was doing exactly what President Madison and southerners wanted. Mathews maintained that he had orders authorizing him to muster and outfit American settlers in their efforts to overthrow Spanish rule in Florida and join the United States. Although officials in Washington later denied such orders, Mathews asserted that his instructions permitted him to occupy any part of Florida provided that local authorities invited him to do so or that the territory was being invaded by a hostile power. This certainly fits the tenor of both Jefferson's and Madison's administrations and is how the United States justified and proceeded in West Florida. Thus began the "Patriot Revolution," a small, unofficial conflict between Spain—a British ally in the war against Napoleon—and volunteers from the United States fought solely for the purpose of expanding American slaveholding territory. Yet once the United States declared war on Great Britain during the summer of 1812, Americans would find themselves fighting two enemies on separate borders, with neither conflict progressing as expected.[18]

Before departing for southern Georgia in August 1811, Mathews met with Spanish officials in Mobile and attempted to persuade them to relinquish their claim to the Floridas. Their steadfast refusal led Mathews to organize a frontier group of Georgia-born settlers into a revolutionary army and furnish them with arms. Calling themselves "Patriots," they planned to revolt and seize control over East Florida and then ask to be annexed to the United States; this practically duplicated the events in the Baton Rouge district during September 1810 when local residents revolted, threw out the Spanish officials, and requested annexation.[19]

Spending the last months of 1811 and early months of 1812 in St. Mary's developing plans for the occupation, Matthews saw the lawlessness that reigned in the region. Slaves fled across the Georgia-Florida border unimpeded. Cattle rustling, slave stealing/kidnapping, smuggling, and even piracy girdled the regional economy. Moreover, rumors abounded about the impending arrival of Spanish black troops from the Caribbean, Napoleon's French troops, and even "a detachment of English troops (blacks)" that would occupy the area. Mathews's plans called for an attacking party of Georgia insurgents to descend quickly on St. Augustine. Meanwhile, U.S. gunboats would patrol the waters off St. Augustine to prevent Spanish reinforcements or a British intervention. The quick strike would presumably catch the Spaniards by surprise, forcing them to surrender the fort and ultimately the province. The insurgents, then joined by Patriot volunteers, would organize a government and request annexation.[20]

This plan rested on the cooperation of the U.S. Army, and local commander Maj. Jacint Laval would not commit troops without directions from his superiors. In order to win the support of the navy, Mathews moved his 180 Georgia Patriots south across the St. Mary's River and occupied Rose's Bluff, some four miles across the bay from Fernandina on Amelia Island. The quick conquest of Amelia Island presumably would rally troops for the forthcoming attack against St. Augustine.[21]

On March 16, 1812, five U.S. gunboats anchored off Fernandina. Carrying 24- and 32-pounders, the largest guns in contemporary naval use, Hugh Campbell's boats had lighted matches, but his commanders were instructed not to fire unless Spanish forces fired first. Additionally, Campbell had provided "a positive order not to fire a shot on any patriot whatever." The commander of the Patriot force, Lodowick Ashley, notified the Spanish commandant at Fernandina, Don Justo López, that he had but one hour to surrender. Should the Spaniard refuse, should he try to arm the blacks of the area, or should he give any appearance of preparing the defenses of the town, Ashley would order the destruction of the dilapidated fort and town. In fact, Ashley further warned that his forces would "give no quarters in the Town" if the Spanish had "armed the negroes on the island, against us." As the Patriots' large boats began their amphibious assault, López quickly took stock of his inadequate force, realizing that his fort could not withstand an attack by armed U.S. gunboats. López had little choice but to surrender the island to the rebels, who immediately raised their flag over the fort. López soon withdrew his troops to St. Augustine, and his free black militia moved south into Indian Territory, where they informed the Seminoles of the invasion. Other slaves and free blacks from nearby lumber camps and plantations also fled south toward St. Augustine.[22]

The Patriots held control over Amelia Island for only one day before Colonel Thomas Smith took possession for the United States on March 18, 1812. Four days later the Patriots began their march south toward St. Augustine, and by the end of the month, they had seized Picolata, the fort that guarded the crossing of the St. Johns River to St. Augustine. This position also controlled the communication routes between the Spaniards and the Seminoles, and once the Americans had severed it, Mathews initiated negotiations with the Indians. Unable to speak the Muskogee dialect, Mathews captured a slave named Tony Proctor who served as a translator at trading stores in the area and was, according to the new East Florida governor Sebastián Kindelán, known to be the "best interpreter of Indian languages in the province."

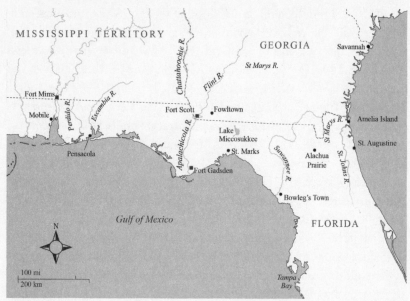

Florida Patriot War, 1812–14. Map by Tracy Ellen Smith.

Mathews took Proctor south to Alachua—near present-day Gainesville—to meet with Chief Payne, the principle chief of the Seminoles,
and to convince them to remain neutral in the struggle between the
Patriots and the Spanish.[23]

When Proctor spoke to the Seminoles, in a language Mathews did
not understand, he told them that the Patriots would emasculate their
warriors and domesticate the elderly and the women; this sobering
claim alerted Seminoles to the transformation already occurring to their
Muskogee kinsmen—the Creeks. The unsuspecting Mathews could not
dispute Proctor's message because he did not understand what the slave
said. He assumed that Proctor would do as told and translate the message that the Seminoles should remain neutral. Payne responded that he
and his people needed time to make an important decision, prompting
Mathews to withdraw. While awaiting a decision, Proctor escaped from
Mathews's camp and returned to Alachua to warn the Indians in direct
terms. This time, he strongly suggested that they should join the Spanish
in the struggle against the American-supported Patriots, and the Seminoles overwhelmingly agreed.[24]

News of the Patriot invasion into Florida spread like fire along the
St. Johns River. In late March free black logger Tony Primus, who had

spent more than two months in the isolated swamps of Julington Creek, learned from his white neighbors of the American encroachment; they warned Primus to flee to St. Augustine or risk being captured and sold as a slave. Having harvested more than 22,000 linear feet of red cedar, Primus believed that the invaders only intended to run him off and seize his timber. Not willing to leave his considerable work behind because of a rumored invasion, Primus and his thirteen free black loggers continued their work. The following day the logging crew heard gunshots nearby. Convinced now that the rumors were true, they quickly abandoned their camp and set off for St. Augustine, arriving late in the evening of March 23, 1812. The following morning they reported to Spanish officials and took up arms in the free black militia.[25]

Late in the following evening, Patriot scouts got their first glimpse of St. Augustine, and the following day the remainder of the invading force arrived on the outskirts of the town. More than one hundred East Florida rebels would join the Patriot force in the days to come. Meanwhile, acting governor Estrada, having taken up refuge in Castillo de San Marcos, observed Patriot forces gathering on the outskirts of the city from the tall stone watchtower inside the fort. Although he had but a limited number of men—less than three hundred inside the fort, of which fifty reportedly were "free Men of Colour"—more than two hundred militiamen had not yet reported for duty; most lived in outlying areas and found it difficult to reach town because of the Patriot presence. Additionally, the Patriots had severed contact with the Indians, so Estrada had no idea as to which side the Seminoles might support. He did anticipate that the Seminoles and the free blacks and slaves would join the Spanish cause, providing him with a potential source of manpower far greater than the Patriots could muster. Thus he intended to hold out until reinforcements arrived or he was forced to surrender, and he tried to bolster the morale of the defenders as well as gather cattle for what could be a prolonged siege. It was, ultimately lasting more than a year.[26]

The Patriot rebels scoured the countryside, looking for cattle and other supplies, and they looted and pillaged deserted homesteads, taking what they believed they deserved; slaves held particular value for rebels trying to provide for themselves. But the military inactivity weighed heavily on their forces. The men wanted a chance for glory and had been promised rewards of land, money, and positions. With no sign that St. Augustine would surrender and no sign of immediate combat, some of the volunteers began melting into the countryside, returning to their homes and farms. Not even the arrival of Col. Thomas Smith and U.S.

Army forces at Fort Mose on April 12 or the appearance of U.S. naval vessels off St. Augustine improved Patriot morale.[27]

In early April Mathews reported to U.S. officials that the Patriots had gained control of East Florida as far as the walls of St. Augustine, and he requested annexation to the United States. He also asked Captain Campbell to use his naval force to blockade the Spanish city. Mathews sincerely believed that he had executed the president's orders and that East Florida would soon be part of the United States. Instead, Secretary of State James Monroe removed Mathews's commission, claiming that the former Georgia governor had exceeded his orders. According to Monroe, Mathews had not been authorized to take the territory of Florida unless that province had been voluntarily offered by the Spanish or threatened by foreign invasion. Since neither situation existed, Mathews had exceeded his instructions. Although Monroe's recall of Mathews expressed an extremely mild tone seemingly not intended as a reprimand, when President Madison wrote to Jefferson, he howled that Mathews had completely ignored his orders, placing the United States in a "distressing dilemma" of having to commit more troops to Georgia if Patriots could not finish the job or if slaves and Indians rose in force.[28]

When Monroe removed Mathews, it temporarily left East Florida in a state of chaos; one widely circulating rumor suggested that Spanish agents had delivered weapons behind American lines to "negroes & the crews of British vessels in port" at Amelia Island "to attack the Patriots in their rear." Other more exaggerated stories had slaves spreading insurrection throughout southern plantations. In an effort to restore order, Monroe appointed Georgia governor David B. Mitchell to arrange a peaceful settlement with the Spanish. Although the decision about removing U.S. troops would be left to Mitchell's discretion, neither Madison nor Monroe wanted to withdraw from Florida or to end the Patriot War. Instead, they wanted to mediate with Spanish officials, hoping that prolonged negotiations would provide ample time for the Patriots to seize St. Augustine or for Congress to give U.S. forces the authority to conquer Florida officially. Failing all else, Patriot pressure on St. Augustine might eventually compel the Spanish to surrender East Florida by diplomacy.[29]

But East Florida's new governor, Sebastián Kindelán, was unwilling to relinquish the province to the Patriots, so he continually requested reinforcements from Cuba and stalled in his negotiations with Mitchell. With each passing week, Kindelán watched as the Patriot force further dissolved outside St. Augustine's walls. By mid-July he received two companies of *morenos* and one company of *pardos*, some 270 fresh soldiers belonging to the Cuban Black Militia. Later that month he also learned that both the Seminoles and their black allies would oppose the invaders. With this infusion of men, Kindelán could thereafter negotiate from a position of newfound strength.[30]

The Georgia governor continually increased his demands of the Spanish. At first Mitchell only wanted amnesty for Patriots involved in the rebellion; Kindelán was prepared to offer that concession. Then he demanded an apology for Spanish forces firing on the American flag; the Spanish governor contended that the Americans bore the burden of this misunderstanding because they shared an encampment with the Patriots. Mitchell raised the stakes further, accusing Kindelán of provoking violence by bringing black troops into East Florida and threatening the southern states—a situation, according to Mitchell, that the United States would not tolerate. Although negotiations broke down at this point, an aide to the Spanish governor responded to Mitchell's accusations in a letter printed in a southern newspaper. Black soldiers did not represent an anomaly in the Spanish Empire, he retorted. In fact, the Spanish government expected that all men, black or white, would serve in time of need. Moreover, Governor Mitchell's complaint about black soldiers rang hollow because it mimicked the objections of a burglar armed with a pistol, who after breaking into a home finds the resident with a loaded blunderbuss. Spanish officials willingly misstated the number of Cuban blacks in the province in an attempt to diffuse the tense situation, and the governor agreed that the Cuban soldiers would not conduct operations north of the St. Johns River.[31]

Granted, black troops in East Florida unquestionably provoked southern outrage, but Kindelán knew that he needed them to defend the colony. Even so, he had misgivings about the recently arrived Cuban militia because most of them had been convicts and, more importantly, were incompetent soldiers. He reported to the captain general in Havana that "there is not one among them that does not shut his eyes when he fires his rifle." Conversely, he had faith in his local black militia because they had gained a reputation as effective bush fighters, they knew the countryside, and they had no desire to accede to the Americans. He had no doubt that they were good soldiers, even though they were black. As such, Kindelán decided to use his Cuban militia to garrison St. Augustine, and he assembled a force of white soldiers and black militia for raids along the St. Johns River, where they could create havoc among the Patriots and Americans and secure food for St. Augustine.[32]

Jorge Jacobo commanded the local black militia during the raids, relying on Juan Bautista "Prince" Witten and Benjamín Seguí as his lieutenants. Governor Kindelán instructed his black militia to descend on a Julianton plantation where reportedly a small group of Patriots had encamped. He explicitly told them not to be "excessively sanguinary" or barbaric in their actions; they should fight a civilized conflict and treat their enemy with respect, a direct contradiction to what Americans would be expected to do. In fact, a few months later, American general Thomas Flournoy, exasperated by lack of success and the racial dimensions of the war, directed "every negro found in arms [to] be put to death without mercy." Kindelán did not want to incur American wrath or drive them into a blinded rage, he only wanted to drive them from his province. Additionally, he directed the militia to destroy cannon and other large weapons; to seize guns, powder, and all available provisions; to burn houses, storehouses, and other buildings; and, finally, to liberate or take all slaves into custody. Once finished, they should leave behind a contingent of men to surprise other Patriots arriving at Julianton, then cross the St. Johns River and attack the rebel outpost at Picolata. Their instructions directed them to take what they needed—including horses, cattle, weapons, equipment, and supplies—and destroy everything else. Since they carried with them only limited supplies, Kindelán expected them to live off the land and appropriate rebel supplies, which would permit the raids to continue indefinitely. Although the Crown claimed all weapons, munitions, and slaves, everything else could be kept by the militia, giving them a monetary incentive for the raids. Should they capture any white prisoners, the governor insisted that they be protected and well treated, as this would not add fuel to the fire of American discontent. Any slaves or free blacks who wanted could be mustered into the black militia after they had demonstrated their loyalty. Not surprisingly, the local black militia raids weakened the Patriots, provided weapons and supplies for the Spanish, and increased the strength of the black militia, while letting Kindelán report to American officials that his black Cuban troops remained in St. Augustine.[33]

When the Patriots initially invaded Florida, the Seminoles and their black allies had remained neutral. But as a result of Spanish persuasion and the Patriots and Americans affording them ill treatment, both groups chose to join with the Spanish. Seminole chief Billy Bowlegs, the younger brother of Chief Payne, had initially wanted to join the Patriots, but he now led the call for war against them, insisting that Indian warriors should strike first at the Americans or risk eventual destruction and slavery. Although Payne preferred peace, the younger Seminoles and several of the upper Creek towns agreed to fight alongside the Spaniards; the upper Creeks immediately contributed some two hundred Indians and forty black "gun men." Before the end of July, the Seminoles and their black allies had descended on the farms and isolated outposts north of the St. Johns River, burning buildings, killing pro-American blacks and whites alike, and liberating more than eighty slaves. They ultimately wreaked havoc on both sides of the St. Johns, raiding as far north as St. Mary's and even threatening U.S. forces. This heightened activity immediately drove many of the Patriots home to protect their families and farms, greatly weakening the siege against St. Augustine and providing Kindelán the opportunity to send out his black militia to make further contact with the Indians; when they returned, they brought cattle to feed the city's besieged inhabitants. Additionally, Kindelán's decision to mobilize the Seminoles and their black allies permitted the Spaniard to profess neutrality—Spanish troops were not fighting the Americans—while breaking the siege and driving the invaders from the colony.[34]

Many Patriot leaders were convinced that the Spaniards had opened Pandora's Box by bringing black soldiers to Florida and encouraging fugitives to take up weapons. Armed blacks set a dangerous precedent that would reverberate across the South. One Patriot leader warned Secretary Monroe that "our slaves are excited to rebel, and we have an army of negroes raked up in this county, and brought from Cuba to be contended with." He also decried that East Florida had emerged as the "refuge of fugitive slaves; and from thence emissaries . . . will be detached to bring about the revolt of the black population of the United States." Governor Mitchell also warned Monroe that the Spaniards "have armed every able-bodied negro within their power" and have received "nearly two companies of black [Cuban] troops!" Should these black troops be permitted to remain in Florida, Mitchell predicted that "our southern country will soon be in a state of insurrection." Since the Spanish "governor has proclaimed freedom to every negro who will join his standard . . . most of our male negroes on the Sea Board are restless and make many attempts to get off to Augustine." Not surprisingly, Mitchell proclaimed, "many have succeeded." Charleston and Savannah newspapers carefully censored their reports on the Patriot War, deleting every reference to black troops in St. Augustine and using asterisks instead "for reasons of local security." The longer black troops held out against white American and Patriot invaders, the more emboldened southern slaves might become. According to southerners, only a quick American victory could restore the proper relationship to the borderlands.[35]

American forces would not secure the quick victory they wanted or anticipated. By August Colonel Smith had only four hundred men outside St. Augustine's walls and a few others along the frontier. Governor Kindelán could count twice as many men within St. Augustine's walls, as well as innumerable Indian and black allies roaming the countryside. Smith's men found Florida "pregnant with sickness and death" or unseen enemies, in addition to "dreadful lurking" Indians and black troops who were not "strangers to fear." Patriot William Kinnear described with horror how a group of Indians and black guerillas tortured and murdered three mail carriers, one of whom had his nose, ears, and genitals cut off. Not even the arrival of Col. Daniel Newnan, adjutant general of Georgia, and 250 militia volunteers could buoy U.S. and Patriot forces. The mutilations prompted Colonel Smith to doubt whether the Patriots "will ever revive again." Additionally, the flow of "several hundred fugitive [sic] slaves" from the Carolinas and Georgia, supported by increased "desertions from Georgia & Florida," had created a "troublesome" situation.[36]

The situation in Florida would become far more troubling than Smith or his officers could have predicted. Marine captain John Williams deplored being kept in an "unpleasant" and "unhealthful" situation in Florida "without the liberty of firing a gun unless we are fired upon." Yet on the evening of September 12, 1812, his detachment of twenty-one marines and Georgia militia would have the chance to return fire. Escorting two wagons, mule teams, and pack animals west from the Patriot encampment near St. Augustine toward the U.S. supply depot at Davis Creek on the St. Johns River, the party reached Twelve Mile Swamp—named such because of its distance from the St. Johns River—without incident despite numerous opportunities for an attack. The motionless pools, darkened swamps, and dusky sky filled the American troops with apprehension. Prince Witten and his group of fifty-seven blacks and six Seminoles, all disguised as Indians, had been lying camouflaged in the dense palmettos for hours, waiting for the column of uniformed white soldiers to approach within volley range. Suddenly out of darkness, Witten screamed for his militia to fire. Almost instantly six privates in the rear of the column fell wounded. As the Americans turned to the rear several shots of the second volley hit Captain Williams, knocking him from his horse but not immediately killing him. In fact, he was shot eight times total during the engagement, dying from his wounds seventeen days later. A shot that wounded a corporal bounced into the knee of Capt. Tomlinson Fort of the Georgia militia as he tried to drag Williams to cover. Attackers armed with axes and knives swiftly pounced on the corporal, scalping and killing the soldier in front of his terrified brethren.[37]

Witten had instructed his men to pick off the officers, pin down the men, and immobilize the wagons, and the first two volleys accomplished these objectives. As the Americans tried to regroup, the ambushers instilled greater fear into those still alive with the continued Indian war whoops and screams. The intense fighting lasted twenty-five minutes, and the entire engagement two hours. Through the dim moonlight the Americans saw Witten and his disguised black soldiers rounding the wagons and bearing down on them with tomahawks, knives, axes, and bayonets. Williams and Fort mustered enough strength to rally their soldiers, who, having run out of ammunition, mounted their bayonets and engaged the attackers in hand-to-hand combat. Witten chose to break off the attack after a stubborn American defense, but his men continued to harass the beleaguered Americans for the next two hours before the black leader burned one of the wagons and used the second to evacuate his seven wounded Indians and two militiamen. While sunrise brought a relief force from Davis Creek who rescued the white soldiers, the previous night had determined the fate of the Patriot War and effectively ended the siege of St. Augustine.[38]

Governor Kindelán learned of the ambush later that evening, and he could not contain his happiness. He immediately dashed off a report to the captain-general, praising Prince Witten and his black militiamen for their service to Spain. Not only had they harassed the Americans continually, during the summer they had risked their lives to bring cattle to St. Augustine; during July–September 1812 they had brought in some 460 head, which prevented St. Augustine from starving. The cattle they secured also deprived the Americans of food, and by mid-September Colonel Smith's forces desperately needed provisions. Without supplies, and with an encampment of sick and dispirited troops and a severed supply line, Smith had little choice. Two days after the ambush he chose to withdraw to Davis Creek under the protection of U.S. gunboats on the St. Johns. The dejected soldiers burned their huts and shelters and left.[39]

Governor Kindelán, knowing that his victory had occurred because of the local black militia, soon promoted the leaders—Jorge Jacobo to captain, Juan Bautista "Prince" Witten to lieutenant, and Benjamín Seguí to second lieutenant. These promotions brought with them social acknowledgment and advancement within the community and increased salaries, as well as participation in the Spanish military pension fund (*Montepío militar*) and insurance program (*Ynvalidos*). The promotions left vacant positions previously held by the officers and thus created opportunities for other local free blacks to advance and fill the void. Men could rise through the ranks and even become officers—Captain Jacobo had once been a sergeant first class and Prince Witten merely a militiaman—and this presumably stimulated recruitment. By January 1813 the black unit numbered eighty-seven men, including three sergeants, twelve corporals, and three black officers. In the months that followed, Kindelán also requested that the Crown award the militiamen, who were family and farming men, contiguous land grants so they could form a defensive barrier on the northern frontier and provide St. Augustine with a source of vegetables and other foodstuffs. By 1815 the Crown heeded Kindelán and began awarding the land grants to the black soldiers.[40]

The Patriot War in Florida had drained military resources from the United States, had destabilized the borderland area, and had not proceeded according to General Mathews's initial plans for a quick American victory. In fact, the conflict had quickly degenerated into a local struggle near St. Augustine with Spanish-supported blacks and Indians brutally raiding Patriot outposts, constantly harassing American supply lines, and preventing the United States from incorporating the region under the Stars and Stripes. By the time American troops gained an advantage against the Spanish and their black and Indian forces during the spring of 1813, the United States had already declared war on Great Britain. American military activities in Florida slowed as British operations during the spring of 1813 along the Niagara River frontier, in the old northwest, and on the seas preoccupied American policy makers. As a result, the brutality of the war continued unabated throughout Florida, with the Spanish officially holding St. Augustine and the Americans struggling to gain control of the surrounding area. Months passed, and with each day it seemed as if the conflict became more contested. Yet in the end neither side could declare victory, as could neither the United States nor Great Britain in their larger struggle.

Georgia militia colonel Daniel Newnan did not want to give up the campaign so easily. He suggested to his militiamen that they should reenlist and join him on an expedition against the Alachua towns, eighty miles into the heart of Seminole country. The raid would permit them to drive the Indians and blacks from their strongholds and destroy their support for the Spanish, as well as survey the area for future white settlement.

The prospect for land motivated many of the 117 American volunteers. On September 24, Newnan's ill-supplied army began its march south and within three days was but eight miles from its objective. As they approached a large cypress swamp blocking their advance, scouts reported the approach of an Indian party of sixty to seventy warriors. Newnan quickly positioned his men to meet the surprised Seminoles. Not expecting an attack, Chief Payne and his braves were stunned by the Americans, quickly falling back into the swamp to regroup. The two sides continued to exchange fire from covered positions for the remainder of the afternoon (more than two hours), with neither side gaining an advantage. At dusk, about 6:30 P.M., the forest suddenly erupted in noise as the Seminoles and their black allies—a force that had grown to more than 250—rapidly stormed toward Newnan's men. Hearing that Payne had been wounded, the blacks fought with such ferocity and bravery that Newnan later declared that the "negroes . . . are their best soldiers."[41]

The Americans held out despite being outnumbered, prompting the Seminoles and their allies to withdraw again back into the swamp. Knowing that he could not retreat in the darkness carrying his wounded without suffering terrible casualties, Newnan had his men cobble together fallen cypress trees and earth into a crude fortification. For the next week, Newnan's starving force huddled inside the makeshift fort, trying not to reveal themselves to sporadic enemy fire. Then an autumn storm blew in cold rain, saturating the beleaguered Americans, and the Indians began targeting their horses. Hungry, cold, trapped on foot, and outnumbered by more than two-to-one, Newnan's men demanded that they retreat. Although Newnan warned them to reconsider, the men overruled him. For the next seven days, they encountered hurricane-like conditions, continued Seminole and black harassment, and extreme deprivation before they finally reached the safety of Fort Picolata.[42]

Newnan's "punitive expedition had degenerated into a desperate retreat," or rather an American disaster that provided additional time for the Seminoles and their allies. The fate of Williams and Newnan and the audacity of the black soldiers demanded retaliation. Governor Mitchell publicly proclaimed to the Georgia Assembly that Spain's "savage and barbarous" use of black warriors produced "utmost indignation and resentment." In order to respond to the crisis, he asked the legislators to outfit a detachment of five hundred mounted soldiers for the conquest of Florida; the "disaffection among the blacks" and their apparent willingness "to commit murder and depredations" had struck fear throughout

Georgia and across the South. The East Tennessee militia responded by assembling almost two hundred mounted volunteers for a new punitive expedition against the Seminoles. By the time they had crossed the Florida border, they had joined Colonel Smith's 220 U.S. troops, 100 Georgia militiamen, and a small group of Patriot volunteers. Commander of the expedition Gen. Thomas Flournoy offered the soldiers simple instructions: burn Indian settlements, destroy crops in the field, seize everything that could be carried off, drive away cattle and horses, execute every "negro found in arms," and take away unarmed blacks as slaves. During the three-week campaign that followed, the Americans burned 386 houses, destroyed or collected 1,500–2,000 bushels of corn, captured or destroyed some 2,000 deerskins, seized three hundred horses and four hundred head of cattle, and captured nine Indians and blacks. Although most of the Indians and blacks had learned in advance of the American approach and had deserted their towns rather than face a numerically superior army, the U.S. raid had destroyed food sources, ultimately forcing the Indians and blacks to relocate. The Seminoles moved westward to the Suwannee River area while many of the blacks migrated further south, founding Pilaklikaha (near present-day Bushnell).[43]

Flournoy's raid during the early months of 1813 devastated Florida and almost determined the fate of the isolated Spanish province, but the U.S. Congress decided not to take possession of East and West Florida. With the withdrawal of U.S. forces from Florida in early May 1813, some anticipated that Patriots would be "exposed to the menaces of free negroes and . . . slaves" despite Governor Kindelán's promises of amnesty. The overt acts of violence that many anticipated did not return. The Spanish governor, not wanting to provoke the Americans again, detached his black militia to the frontier with strict instructions to defend, and only defend, the colony. Prince Witten's militia detachment surveyed the damage along the St. Johns River and took up defensive positions. Yet not surprisingly, the presence of these black troops so close to the United States troubled Georgians who believed that not even Spanish officers could control them. Reportedly, black troops were there to protect runaways from Georgia and incorporate the fugitives into their ranks. Kindelán quickly realized that he needed to recall the *morenos* from the border in order to maintain peaceful relations with Georgia.[44]

In early August 1813 a Spanish force attacked the Patriot stronghold at Waterman's Bluff, but the twenty-minute battle settled nothing, as neither side could declare victory. During the following months Patriots raided Spanish farms and settlements in the region. They stole blacks from Florida and reenslaved them in Georgia and other southern states. In effect, the region between the St. Mary's and St. Johns Rivers became an armed camp of Patriots and interlopers—not necessarily supporters of the Patriots but men willing to use the discord of Patriot rule to raid and maraud. Kindelán sent black soldiers to the northern frontier to try to curtail the raids, but the Spanish had little success. A group of Patriots led by Buckner Harris eluded Spanish sentries and relocated the Patriot movement south to the Alachua region, where they built a fort, surveyed the lands, and soon requested annexation to the United States. But in a blow to Patriot efforts, in late April 1814 the Madison government refused to recognize the Patriot settlement at Alachua or to annex it into the United States. Some two weeks later, on May 5, 1814, a Seminole party enlisted by Kindelán ambushed Harris, killing and scalping him. The Indians sent Harris's scalp and his possessions on to the Spanish governor to receive the reward for his death. Afterward, the Patriot movement began falling apart, and most of the interlopers limped back to the United States. Seminoles and maroons soon reestablished their villages south of Alachua. With Harris's death and the return of the Seminoles and their black allies, the Patriot War had ended.[45]

As the Patriot War raged in Florida, hostile Native Americans took the violence north across the border to present-day southern Alabama. On August 20, 1813, Red Stick Creek warriors of the Creek Confederation attacked the isolated American outpost of Fort Mims, located a few miles north of the mouth of the Alabama River in the Mississippi Territory. The savage three-hour attack resulted in the death or capture of more than 250 of the settlers, soldiers, friendly Creeks, and slaves inside. The Red Sticks had feigned peaceful intentions to gain easy access to the American fort, rushing into the stockade at noon when the gates were open and the soldiers distracted. The Indians set fire to a house in the inner stockade that quickly spread. Once the Red Sticks had forced their way into the inner enclosure, they killed and scalped men, women, and children indiscriminately. The massacre represented a conscious choice by the Creeks to reject the white American ways of life. Almost immediately news of the savage massacre circulated throughout the South and reverberated intensely across political boundaries. In southern Georgia Patriots propagated stories that black Spanish soldiers, Seminoles, and their maroon allies, assisted by Spanish sympathizers, had embarked on plans for a similar massacre. The specter of an Indian-maroon-Spanish Fort Mims–style massacre had existed in the Florida borderlands for years. In fact, during the fall of 1812 the Patriot government on Amelia

Island had condemned two free blacks to death; the father and son who had been free for more than fifty years and who had moved freely around the island, a Spanish observer remarked, "were guilty of no other crime than being free blacks." The Patriots had apparently decided the time had finally come to "not leave free any black or colored person who falls into their hands." Blacks allied with Indians had always created anxiety, and after the Fort Mims massacre of August 1813, white southerners were hypersensitive to anything that seemed unusual.[46]

The British war with the United States came to the Florida borderlands when Adm. George Cockburn's British squadron entered the St. Mary's River in May 1814 and landed troops on Amelia Island. That summer, the British agents set off west overland toward the Apalachicola River, where they planned to recruit Indians and maroons for British operations against Georgia and the Gulf South. Although Indians and maroons armed and encouraged by the British would not reshape the war in Florida, they did create a new intensity for the Anglo American war that could, in fact, determine the fate of the United States.

Black soldiers had saved Florida for Spain during the Patriot War, a conflict of American expansion spurred by the desire for more slave-holding territory. They had protected the isolated frontier, fought in ferocious bush-style combat that discouraged Americans, and constantly secured food for St. Augustine and other Spanish outposts. In effect, without the local black urban militia and the black Cuban soldiers from Havana, Spain might not have withstood the onslaught of Patriot and American forces. Yet the Spanish decision to employ these soldiers created consternation and great alarm in neighboring Georgia and produced intense fear and anger in much of the southern United States. The prospect of armed black soldiers so close to the United States convinced most southerners that there was an impending slave rebellion. American blacks had not been encouraged to think of themselves as potentially successful soldiers, as that would almost guarantee a slave revolt, or so southerners thought. Governor Mitchell, other Georgia leaders, and those in neighboring southern states protested vehemently to Spanish authorities about using these troops, yet their rhetoric seemingly mimicked their fears. Ultimately Spanish officials had no choice other than to employ these soldiers; the captain general in Havana never sent enough men, money, or supplies to forestall the inevitable. Black soldiers represented the best soldiers that Spanish governors could put into the field to maintain control over their colony. Moreover, they had been fighting for themselves and their own purposes—fighting to maintain their freedom as they knew it from the encroaching American plantation system; likewise, the Seminoles fought for their lands, cattle, and freedom. For more than two hundred years Florida had remained a safe haven for fugitive slaves, free blacks, and Indians, yet within a few years after the end of the War of 1812 that would change forever.[47]

THE LARGE NUMBERS OF BLACKS WHO FLED to the Spanish should not have surprised Americans. When Spain resumed control over the Florida peninsula in 1783, the isolated province again became a haven for fugitive slaves and free blacks seeking to escaped the ever-expanding slavery plantation system developing in the southern United States. Moreover, since the Spanish colony lay contiguous to Georgia, slaves found many easy routes into Florida. Once there, they encountered a colonial government willing to accept them and employ their services. Co-opting blacks into the colony's Catholic religion, its social and economic system, and its compulsory military structure created a loyalty that Americans did not recognize or understand. That nurtured loyalty paid Spain tremendous dividends during the Patriot War and attempted American occupation, as Spanish governors marshaled black militiamen to meet and turn back the invading forces. These soldiers willingly confronted hardship and danger because they knew that any defeat or setback could erase the hard-gained freedoms they had secured.

Reaching Florida did not represent the ultimate goal or simply "notions of liberty and happiness." Instead, it embodied only one step in a continuing journey to secure and maintain their freedom, and Prince Witten's story provides a cogent example. Having secreted his family to Florida in the 1780s, he earned a place in Spanish society and in the local militia, helping to drive off Patriots and Americans during the era from 1812 to 1814. Although he gained recognition from the Spanish Crown, Witten soon fell victim to the shifting geopolitics and imperial ambitions affecting the Gulf region after 1815. Unable to maintain order in the peninsula and confronting an increasingly expansionist United States, Spain traded Florida's sovereignty for the security of Texas. On July 10, 1821, the Spanish flag came down for the last time over St. Augustine, leaving the sixty-two-year-old Prince Witten facing an uncertain future. He had escaped slavery in South Carolina and Georgia and devoted more than twenty years of faithful service to the Spanish Crown. For him there was no dilemma—he would not stay in a Florida ruled by the United States and controlled by Americans. During the months following the transfer, Witten and his large extended family boarded ships for Cuba, where the Spanish government granted them homesteads and daily rations for the dutiful service. While it was not Florida, Witten and his family retained the freedom that they had fought so hard to secure.[48]

CHAPTER 4

TERROR IN THE CHESAPEAKE, 1813–14

"Negroes who were anxious to join us"

Born about 1780, slave Charles Ball lived on a Calvert County, Maryland, tobacco farm until he was four, when the owner's death forced the liquidation of the estate. His mother was sold to a Georgia trader, his siblings to Carolina planters, and a local Marylander bought Charles, dressing him in a child's frock as they rode away from the sale. Ball vividly remembered that as the family was being split apart, his mother pleaded with the Maryland planter to buy the entire family. She ran after the horse, pulled Charles down, "clasped [him] in her arms, and wept loudly and bitterly over [him]." The "hardened fiend into whose power she had fallen" chased after her, giving her a couple of "blows on the shoulder with his raw-hide," and angrily dragged her by one arm back to the place of sale. As Ball and the Maryland planter rode away, he distinctly recalled hearing his mother's voice become faint, until it faded into silence. The "horrors of that day sank deeply in [his] heart, and even . . . though a half century [had] elapsed, the terrors of the scene return[ed] with painful vividness upon [his] memory." A short time later Ball's father, who lived on a nearby plantation, learned that his "penurious" and "exceedingly avaricious" master planned to sell him south as well. But before the transaction occurred, Ball's father fled to freedom, and the young man never saw him again. Ball's elderly grandfather, an African warrior brought to the Chesapeake during the 1730s and who lived on another nearby plantation, was now the only family that the young man had.[1]

The forced sale of Ball's mother and siblings and the flight of his father had a profound effect on the young man. His master's family became his surrogate family. Serving as their waiter, he was given abundant clothing and food and apparently even received promises to be the farm's future overseer. Unfortunately when he was about twelve his master suddenly died, and the adolescent Ball became the property of his dead master's father. The "old gentleman treated [him] with the greatest severity, and compelled [him] to work very hard on his plantation." Around 1800 the old master hired out the then twenty-year-old Ball to the Washington Navy Yard for a year, and the slave became a cook aboard the U.S. frigate *Congress*. On board, officers and sailors treated him well and gave him clothing and money. On Sunday afternoons he had the freedom to walk around Washington and the surrounding communities. During his time aboard the frigate he also met a host of black sailors who told him stories of freedom in the North. At one point, Ball even conspired with a black Philadelphia sailor aboard a merchant ship to steal away among a cargo of loose tobacco; at the last moment the ship changed its cargo to flour and its destination to the West Indies, forcing Ball to await another opportunity. Unfortunately, Ball's master soon retrieved him from the Navy Yard and sold him to another farmer, ending his immediate opportunity to secure his freedom.[2]

Ball returned to Calvert County, married a woman named Judah who served as a ladies' chambermaid on a nearby estate, and worked as a slave for some three years on Levin Ballard's farm. And while Ballard was far from an ideal master, providing Ball with few clothes, making unreasonable demands of him, and overwhelming him with coarse and abusive language, the slave nonetheless lived near his wife and children. But this degree of contentment soon passed as Ballard sold Ball to a slave trader who placed him in shackles and marched him to a new owner in South Carolina. This owner sold him to a particularly abusive master further south in Georgia, exasperating Ball: I "knew that my case was hopeless, and that resistance was vain," Ball recalled. He was "incapable of weeping or speaking . . . in [his] despair [Ball] laughed loudly." In 1808 Ball finally escaped from Georgia and spent a year living off the land and following the night stars north to Maryland. When he finally returned to his family in Calvert County, his wife's master and mistress kindly encouraged him to work locally as a free man. Ball hired himself out to area farmers and worked as a fisherman until 1813, when the war with Britain disrupted his livelihood.[3]

In May 1813 Ball joined a party of white Americans who visited the British fleet in the Chesapeake, and he tried unsuccessfully to convince slaves to return to their masters. By the time British operations intensified during the spring of 1814, Ball had already enlisted in Joshua Barney's Chesapeake flotilla, serving aboard a gunboat until the Americans scuttled them. He served in the artillery alongside Barney's flotillamen at Bladensburg and later helped man the defenses at Baltimore. Once the war ended Ball chose to remain in Baltimore, and through his economy and hard work, by 1830 he had accumulated money and property; his first wife had died, but he and his second wife had four children together. Ball "looked forward to an old age of comfort, if not of ease; but [he] was soon to be awakened from this dream."[4]

"[F]ULL OF NOTIONS OF LIBERTY AND HAPPINESS": 1813: BRITISH RAIDS IN THE CHESAPEAKE

Since the beginning of the war between the United States and Great Britain, British policy makers had considered the conflict only a secondary theater of operations. After weathering American attacks against Canada during the late summer and fall of 1812, British leaders as well as naval and military officers focused on how they could quickly force the Americans into submission while protecting their colonial holdings in the Western Hemisphere. In November 1812, only five months after the United States had declared war, Sir John Borlase Warren, then British commander of the North American squadron, proposed an operation against New Orleans to divert the American attack against Canada. He had insisted that such an operation would close the Mississippi River as well as "cut off the resources of the American Southern States . . . who are now actively employed against the Canadas." Instead, Earl Bathurst, Secretary of State for War and Colonies, instructed commanders to conduct diversionary raids against the American coast, and the orders demanded that British raiding parties destroy all public property within their reach. Yet, more importantly, Bathurst broadened the scope of the war, suggesting that British forces could liberate American slaves and enlist them in the British black corps in the Caribbean, which would permit the reallocation of other forces to North America for the war against the United States. Such a possibility prompted Warren to suggest another attack against New Orleans in late 1813, but in this case he suggested bringing "forward the Indians and Spanyards [sic] . . . and a division of black troops to cut off the resources of the Mississippi." Bathurst did not initially embrace the use of slaves as combatants, but rather wanted to employ them as guides and scouts. Instead, Warren suggested that arming and training slaves deeply scared southerners and gave the impression of a full-scale slave insurrection. The "Terror of a Revolution in the Southern States . . . [would] produce a good effect in that quarter."[5]

Expanding the scope of the war with major operations against New Orleans and the Gulf Coast was also on the minds of other naval officers in 1813. Capt. James Stirling wrote a detailed memorandum on the geography of the Gulf of Mexico region. The conquest of Louisiana by British forces supported by Indians, blacks, and "displeased" Spaniards would place Virginia and the interior states "at the mercy of Great Britain." All of these options seemed expedient considering the limited British resources available for the American war and the American naval victories against the British during the fall of 1812. As such, Warren chose to use a "flying army" or mobile corps to harass the American coastline.[6]

British admiral George Cockburn arrived off the Chesapeake Bay in early March 1813, and with Col. Sir Thomas Sydney Beckwith, they began launching hit-and-run diversionary raids designed to demoralize the Americans. They also had orders to recruit slaves to join British ranks. The possibility of inciting a slave revolt appealed to military commanders in hostile territory running short of men and supplies, but it did not tempt British leaders in London. Bathurst had included strict guidelines for dealing with American slaves in his secret March 1813 orders to Beckwith, and these instructions firmly ruled out inciting slave revolts. Bathurst's directive permitted individual slaves who became involved in British operations to be removed from the United States for their own safety and to be given protection and granted freedom. Yet Bathurst clearly hoped that the number of slaves would be small since "the Public became bound to maintain them." These orders ultimately proved inadequate because they underestimated the considerable number of slaves who would escape their bondage; some slaves boldly stole canoes or boats to meet British patrols in creeks or offshore while others used the darkness of night to slip off quietly to British lines. In some instances slaves started fires ashore to get the attention of overcautious British

Chesapeake Bay, 1813–15. Map by Tracy Ellen Smith.

patrols, while other times they barged into a British camp offering information regarding a community or American forces. Even though the method by which slaves arrived in British camps varied, slaves' escapes revealed an undeniable fact—that many willingly challenged their status of servitude and bravely sought out the freedom that seemed within their reach.[7]

Although the British had raided at will and had terrorized slave-holding American citizens throughout the Chesapeake region, Cockburn wanted to sack the city of Norfolk, which protected the American frigate *Constellation*. Despite securing a wealth of information, Cockburn did not understand Norfolk's weak defenses. Capt. Charles Stewart, commanding the *Constellation*, claimed his gunboats did not have adequate sailors and the reliance on the local militia "has proved abortive" at best. In fact, amid "a gloomy prospect of security," many citizens fled the city. Local leaders secured the assistance of sixty free blacks who volunteered for one week of manual labor to help bolster the city's defenses, and these works withstood a first British attack in March 1813.[8]

Stymied in his attempt to sack Norfolk and destroy the *Constellation*, Cockburn began a series of devastating diversionary raids against merchantmen and coastal towns, while Warren took a squadron of ships to the northern end of the bay. On April 2, one of Cockburn's cutting-out operations on the Rappahannock River netted several vessels and also emboldened slaves near Hampton. One early April evening, a canoe of slaves hailed an American vessel in the James River, believing it to be British. Once aboard, the slaves requested arms to "massacre the whites," boasting they could mobilize some "2000 negroes [that] were embodied and exercised in squads at night." The ship captain continued the ruse by providing them with some swords and drilling them until he learned the full scope of the plan, including the intended victims. After he had gained information on the conspiracy, the captain turned them over to officials who soon imprisoned them in Williamsburg. At nearby Gloucester Court-House a group of blacks attempted to murder three slaves who would not join the British conspiracy, and in adjacent Matthews County another "eight negroes had been condemned to hang" for impersonating an Englishman and robbing a man.[9]

British forces had encountered no opposition as they raided Maryland and only sporadic opposition when they went ashore in Virginia. Such ease of movement obviously was not lost on local slaves, prompting Warren to report to his superiors, "the Black population of the countries evince . . . the strongest predilection for the cause of Great Britain, and a most ardent desire to join any troops or seamen acting in the country." Yet one southern apologist retorted publicly that the South had no reason to fear a British-sponsored slave insurrection because southern slaves "are in general a peaceable inoffensive race; content to do the duty to which they were born, and attached to the families from whom they respectively receive protection and support." Furthermore, the southerner assured readers slaves would not flee but would instead perform their duty even with British troops in the area. In reality, the absence of the militia frequently forced locals to accept British demands or suffer accordingly. During the spring of 1813, state officials also learned, much to their chagrin, that federal officials refused to pay the costs of calling out the militia unless the national government authorized their use. So Cockburn's presence threatened locals, state government, and federal authority, with each feeling abandoned by the other.[10]

As Cockburn's squadron anchored off Spesutie Island in late April, overconfident Americans in Havre-de-Grace, Maryland, who had brazenly hoisted the Stars and Stripes, fired on his vessels. Such boisterous action, he concluded, deemed the town worthy of attacking. On May 3, Cockburn's black and white marines overran the town, encountering little resistance. In fact, the Maryland militia had begun running immediately, and the townspeople fled with only the clothes on their backs. Within minutes, British marines took the little town, ransacking and torching buildings. Cockburn personally led a party to the nearby Principio Foundry, one of only three cannon factories in the United States, where they destroyed some 130 small arms and forty-six cannon, and they burned the foundry itself, which represented Cockburn's greatest 1813 strategic victory. Meanwhile another British party moved up the Susquehanna River to Lapidum, where they burned five vessels and some five hundred barrels of flour. Although reports indicate that the British burned two-thirds of Havre's houses and even pillaged St. John's Episcopal Church, Cockburn maintained that he did so because the people had brought it on themselves.[11]

A few days later Cockburn moved against Georgetown and Fredericktown on the Sassafras River, destroying war materials and ships and burning the towns because they too offered resistance. First, he offered them the chance to avoid destruction if they submitted peaceably. But when they did not, Cockburn used former slaves as messengers during the attacks because their local knowledge and innocuous presence did not alert Americans to anything unusual. Nearby Charlestown on the North East River accepted Cockburn's offer and was thus spared. In less than a month, Cockburn had demonstrated the vulnerability and racial instability of the Chesapeake region and the American inability to provide defense to the countryside.[12]

Throughout the Chesapeake British raids had mobilized slaves who saw the redcoat presence as a way to secure their freedom. During early May in Princess Ann County, Virginia, several slaves "eloped" to the

British, prompting the venomous newspaper *National Intelligencer* to charge that "the unfortunate beings who have run away to the British are kept . . . constantly at hard labor, in doing all the drudgery and dirty work on the ships; that they are whipped like dogs, and if any of them should be taken sick, they are immediately thrown overboard." Undoubtedly, as the paper contended, the British would take the slaves to the Caribbean and sell them into slavery just as Lord Dunmore had reportedly done to "the fathers of these deluded wretches." Responding to an American officer about these charges, Warren retorted that the British had not reenslaved them, but that the "Black people are . . . at liberty to follow their own inclinations." Former slave and fisherman Charles Ball soon learned exactly what Warren meant.[13]

In Calvert County, Maryland, plantation mistress Mrs. Wilson had kept her slaves under close surveillance during British activities in the area. Despite never treating them poorly, the British presence almost assured that some of her slaves would desert. On a spring 1813 evening, a couple of slaves stole a canoe and paddled out to the British fleet, informing them of the presence of more than one hundred slaves on a nearby plantation. According to the newly devised plan, the slaves would return to the plantation and the following evening lead them to the shore, where a British detachment of boats would "bring them off." The escape occurred around midnight the following evening "partly by persuasion, partly by compulsion." According to Ball, this defection represented "the greatest disaster that had befallen any individual in our neighbourhood, in the course of the war," prompting one American officer to attempt to ransom the slaves. Warren refused to negotiate for the former slaves, instead permitting them to decide for themselves whether they would return.

Ball joined the party that visited the British fleet under a white flag to retrieve slaves. While Lt. Col. Kendall Addison and other white gentlemen met with British officers about the slaves, Ball circulated among them, extolling the virtues of returning. They unsurprisingly refused because "their heads were full of notions of liberty and happiness in some of the West India islands." When the American commissioners departed, a white man and Ball remained behind, with Ball having instructions to exert himself "to the utmost, to prevail on the runaway slaves to return to their mistress." Ball spent two days trying to persuade the "mass of black fugitives" to return, but he could not convince them. As the fleet hoisted anchor, a British officer reportedly even suggested that Ball leave with the others, but he respectfully declined, falsely claiming that he was "already a free man, and though [he] owned no land [him]self, yet [he] could have plenty of land of other people to cultivate." Technically, though, Ball was a fugitive slave from Georgia.[14]

Before the end of May, another sixty to seventy slaves had escaped to the British squadron. The numbers continued to grow throughout early June, as the *Narcissus* reported that it picked up "6 Black Men, 3 Women & a child from the main." Although Warren found that American slaves "evince upon every occasion, the strongest predilection for the cause of Great Britain," the increased number of refugees strained his resources greatly. The Admiralty Office had instructed officers not to "give encouragement" to the slaves "to rise against their masters" because, among other things, such insurrections would inundate the British squadron with refugees. Warren did have the authority to "enlist them in any of the Black corps" or to evacuate them. As they came aboard British ships Warren tried to have them "employed in the mode which seems . . . most beneficial." Not surprisingly, the prospect of evacuation appealed far greater to slaves than labor or combat, and the possibility of evacuation also spurred continued flight. The Admiralty Office warned officers that every slave evacuated would become the responsibility of the British government to maintain, so Warren had to be cautious as to how he fulfilled his directives. Despite his prudence, once slaves learned that they could find safe haven with the British fleet, the proverbial floodgates opened.[15]

Warren's return in mid-June 1813 momentarily solved the British manpower shortage, as he brought with him additional troops, including "two companies of Foreigners" labeled as "Canadian chasseurs"—these three hundred Frenchmen captured in Spain had volunteered to fight in America rather than languish in British prisons. With these supplements Cockburn and Warren again attacked Norfolk. When Warren sent his troops ashore on June 22, the island's geography and the shallowness of the water limited their approach. British boats soon ran aground, piling up on one another, making easy targets for the American defenders. One of the boats carrying thirty of the French soldiers capsized before reaching shallow water, and American troops reportedly waded out into the surf to shoot at the drowning men. While the British attack at Craney Island had caused a great "degree of alarm," the American vengeance during the engagement would come full circle, much quicker than anyone expected.[16]

Three days later, Warren sent his troops across the bay to Hampton on the north bank of the James River. Cockburn's troops encountered light opposition and quickly stormed the little village that commanded the communication routes between Norfolk and the up-country. British forces swarmed the adjacent militia camp, destroyed all potential military stores, and seized the city, where they remained for the next three days. During the early stages of the occupation, the "company of French prisoners . . . proved to be so unmanageable, and in every way so bad," that Cockburn believed he would have been better off without them. They pillaged, looted, burned buildings, and killed indiscriminately. Dead bodies reportedly remained on the ground days after the battle. Once the French troops had eliminated American forces, they descended on old and young women unable to escape. Many females "suffered to be abused in the most shameful manner, not only by the venal, savage foe but [also] by the unfortunate and infatuated blacks who were encouraged by [the French soldiers] in their excesses." Reports of black soldiers participating in the episode only heightened the American fear and trepidation, yet were unproven. In one instance, a woman remembered being attacked by six soldiers, some of whom wore redcoats—as opposed to the French greencoats—who raped her repeatedly even in front of her young daughter. In another instance, four soldiers dressed in green robbed and accosted a young woman with her infant child; one of them "gratified his abominable desires." Numerous other stories, many of which were about the blacks, were simply fabricated hyperbole.[17]

British encouragement of slaves appeared to Americans as despicable and frightening because it undermined the entire social order and economy of the South. The "discovery of parties of negroes . . . exercising with arms in the night," Warren reported, produced "great alarm" bordering on paranoia. After the Hampton episode, rumors quickly spread that the British would land black regiments and "chosen rogues" to burn, pillage, and plunder. That slaves had "a most ardent desire to join any [British] troops or seamen acting in the country" prompted the American newspaper *Niles' Register* to label Warren as the "spoiler in the Chesapeake." After the Hampton affair the paper also likened Cockburn to "Satan in his cloud . . . treating the suppliant females with the rudest curses and most vile appellations." Yet Cockburn felt it necessary to take extreme actions against a populace who would go to any lengths to harass his forces. He intimidated the American people with deliberate acts of "frightfulness," including the possibility of slave insurrections, and destroyed the material things that Americans needed to retaliate. As a result the fighting devolved into "a vicious little war," with both sides perpetrating numerous outrages.[18]

The prospect of a slave insurrection, with all of its inherent horrors, weighed heavily on the minds of southerners. Citizens pleaded desperately with state and federal officials to provide more coastal protection. North Carolinians reportedly agreed to raise troops to help defend the coasts of Virginia, which would prevent their slaves from fleeing north to seek out British forces. In nearby Norfolk, Gen. Robert Taylor acknowledged that the presence of a large and armed American force in the region would discourage "any movement of slaves" as well as prevent their cooperation with the British. Likewise, Maryland governor Levin Winder warned his militia to secure all small boats that the slaves frequently used to flee to the British. Local areas also created slave patrols because "the blacks in some places refuse to work and say they shall soon be free. . . . Should we be attacked, there will be great danger of the blacks rising, and to prevent this, patrols are very necessary, to keep them in awe." But in no case did slave owners believe that large armies, state militias, or even dedicated local armed patrols thwarted determined slaves from escaping, nor could such forces prevent the British from landing and liberating the slaves. There was little that officials could do to restrict "the migration of colored people."[19]

Aggressive British action in Hampton Roads during July had increased the influx of slaves to the British fleet. Late that month some twenty-five women and children stole canoes and hid near a grove of waterside trees, waiting to flee to a nearby British ship. But the owners of the canoes had discovered the slaves, hid among the undergrowth, and began firing on the overloaded crafts as their occupants rowed feverishly toward the British ship. The shots struck two, and the other twenty-two surrendered. When the fishermen marched the slaves back to Hampton, the locals lauded their bravery. A few months later, a slave patrol hid among some sand dunes near Cape Henry while two of their members with blackened faces and hands waved their handkerchiefs at a nearby British vessel. The British dispatched three small boats to rescue the slaves. When one of the British sailors coming ashore noticed the white ankle of the disguised black man, he screamed, "White men in disguise by _____!" The boats beat a hasty retreat but not before the American patrol had killed two British sailors.[20]

Slaves braved the possibility of being wounded, killed, or captured and punished. They left behind everything they knew for the rumor of freedom, and the number of fleeing slaves arriving at British positions increased daily. During the British operations against Norfolk and Hampton in late July, a Virginia militia officer reported that "about one hundred & twenty negroe slaves" had fled from the area of Northampton in the northern Chesapeake Bay. Near Washington, people left the countryside for the capital city, convinced that the "few scatter'd s——s about our neighbourhood" would descend on the capital city where they could join with those slaves from the city. A month later British forces took "42 slaves, men, women, and children" from Kent Island. Some thirty British soldiers landed at St. Jerome's Creek in St. Mary's County, Maryland, and took all of Caleb Jones's "Negroes and a quantity of stock chiefly poultry." One of Jones's slaves later returned to seek his "vengeance" by leading a British force, who again looted the plantation. The slave now armed with pistols and a sword, verbally tormented Jones throughout the night, before leaving with the British and the plantation's other slaves the following morning. A St. Mary's County militia officer confirmed that with such episodes, "nine-tenths [of the area's slaves] will abscond unless the enemy can be driven" from the region. Even Nicholas Faulcon, known as "one of the most humane and indulgent masters on earth," found his former slaves leading British troops back to his plantation, where they destroyed virtually everything and freed those still in bondage. That slaves fled to the British weighed heavily on American minds, but that they could also return armed and guiding enemy forces created an unsettling and all-encompassing angst.[21]

Although the summer 1813 campaigns had not resulted in many British casualties, the heat and mosquitoes certainly took their toll. Scurvy appeared among the sailors, and fever ravished the marines. The presence of disease spreading through the fleet combined with hurricanes—one of which blew through in late September—prompted Warren to call an end to the campaign season. He departed Kent Island for Halifax with "all the negroes that were not too old and infirmed," prize captures, and supplies requisitioned from the American coast. Cockburn departed for Bermuda, leaving behind Capt. Robert Barrie with a small squadron to continue the blockade. Despite the fleet's departure, wealthy Virginia planter Joseph Cabell confirmed that the remaining British plundered, burned ships, and even liberated some two hundred slaves from Northumberland and Westmoreland counties. Slaves also flocked to the British standard in increasing numbers, prompting Americans to plead for their return and leaving British officers wondering how to deal with the refugees.[22]

Many Americans mistakenly believed that if they visited British ships, they could persuade their own slaves to return to servitude. Yet the presence of American planters rarely, if ever, made a difference.

Wherever British ships anchored, Admirals Warren and Cockburn received numerous requests from American slaveowners to board British ships in an attempt to reclaim their property. While permitting slaveowners to appeal to the refugees in person, British commanders maintained throughout the war that the refugees were free people who could decide their own fate, and they did. In one instance a black man named Ben George, who had been sentenced to three years in prison for larceny, escaped to the British; after meeting with Americans he reportedly chose to return and "submit to his confinement." In another instance, an American who boarded the *Barossa* during the summer of 1813 claimed that the British had sent the refugees to Bermuda a couple of days before his arrival, "no doubt to be treated or sold as West Indian slaves." The slaves had not been sold. In fact, the refugees had been sent instead to Bermuda because the continued influx of refugees strained British local resources, forcing a constant resupply. After a few days aboard British ships, commanders generally sent most of the slaves in emptied vessels to Bermuda or Halifax, where the Admiralty Office anticipated that they would be apprenticed in useful occupations. Although Americans could not prevent the flight of slaves, their fictitious propaganda alleged that the refugees would be reenslaved in the Caribbean.[23]

By the end of 1813 British commanders as well as the Ministry understood the potential manpower that slaves offered and instructed officers to provide shelter, protection, and evacuation to refugees. Americans, unaware of the true British policy regarding refugees, certainly believed that the predatory raids and willingness to liberate slaves were designed to destroy the fabric of the southern economy and society. In reality British policy makers simply tried to manage the war in American waters with limited resources. As news of the continued influx of refugees arrived throughout 1813, it convinced Lord Bathurst that slaves enlisted into the marines could alleviate British manpower shortages. And, while Captain Barrie had not received new ministerial directions regarding slaves, he had gained the wisdom of using the "very intelligent" slaves as guides. Their knowledge of local terrain, combined with their informational networks within the slave communities, convinced the British officer that "there is no doubt but the blacks of Virginia & Maryland would cheerfully take up arms and join us against the Americans." Capt. Charles Napier, also serving in American waters, confidently proposed that with a handful of British soldiers he could within twelve hours assemble a slave army of more than one hundred thousand that could seize control of the area between the Chesapeake and Delaware Bays. Finally, Napier suggested that his plan would "have dictated peace and abolished slavery in the United States." While the British government did not adopt Napier's plan for a grand slave army, they did encourage officers to enlist slaves into the ranks. [24]

"[G]REATEST POSSIBLE ALARM, AND ANNOYANCE AMONGST THE AMERICANS": 1814: DESTRUCTION IN THE CHESAPEAKE

Although new commander British admiral Alexander F. I. Cochrane did not arrive in American waters until April 1814, he spent much of the early spring in Bermuda drawing up plans for assault. He wanted his officers to "act with the utmost hostility against the shores of the United States" and to show the Americans that they were "at the mercy of an invading force" who could reduce American seaports to ashes and waste the surrounding countryside; this would provide some "retaliation for their [American] savage conduct in Canada." Two years earlier—even before the United States had declared war—Cochrane had drafted a strategic blueprint, suggesting that New Orleans and Virginia were the two most vulnerable places in America and that the British could take both. The resulting internal pressure would topple the American government. In Virginia, he proposed two targets: the state's few cities and the black slave population, who he asserted were "British in their hearts, . . . [and] might be of great use if war should be prosecuted with vigor." Cochrane knew slave labor girded the southern economy and provided the underpinning and structure of society, and any disruptions would leave Virginians in a state of panic.[25]

Cochrane had learned from Captain Barrie that there were some 120 slaves from Virginia and Maryland aboard HMS *Dragon,* and he was convinced that even more would "cheerfully take up arms and join us against the Americans." Among the group, Barrie reported, were "several very intelligent fellows . . . willing to act as local guides" in addition to those eager to fight. And despite repeated American attempts to persuade the refugees to return, Barrie insisted that "not a single black would return to his former master." Buoyed by optimism, Cochrane was instructed to recruit "negroes and coloured inhabitants" into His Majesty's Service and, if they would not fight, then evacuate all who wished to leave the United States as "free settlers [to] some of H.M. colonies." Once refugees had been relocated, the Admiralty Office anticipated that local officials would have them "apprenticed in such manner" as benefited the local economy.[26]

In late February 1814, Adm. George Cockburn returned after six months in Bermuda to resume his Chesapeake raids. He also brought with him orders to "find and get possession of some convenient Island, or point within the Chesapeake . . . which might also serve as a place of refuge for the negro slaves from the surrounding shores." Admiral Cockburn began surveying for such a location, and he sent Cochrane information about local conditions, highlighting the shortage of British troops for future operations. The sobering news did not discourage Cochrane, but rather reconfirmed in his own mind that the refugee slaves could greatly supplement British forces. Yet he acknowledged that the infrastructure to manage such an influx of refugee soldiers—an anticipated five thousand men—did not exist. He asked Warren to send agents from the black West India regiments to Bermuda, where they would recruit and train refugees. Additionally, he requested that Warren construct temporary wooden barracks on the island of Bermuda to house black soldiers, along with their wives and families; the British government would support refugee dependents in the same manner as they did for other British soldiers. According to Cochrane, the only immediate problem was that Bermuda law prohibited "the introduction of colored persons into" the island. Pleading for Warren to use his influence to secure a temporary suspension of the act, Cochrane warned that it would be "an opportunity lost that never may return." If British ships could not land the "emigrants" quickly, then loaded supply ships could not immediately return "to the Coast of America for others."[27]

Soon after his appointment, Cochrane had boasted that with "15,000 of Lord Wellington's Army all the country south west of the Chesapeake might be restored to the dominion of Great Britain." Yet this audacious pronouncement did not reflect current conditions in the Chesapeake but rather Cochrane's hopes for acquiring additional soldiers. Knowing that the war in America did not resonate as strongly as or have the urgency of the French war against Napoleon, Cochrane would have to construct his army creatively. He proposed an operation against New Orleans using a small force of regulars, Indians, slaves, Baratarian pirates, and disaffected citizens. Cochrane had also sent Capt. Hugh Pigot to the Gulf Coast with some two thousand stands of arms, acknowledging that equipping Indians would be "by far the cheapest and most effectual way . . . [for] draining off the attention of the American government from . . . Canada." He also devised plans

By the Honorable Sir *ALEXANDER COCHRANE, K. B.*
Vice Admiral of the Red, and Commander in Chief of
His Majesty's Ships and Vessels, upon the North Ameri-
can Station, &c. &c. &c.

A PROCLAMATION.

WHEREAS it has been represented to me, that many Persons now resident in the UNITED STATES, have expressed a desire to withdraw therefrom, with a view of entering into His Majesty's Service, or of being received as Free Settlers into some of His Majesty's Colonies.

This is therefore to Give Notice,

That all those who may be disposed to emigrate from the UNITED STATES will, with their Families, be received on board of His Majesty's Ships or Vessels of War, or at the Military Posts that may be established, upon or near the Coast of the UNITED STATES, when they will have their choice of either entering into His Majesty's Sea or Land Forces, or of being sent as FREE Settlers to the British Possessions in North America or the West Indies, where they will meet with all due encouragement.

GIVEN under my Hand at Bermuda, this 2nd
day of April, 1814.

ALEXANDER COCHRANE.

By Command of the Vice Admiral,

WILLIAM BALHETCHET.

GOD SAVE THE KING.

Adm. Alexander F. I. Cochrane Proclamation. Adm. Alexander F. I. Cochrane's
April 1814 Proclamation promised British forces would liberate those willing
to depart the United States. Slaves could join the British military or be
relocated as free settlers to other British colonies. Image from the National
Archives, Public Records Office, Admiralty Office Papers, 1/508, fol. 579.

for mobilizing slaves and entrenching them in the Chesapeake—he had requested "five hundred stand of arms," an engineer, "entrenching tools," and a black regiment from the Caribbean—because the presence of a slave bastion would weaken and demoralize American defenses in that region.[28]

To ensure that slaves fled to the British standard and his new army, Cochrane printed one thousand copies of a bold proclamation for distribution among slave populations. It stated that British ships and troops would accept all "those who may be disposed to emigrate from the United States . . . [along] with their families." Like Virginia governor Lord Dunmore, who had issued a similar edict in November 1775, Cochrane's addressed black residents of the United States. Once under the protection of the British flag, the admiral offered the "choice of either entering into His Majesty's Sea or Land Forces, or of being sent as FREE Settlers to the British Possessions in North America or the West Indies." Convinced that the broadly worded proclamation would provide protection to runaways, "annoy [Americans,] and bring the consequences of the war home to their own doors," he recognized that putting arms in the hands of slaves could very well have an adverse effect. The American government, he predicted, would "order the blacks to be sent into the interior," depriving Cochrane of the soldiers he anticipated. In fact, Richmond's mayor and aldermen did consider evacuating all blacks except those deemed absolutely necessary, while the state legislature introduced repressive bills restricting slave and free black movement and abolishing schools for blacks. Cockburn, who had been liberating slaves for the better part of a year, believed that few slaves would actually enlist, suggesting instead to Cochrane that when given the choice between freedom and "joining us in Arms," they would obviously choose the former. Since "Blacky . . . is naturally neither very valorous nor very active," Cockburn planned to mention only British willingness "to receive and protect them, and to put arms in their hands if they chuse to use them in conjunction with us."[29]

Cockburn immediately landed slaves with copies of the proclamation to infiltrate American plantations and spread news of the British presence and willingness to "receive, protect, and assist them and put arms in their hands." Within four weeks, more than one hundred men, women, and children had fled to British protection on Tangier Island, located in the southern Chesapeake Bay off the Potomac River. It had a number of strategic and geographic advantages, and Cockburn emphasized its most important quality—the island was "surrounded by the

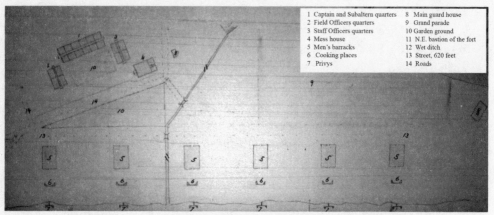

1 Captain and Subaltern quarters	8 Main guard house
2 Field Officers quarters	9 Grand parade
3 Staff Officers quarters	10 Garden ground
4 Mess house	11 N.E. bastion of the fort
5 Men's barracks	12 Wet ditch
6 Cooking places	13 Street, 620 feet
7 Privys	14 Roads

British Base on Tangier Island. Tangier Island became the British base for training refugee slave soldiers during the spring of 1814. Isolated in the Chesapeake Bay and adjacent to deep water, Fort Albion, as it was called, served as a staging area for operations, a training facility for Colonial Marines, and a depot to transfer evacuees to British ships bound for Bermuda. Courtesy of the trustees of the National Library of Scotland, Alexander F.I. Cochrane Papers, MS 2326, f 288 B.

districts from which the Negroes always come," providing enough ratio-nale for choosing Tangier Island as a refugee depot.[30]

In early April, Cockburn landed two hundred military laborers with marine guards on the southern tip of the island, instructing them to clear ground for the construction of Fort Albion. The bastion was built quickly and included two redoubts three hundred yards apart, a parade ground, and a garden. The soldiers, with only one saw, one hammer, and one bucket of nails, then erected a storehouse and barracks. They spared a grove of nearby trees, pitched their tents instead in a semicircle on the north side of the fortification, and complained of the "sand and swamp and . . . myriads of mosquitoes" that covered the island. By the end of May, British troops had completed the base and "depot for run-away slaves," which increased the "inconveniences the Americans in this neighborhood already suffered from the War."[31]

Even with the depot "in the centre of the Chesapeake," Cockburn did not anticipate large numbers of recruits until the British established a mainland position. In mid-April, he had sent the sloop *Jaseur* to hover near the mainland in anticipation of rescuing evacuees. Instead, the ship's presence alerted Americans and discouraged slaves from trying to escape. Then Cockburn sent raiding parties up the rivers with in-structions to capture food and supplies, burn ships, and liberate slaves.

A week later, British troops moved up the Rappahannock in Lancaster County where they freed more than 130 slaves and captured two schooners, some 250 barrels of flour, and sixty sheep. Even with the additional supplies, the need to secure food for the soldiers and sailors of the fleet and for the increasing number of runaway slaves unexpectedly strained British resources. Lieutenant Scott recalled that virtually every night, canoes and small boats loaded with these "poor creatures came off to us." One particular episode tugged at Scott's emotions: a "negress who came down with an infant in her arms," put the child in the boat, and suddenly ran back into the woods to retrieve "something she had forgotten"; the mother never returned, and the infant was later adopted by Capt. Charles Ross. Most of those who made it to the British fleet generally arrived without any personal effects, with little if any clothing, or without any family. "Crowds of refugees of colour, of all description, ages, sexes, and condition" suddenly inundated Fort Albion, so much so that by early May Cockburn reported that he had more than 225 mouths to feed, potentially threatening British operations in a way American defenders could not.[32]

Faced with a deluge of humanity, Cockburn devised what he believed to be a simple formula for providing provisions to the "Refugee Negroes." He proposed giving men two-thirds of a seaman's allowance of bread or flour, plus a serving of corn, rice, or Indian meal. Women would receive a half allowance, and each child would warrant a one-quarter allowance. Not surprisingly, most of the refugees did not "seem to be quite satisfied with it or to think it enough" food. Refusing to increase the allowances, Cockburn suggested that the food allotments were sufficient and often supplemented with "a considerable quantity of fish." "It ought to content them, if it were in their nature to be contented," Cockburn bellowed, but he would offer additional food to "those who volunteer for the service." Cochrane approved Cockburn's plan for feeding the refugees and later suggested providing them "with their usual food" of vegetables, fish, and rice. Yet dispensing rations to refugees caused increased trouble for those responsible for balancing the ship's books with the commanding admiral and with the Admiralty Office because the refugees drained considerable resources, and much of it could not be accounted for in the ledgers.[33]

Clothing the refugees also proved to be a financial drain, but without the new clothing, the slaves posed a potential health risk. Of the first 225 refugees who had found their way to Tangier Island, Cockburn found that without exception, "those who come off to us have only the few dirty rags of covering in which they escape." Fearing that "they will breed disease amongst us," he instructed officers to provide the refugees with "slop clothing" and keep detailed records of the transactions. Clean clothing would reduce the risk of spreading disease and would also be a "very considerable and effective inducement to draw them over to us," Cockburn proclaimed. Cochrane concurred, wanting to provide them with "Red Jackets," which he believed would give them a "gay appearance [and] act as an inducement to others to come off."[34]

By the end of May 1814, British forces had transformed Tangier Island from a remote, isolated outpost to an easily accessible military training base and runaway slave depot. Wanting to transform the bondsmen into soldiers so they could earn the freedom they sought, Cockburn enlisted almost fifty recruits from the first group of refugees. He issued them additional food and clothing, convinced that uniforms would help to convert these men into soldiers. Granted, he did not initially think they would immediately become proficient soldiers, but he was convinced that they would be capable of carrying weapons and participating in combat. Selecting only strong, able, and motivated men for his new unit of Colonial Marines, he commissioned Sgt. Maj. Charles Hammond as an ensign (confirmed permanently by the Prince Regent) and gave him the responsibility of transforming the raw recruits into soldiers. Initially, Cockburn asserted that the refugees were "naturally neither very valorous nor very active." They "pretend to be very bold and very ready to join us in any expedition against their old masters," but Cockburn still remained skeptical of their ability and motivations. As Hammond transformed these men, the Colonial Marines soon created "the greatest possible alarm, and annoyance amongst the Americans." Surprisingly, Cockburn proudly boasted, these soldiers "are getting on astonishingly and are really very fine fellows." He also admitted he had underestimated their abilities—"they have induced me to alter the bad opinion I had of the whole of their Race and I now really believe these, we are training, will neither show want of zeal or courage when employed by us in attacking their old Masters."[35]

The Colonial Marines responded so well to British training that Cockburn soon claimed he preferred them to his own marines. Hammond, acknowledging their "steadiness," reported they "only require a little instruction" and will soon "equal their brother soldiers in the performance of every part of their duty." The soldiers proved their value, as they were fitter and stronger; in operations ashore they committed no outrages; accustomed to hot weather, they withstood long marches and arduous labor better than the average marine. They had knowledge of local terrain, making excellent scouts and reliable guides, particularly in night operations, where their knowledge and experience made it easier for small raiding parties to elude or surprise American forces.[36]

Cockburn had sent many slaves ashore to disseminate information about British activities in the bay, and they told a "good tale and their comrades kept so faithfully their secret that they escaped condemnation." True, the Americans captured many of the infiltrators, but they still conveyed information about the slave soldiers training at Tangier, about Cochrane's proclamation of freedom, and about the possibility for a new home in a British colony. Combined with the Colonial Marines, this clandestine group became a tough and loyal auxiliary force that created an indelible mark on the psyche of Americans, causing "a most general and undisguised alarm." Cockburn declared the Americans "expect Blacky will have no mercy on them and they know that he understands bush fighting and the locality of the *woods* as well as themselves and can perhaps play at hide and seek in them even better." In any case, the British benefited, and Cockburn took great pride in noting the alarm among planters as revealed in the local press.[37]

The Colonial Marines, who by mid-May numbered about eighty, saw their first action on May 30, 1814, when Cockburn sent a small force under Captain Ross to take an American battery on Pangoteake (Pungoteague, Virginia) Creek, twelve miles to the east of Tangier Island. Rowing throughout the cool night, by sunrise the boats were within three miles of the American position when an alarm gun fired, warning of the British approach. Almost immediately, an American battery fired on the boats, which had run aground in shallow waters. British marines quickly spilled out, wading in water up to their waists and struggling to get to a protected position on shore. Some of the British flotilla, undetected, landed toward the rear of the Americans, crossed a wet marsh, took up a position in the woods, and began firing on the battery from behind. After only a few minutes the Americans retreated, leaving their artillery and supplies. Ross reported that the "new[ly] raised Black Corps . . . gave a most excellent specimen of what they are likely to be, their conduct was marked by great spirit and vivacity, and perfect obedience." During the attack "though one of them [Michael Harding] was shot and died instantly . . . [and another Kennedy Breto was wounded], it did not daunt or check the others, but on the contrary animated them to seek revenge." Moreover, they did not commit "any improper outrages" as they burned barracks, captured a small-caliber field gun, and robbed and pillaged a house. Cockburn later awarded the gun to the Colonial Marines for their "steady and good behaviour," and apparently the reward "made them very proud." While an American newspaper reviled the "barbarisms" of the "ruffian Cockburn" and his "negroes in uniform," the British admiral praised "the Colonial Marines, who were for the first time, employed in Arms against their old Masters, and behaved to the admiration of every Body."[38]

In early June, Captain Barrie acknowledged that during a night operation up St. Leonard's Creek, the "Colonial Marines . . . evinced the greatest eagerness, to come to Action with their former Master." They raided the plantation of a Mr. Sewell, carrying off livestock and liberating slaves. During the next few weeks, Barrie tried repeatedly to lure Joshua Barney's American gunboats out of the shallow waters of St. Leonard's Creek with no success, prompting the British to launch a series of vicious diversionary raids. In raids against Benedict (June 15), Lower Marlboro (June 16), and Magruder's Landing (June 17), Maryland, the Colonial Corps burned more than 3,150 hogsheads of tobacco, seized hogs and sheep, liberated slaves, and "conducted themselves with the utmost Order, Forbearance and Regularity," even though they "might expect to meet their former masters." Despite the destruction, Barney still refused to take the bait.[39]

Cockburn also sent twenty Colonial Marines on a special mission to capture Maryland militia captain Ignatius Jarboe. In early June British lieutenant George Urmston had gone ashore under a flag of truce near Cedar Point to secure water and food. While he was intending to pay a fair price for provisions, a group of American militia officers accosted and verbally insulted him. Jarboe, the most insolent of the group, brandished his pistol at the lieutenant and threatened to stand him up like a scarecrow. Urmston quietly returned to his ship without responding to the outrageous insult, where he asked all of the runaways whether anyone knew of Jarboe. A former slave of Jarboe's was enlisted to lead a "very steady party" of Colonial Marines to Jarboe's house, located eight miles from their landing location and near an American militia camp. Upon reaching their destination late at night, British forces discovered Jarboe shivering in his bed with his new wife. Sensitive to the young bride's plea to release her husband, Urmston seized Jarboe and returned to his launch just ahead of pursing American militiamen. Taking him aboard ship, the British respectfully treated Jarboe as an American officer and gave him the same privileges as British officers, despite his previous display of contempt. U.S. Commissioner for Prisoners Gen. John

Mason made a special request for the captain's release, going so far as to provide a heart-wrenching emotional appeal from Jarboe's wife, but Cockburn remained unmoved by the pleas. Instead, Cockburn had the American released on parole in England.[40]

Having driven Barney's American gunboats far upriver, British ships moved off Benedict, where troops stripped everything of value from the countryside. They loaded as much tobacco as they could on board prize schooners, barges, and ships. They seized cattle and sheep to replenish their food supply, horses and oxen to carry their baggage, and in some cases even furniture and personal effects. British soldiers attracted a horde of slaves, who followed behind them begging for their liberation. One estimate calculated that the "royal firm, Cockburn and Barrie," had liberated hundreds of slaves, seized livestock (cattle, sheep, horses, and oxen), and confiscated some four thousand hogsheads of tobacco valued at approximately $250,000.[41]

Isolated in Chesapeake waters and surrounded by enemy territory, British forces relied on a long supply line from Halifax or Bermuda and the bountiful yet uncooperative Chesapeake countryside, as well as on the willingness of some Americans to barter or sell provisions, food, and water. Yet finding Americans willing to deal with his forces proved increasingly difficult for Cockburn as the summer progressed. The raids through the countryside and the flight of slaves to Tangier Island made Americans resentful, including many who did not own slaves or even support the institution. The anger and frustration unavoidably seeped into negotiations between local officials and British officers. In early June, for example, Cockburn offered to exchange an American prisoner of war for a "British subject of colour, a native of Jamaica" who had been held in prison for more than a year, yet he never received a response from the American deputy marshal. Not surprisingly, the exchange, parole, or release of prisoners relied exclusively on the willingness of local officials, and both sides became far more reluctant as the instances of British and American depredations increased. Conversely, as British operations continued throughout the summer, Cockburn found an increased and almost debilitative problem as white British sailors and marines deserted their harsh military service, hoping to find an easier life as civilians in the American countryside. By late June 1814, the frequency of Cochrane's Royal "Marines walking over to the enemy" had convinced him to rely on the Colonial Marines, who were "stronger men and more trustworthy for we are sure they will not desert."[42]

In late June 1814 Joshua Barney's flotilla finally fought through the British blockade, slipping into the Patuxent River. The brazen American attack badly damaged two British frigates, angered British officers who had to exercise greater caution in future operations, and prompted Cockburn to assess the situation for himself. Tangier Island had enough strength to repel any force that might attack, but Cockburn learned that Barney's gunboats had retreated so far up the Patuxent River that they no longer offered a threat to future British operations in the area. The influx of additional runaways also convinced Cockburn that they would need to build an additional depot just to meet the growing demand. He authorized Capt. George Watts of the *Jaseur* (also the commanding officer of Fort Albion) to keep blacks and whites busy expanding the fortifications and the camp's living areas for the refugees, and in early July a prize ship arrived with lumber for the projects. British officers then carefully separated refugees suitable for work from those wanting to join the Colonial Marines. Those who were capable, who were willing to enlist, and who signed an oath attesting to their good physical and mental health received an $8 bonus and an extra half ration of rum to drink to the King's health. Many of the slaves who found their way to Tangier Island wanted to enlist immediately, some boasting "me free man, me got cut massa's throat, give me musket." Unless they enlisted, all refugees would have to earn their keep on Tangier Island until ships arrived to evacuate them to a British colony.[43]

Cochrane instructed Cockburn to intensify the attacks against the American shoreline, if for no other reason than to protect "the desertion of the Black Population." He sent marine transports and additional ships from Bermuda to the Chesapeake to increase British operations; once unloaded, the transports could ferry refugees away from the United States. He also told Cockburn to secure pilots and guides and to pay them well because their services remained essential for successful operations. Granted, Cockburn had only a small contingent of troops in the Chesapeake, but Cochrane assured him that additional soldiers would arrive soon. Until that time, Cochrane suggested that the "desertion of the black population . . . properly armed and backed with [the] 20,000 British troops" soon to arrive would hurl Madison from his presidential throne. Capt. David Milne, commanding off Boston during the summer of 1814, remained more guarded, convinced that "the blacks in the Southern States would certainly join any force that might be landed there to get rid of their masters, who they detest." Cochrane instructed

Cockburn to gain "the cordial support of the Black population," which would give his small army easy access into the interior.[44]

The news of additional soldiers buoyed Cochrane's optimism for the remainder of the campaign season. After reviewing reports from officers stationed throughout American waters, he suggested to the Ministry that the first major attack of his campaign would focus on Baltimore—where he would arm a "Number of Negroes" to fight and serve as guides—followed up with assaults against Philadelphia, Annapolis, and Washington. Believing that these quick-strike operations would permit him to raise a great "Number of Black troops for the prosecution of the War," he also believed Chesapeake raids would drive state and federal officials to concentrate their soldiers in the region rather than on the Canadian frontier. "The Blacks are all Good Horsemen," Cochrane boastfully predicted, "and thousands will Join upon their Masters['] Horses." He even offered a $20 bonus for each horse that slaves brought to the British. Once this groundswell of runaway support had donned red jackets, Cockburn could continue "annoying the Americans a good deal."[45]

With new motivations, Cockburn divided his fleet into two squadrons: one on the Patuxent, commanded by Capt. Joseph Nourse of the *Severn*, and one on the Potomac, personally led by Cockburn. They had simple objectives: to liberate slaves and recruit as many as possible for the Colonial Marines; "to destroy and lay waste" to all towns within their reach; to continue the blockade of the American flotilla in the Patuxent; to reconnoiter so they would have accurate geographical information for future operations; and, finally, to serve as diversions obscuring true British intentions. Cockburn's previous raids had fulfilled all of these objectives, as his soldiers had plundered, burned structures, liberated slaves, requisitioned livestock, mapped the Patuxent as far upriver as Benedict, and convinced Americans that the raids had but financial objectives. They had also thrown "the weight of suffering . . . upon those persons who are more immediately attached to the president's party," for the "wanton and unjustifiable outrages on the unoffending inhabitants" of Canada. Reportedly British troops even frequently marched miles inland only "after negroes and stock."[46]

Nourse's squadron struck quickly, and within a few days in mid-July, his men brought back five hogsheads of tobacco to the fleet along with thirty-nine slaves who had fled from the plantation of a Colonel Plater. During the first week of August, Nourse's men again vented themselves, torching tobacco, houses, and boats along Slaughter Creek off the Eastern Shore, taking a schooner with eight thousand feet of plank, twenty-two hogsheads of tobacco, and "Black Refugees [who] increase so fast that I begin to be somewhat puzzled about them." Not wanting to be burdened with extra mouths to feed, Nourse quickly sent off "all our Blacks except" those used as guides and those "in training for Soldiers."[47]

Cockburn had chosen to operate on the Potomac River for two reasons: it drained the area surrounding the U.S. capital, Washington, DC, and "the Black Population inclined to join us is more numerous on the shores of the Potomac than anywhere else within the Chesapeake." After taking Leonard's Town and Nomini Creek in mid-July, Cockburn sent small parties of troops into the countryside to help slaves find freedom. By the time his army returned to their ships, they had brought back 135 "Negroes who were anxious to join us."[48]

Some years later Lieutenant Scott recalled a meeting under a flag of truce with one particularly uncouth American officer who chided him about recent British night attacks. The American boldly challenged Scott to try to steal cannon from a fort he commanded, adding, "but tarnation seize me in the bramble-busy if I don't blow you to hell within a mile of my command. . . . I would give you such a whipping as would cure you from rambling a-night, like a particular G-d-d tom-cat." Using a former slave as a guide, Scott led a party of seamen and Colonial Marines to the fort and took it by surprise. After only a few shots the Americans fled, their commander in his shorts. Scott later gave the American officer's clothes and regimental colors to a sergeant in the black regiment. The American officer, outraged and insulted that his clothes were being worn by a "G-d-d black nigger," declared this "the unkindest cut of all." Although the story may be apocryphal, it sheds light on the attitude of British officers concerning the relationship of the American combatants and the Colonial Marines they faced.[49]

British raids had left the Chesapeake region completely exposed. The "whole country is now alarmed," Cockburn reported, even as far inland as Washington. During the last ten days of July, British raids, moving against St. Clement's Creek (July 23), Machodoc Creek (July 26), Hamburg (July 28), and Chaptico (July 30), seized spoils, destroyed American morale, liberated slaves, and convinced the locals that any opposition would be useless. On August 4, Cockburn personally led five hundred men, including the 120 now-experienced members of the Colonial Marines, against an entrenched American militia force near the mouth of the Potomac; American general John Hungerford confirmed that British attacking forces included "several platoons [of] uniformed negroes." Although Cockburn achieved another quick victory with few casualties (two Colonial Marines died and one suffered wounds), he acknowledged it could have been far different because his army ventured through well-wooded country, ideal for an enemy ambush. Instead it was operations as usual—British forces burned and seized tobacco, and "the Negroes . . . flock[ed] to them from all quarters." Moreover, Cockburn's extensive marches into the interior convinced Admiral Cochrane that British troops could attack against larger targets in the interior, including the U.S. capital.[50]

The most difficult objective Cockburn had to overcome was not his American opponent, but how to convince Cochrane and Gen. Robert Ross that the city of Washington should be their primary objective. Meeting with the two men, Cockburn described the success of previous raids, including Captain Barrie's mid-June expedition against Benedict where his army of but forty marines and thirty Colonial Marines marched to Marlborough, only eighteen miles from Washington. Cockburn convinced Ross and his staff that a British force could execute a successful attack against Washington, but he insisted the operation should begin with a diversionary assault against Barney's gunboats on the Patuxent, which would distract Americans from the British objective of Washington.[51]

Cockburn had transferred all of the refugees to Tangier Island, where he now had some 120 men enlisted in the Colonial Corps, and these black soldiers "alarm[ed] the Virginians more than Lord Wellington's Army." Reporting that they were "indeed excellent men, and make the best skirmishers possible for the thick woods of this country," Cockburn had no doubt that he could quickly increase the size of the Colonial Corps. The size of Cockburn's black force would eventually reach more than 250, but Cockburn soon found that the great majority of refugees fleeing to the British were instead women and children. Certainly, there "would be no getting the men without receiving them," but women and children proved a costly drain on scarce resources with few other benefits. Cockburn directed that refugees be loaded aboard the *Thistle* transport and the *Jaseur* and immediately taken to Halifax for resettlement.[52]

By August 1814 the Ministry had again reconsidered the question of liberating slaves, warning Ross "not to encourage any disposition which may be manifested by the negroes to rise upon their masters." Indeed Melville feared a corps of slaves might foment a general slave insurrection. Bathurst still believed, however, that British forces should accept only those fearing for their safety or wishing to enter British colonial

*Private of the 5th West India Regiment. Black soldiers, such as this private
of the 5th West India Regiment mustered from the Caribbean, served in the
Chesapeake Bay operations, along the South Atlantic Coast, and during
the wintery New Orleans campaign, where they suffered greatly from the
unexpected cold and damp weather. Courtesy of the Council of the National
Army Museum, London.*

regiments—a number he hoped would be manageable. Cochrane, himself a slaveowner in Trinidad, held high hopes that slaves recruited from
the southern plantations to bolster his West Indian Regiments would determine the outcome of the conflict. Only later did he discouragingly report that refugees would not "volunteer their services to the West India
Regiments." They would willingly join Colonial units, but they would
not join the West Indian Regiments for fear of being reenslaved in the
Caribbean. Even so, Cochrane and other British commanders believed

that using slave combatants would be "more terrible to the Americans than any troops that could be brought forward."[53]

BRITISH NAVAL AND MILITARY OPERATIONS in the Chesapeake region created the opportunity for slaves to escape their bondage and find freedom in a British colony elsewhere. Yet slaves experienced great obstacles in reaching British forces, boarding British ships, and leaving America. Throughout 1813, Virginians and Marylanders kept attentive watch in the areas where British forces operated, trying to prevent slaves from absconding to the enemy fleet. In many instances, Americans boarded British ships, thinking that they could persuade slaves who had reached the fleet to return to their servitude, and that virtually never happened. As the numbers of refugees swelled throughout the year, British officers developed methods of incorporating some of them into their operations, employing the former slaves as messengers, scouts, spies, and guides, and even giving them weapons. The more responsibility the British granted to refugees, the more they embraced their duty. In effect, the British vested the refugees into the British experiment of fighting for their own freedom—employing slaves in the ranks benefited both slaves and the British.

British campaigns during 1814 in the Chesapeake region realigned the interracial relationship between white and black Americans. Virginians and Marylanders witnessed the greatest exodus of slaves from the coast of America since the American Revolution. Some slaves simply fled to the British, some of them took up arms against the Americans, and others chose to remain at home. The fact that they made choices that affected their own lives placed their destiny in their own hands for good or bad. Although Americans had no logical argument for why slaves should not abscond to the British, they instead played on fear and emotion, charging that British liberation did not guarantee freedom, only a new taskmaster. The slaves saw the difference clearly enough, and several expressed identical sentiments: "S'pose [the British] sell me to West Injee planter to-day, what difference 'tween dat an' Yankee sell me to Carolina planter to-morrow?" Slaves also understood what the difference meant to their future, knowing that as long as they were in American bondage someone else controlled their destiny. Fleeing to the British offered the possibility of a different existence and a life of freedom where they could make their own choices.[54]

Charles Ball's story highlights the choices made by slaves and free blacks during the war. He had been born into slavery and escaped from a Georgia plantation, returning to Maryland to be near his wife and children. But the war gave him options. He was not technically free, but he acted as a free black and told British officers he was free. After the war Ball remarried, purchased property, and lived the life of a free black farmer and entrepreneur. Yet in 1830 Charles Ball's dream came to a shattering end, when a Georgia slave trader finally tracked him down and dragged him back to the brother-in-law of his previous owner. Ball escaped again, stowing away on a merchant ship bound from Savannah to Philadelphia. He traveled to Baltimore only to find that his second wife and children had also been seized and taken to Georgia. Ball concluded his abolitionist autobiography with plans to recover his lost family. Had he taken advantage of the British offer during the spring of 1813 rather than falsely proclaiming his freedom, Ball and his family could have escaped slavery altogether.[55]

CHAPTER 5

WASHINGTON, BALTIMORE, AND OTHER TARGETS

"Our enemy at home"

Georg Roberts's story reveals the full gambit of Atlantic World experiences that African Americans endured during the War of 1812. By the time the war began, the then-forty-six-year-old Roberts from the waterfront Canton neighborhood of Baltimore, Maryland, embraced that maritime heritage, signing aboard Capt. Richard Moon's privateer *Sarah Ann;* the ship departed Baltimore in late July, only a month after the beginning of the war. While cruising off the Bahamas in late August, the *Sarah Ann* encountered a British ship bound from Kingston for London and laden with coffee and sugar. Since the British ship outgunned the privateer and the Americans didn't want to get too close, they engaged the vessel for hours in a long-range artillery duel. Then suddenly the American privateer descended on the British vessel, and Roberts and his fellow sailors swept aboard, taking the British vessel as a prize within minutes. After convoying the prize to Savannah, the *Sarah Ann* quickly left to seek other victims.[1]

On September 13, 1812, while cruising again off the coast of the Bahamas, the *Sarah Ann* this time encountered the British frigate *Statira,* which quickly subdued the privateer. Forcing the Americans to muster on deck, British officers singled out six sailors and accused them of being British. George Roberts was one of the six taken to Jamaica in irons. The privateer captain reported to the ship's owners in Charleston that he feared the men would be tried as deserters, which could mean execution. Roberts, "a coloured man and seaman," Moon demonstrated, "I know him to be native born of the United States." While the American captain had not questioned Roberts personally, the sailor apparently "had every sufficient document together with his free papers," and the British still took him. Furthermore, the American captain swore that Roberts had enlisted "on board the *Sarah Ann* at Baltimore where he is married." The Charleston owners responded by seizing twelve British sailors and holding them hostage in confinement. The threat worked, and the British eventually released Roberts and his fellow prisoners.[2]

George Roberts. George Roberts, pictured later in life, served aboard many American privateers during the War of 1812, including Thomas Boyle's Baltimore-built Chasseur *in 1814–15. After the war he participated in Defenders' Day celebrations in Baltimore until his death in January 1861. Courtesy of the Maryland Historical Society.*

Securing his freedom, Roberts eventually signed aboard other vessels before finding his way back to the United States. In late July 1814,
he signed as a gunner aboard the Baltimore-built privateer *Chasseur,*
later hailed by Hezekiah Niles as the "Pride of Baltimore." The privateer
slipped by the British blockading squadron and then unexpectedly sailed
east, directly toward the British Isles. There Capt. Thomas Boyle preyed
on merchant shipping, and in late August he boldly proclaimed the entire British Isles to be under the blockade of the *Chasseur.* Boyle also
demanded that his proclamation be posted on the door of the shipping
underwriter, Lloyd's of London, driving up insurance rates and forcing
the Admiralty to transfer vessels to guard merchant ship convoys. Regardless, *Chasseur* captured or sank seventeen vessels, and, as Roberts
recalled, they had "many hairbreath escapes."[3]

Roberts and the *Chasseur* returned to Baltimore on the evening of
April 8, 1815, and as the privateer passed Fort McHenry she fired her
guns in a salute. Granted, the privateer had not contributed to the American victory at Baltimore, but the city nonetheless embraced the *Chasseur*
and her crew as true heroes of the battle. During the years that followed,
Roberts, being "allowed to parade with the military of the city on all
occasions of importance . . . was generally mounted as servant to the ma-
jor-general of the division." He marched in uniform on each September
12, Defenders' Day, for its annual commemoration. And "throughout
his long life [he] was always highly thought of by the citizen soldiery."
As shown in his photographic portrait, he always carried himself erect
and "never appeared on parade except in uniform." Roberts's patriotism
exuded from him; "though laboring under the weight of so many years,"
he considered it "one of his highest aspirations to still be considered one
of the defenders of his native city." Moreover, throughout his life he
maintained that he would gladly volunteer again, if necessary, to defend
Baltimore. Remaining a lifelong resident of Canton, Roberts died quietly
at his residence on January 16, 1861, at ninety-five years old, and the
Baltimore Sun offhandedly proclaimed "Another Old Defender Gone."[4]

George Roberts's maritime career had taken him to a multitude of
foreign ports, brought him thrills and excitement, and resulted with him
becoming an acknowledged contributor to the city of Baltimore's priva-
teering heritage. Yet he never assumed a central role in the city's postwar
celebrations. Later in life, Baltimore's racial composition changed, and
this undoubtedly impacted Roberts. Between 1850 and 1860 the city's
free black population found its rights greatly circumscribed, revealing
an increased racial prejudice toward black residents. Because George

Roberts had gained recognition as a War of 1812 hero, he had the ability to transcend that racism and prejudice at least for one day a year, when he put on his uniform and marched with other veterans during the Defenders' Day celebrations. Having helped his country maintain its independence, men like Roberts had disregarded the fear and danger of war, fighting for a greater cause—social and economic equality and freedom for slaves. During the conflict Roberts may have been equal and free, but afterward armed and proud black men simply threatened the white status quo and undermined the established racial hierarchy of American society. Once time had passed and black combatants like Roberts died, the stories of their contributions quickly faded and were forgotten.[5]

"NEGROES, DRUNK WITH LIQUOR AND MAD WITH EMANCIPATION": THE RAID ON WASHINGTON

By early 1814, petitions had begun to flood the Virginia and Maryland governors' offices, with constituents begging for help. Virginians readily admitted that they wanted to rebuild Fort Powhatan on the James River simply "in case of an insurrection of negroes." British troops had seized tobacco, fired warehouses, and "taken off a number of negroes," the citizens generally remarked. Some complained that "there are some neighbourhoods, and . . . many parts of the country, in great danger from the negroes; some of whom . . . have uttered threats." Even worse, some citizens charged that the slaves "[leave] us as spies upon our posts and strength, and they return upon [us] as guides and soldiers and incendiaries," leaving the country "infested in the persons of these blacks with the most dangerous spies and traitors." Throughout, these petitions and memorials addressed an all-too-common theme—neither local, state, nor federal officials could provide any defense to protect the Chesapeake or prevent slaves from fleeing to British lines.[6]

Near Fredericktown, in north central Maryland, local officials began to hear a dangerous rumor. The story insisted that slaves planned to arm themselves with knives and attack the town once the militia responded to the British invasion. The slaves had been informed of the British presence in the Chesapeake region and had therefore nominated "a captain and other officers for their company" and would flee to the southeast to join with the invaders after sacking the town. Such a story seemed plausible. That the slaves planned to organize themselves in such a military manner proved too realistic to local officials, who immediately imprisoned eight of the supposed conspirators. Meanwhile, closer to the bay other stories circulated of "the place swarm[ing] with fugitives from below, and . . . it a melancholy scene." Reportedly many of "the negroes, old ones on foot, women and children in carts or wagons" were fleeing into Washington, perhaps to reconnoiter for the British, while many others fled to the protection of redcoat units. The dichotomy proved too troubling. Slaves supposedly fleeing from British forces could pave the way for the invasion of Washington. By giving protection to the fleeing refugees, some believed that they were sealing the capital city's fate. For those slaves who absconded to the British, taking advantage of the chaos and turmoil proved but one effective way to secure immediate freedom.[7]

Defending the U.S. capital from enemy invasion created another dichotomy for American leaders. The country's reliance on the militia had not fulfilled the expectation of Republican leaders, who had anticipated that thousands of citizens would willingly grab their muskets to meet the British invaders and protect their homes. Instead, Mayor James Blake of Washington pleaded for "all able-bodied citizens" as well as for "all freemen of color . . . to proceed to a site near Bladensburg to throw up a breastwork or redoubt." That Blake publicly called for the assistance of the freemen of color truly revealed the city's fear. Washington's black codes of 1808 and 1812 had greatly restricted the actions of free blacks and slaves in an attempt to keep them in a position of servility. While Blake's appeal provided free blacks the opportunity to demonstrate their civic obligation, he rounded up some two hundred free people of color who became "patriots . . . conducting themselves with the utmost order and prosperity." Government agencies and local families had enlisted most men, black and white alike, and every available wagon and carriage to transport records, materials, and family belongings away from the city. Instead of defending their homes, those who could afford it fled into the countryside, taking all of their valuables with them. Many slaveowners sent their slaves deep into the country to prevent them from revolting or falling into British hands. While Washington appeared virtually defenseless, in nearby Baltimore "a company of mariners," more than one hundred men, many of whom were black, voluntarily formed the "First Marine Artillery of the Union" and mustered to defend that city.[8]

On the morning of August 24, 1814, American political and military leaders finally confirmed that British troops were advancing toward the capital city. Commodore Barney had scuttled his gunboats on the upper Patuxent River the day before to prevent their capture and had fashioned carriages so that the boats' heavy guns could be moved overland. Within a few hours Barney and four hundred black and white sailors had arrived in Washington, waiting for instructions as to where they would make their stand. They soon received orders to engage the invaders as they crossed the bridge at Bladensburg, an old tobacco port with a small bridge crossing the Anacostia River, so Barney moved his exhausted sailors, marines, and artillery toward the town; the commodore warned that his men had been "very much crippled from the severe marches we had experienced the preceding days." Joining almost six thousand militia, volunteers, and soldiers who had converged at Bladensburg, many of Barney's men—"tall, strapping Negroes, mixed with white sailors and marines"—initially received orders to protect a small bridge to the rear of the American position. But just as the battle began, President Madison rode by Barney's troops, and the commodore angrily protested his orders to hold a bridge behind the American lines. He wanted to be in the thick of the battle. Madison asked if the commodore's "Negroes would not run on the approach of the British." Somewhat astonished by the question, Barney retorted, "No sir . . . they don't know how to run; they will die by their guns first." Madison gave Barney's men permission to join the battle, and they quickly ran forward to man five cannon positioned on a modest rise just behind the American line to the west of the town.[9]

Charles Ball, who had run away from slavery in Georgia and South Carolina, did not intend to run in the face of this British attack. Instead, he had joined Barney's force as a cook and volunteered to work on an American gun crew, where he had a "full and perfect view of the British Army as it advanced" toward the American position at Bladensburg. On this morning, Ball and his companions had dashed six miles, and many were exhausted as they hauled their heavy naval guns into their battle positions. By the time they had finished, Barney's men could see Gen. Robert Ross's British troops advancing on the east side of the Anacostia River. What they did not know was that Ross's soldiers were equally tired because they had spent almost five hours hacking their way through dense thickets before reaching clear farmland and meadows. Once they had emerged into the clearings, they had spent two hours marching under an unusually hot early morning August sun. Dust also rose from their lengthy ranks, choking almost every soldier. Some redcoats cramped from dehydration. Others dropped by the wayside, too tired to keep up with the quick pace set by regimental buglers. Although a ninety-minute respite revived British soldiers for a few moments, when they began advancing against the American lines at 12:30, most of the soldiers were running on discipline and pure adrenalin.[10]

British colonel William Thornton's Light Brigade made a hasty attack through Bladensburg and onto the bridge crossing the Anacostia. Heavy American artillery fire scattered the initial assault, forcing British soldiers to seek cover. Thornton rode down to the bridge with sword drawn and extolled his men to follow, galloping across to the American side. Other officers, even including General Ross, helped to rally the soldiers to cross the river. "Dreadful" American grape, round shot, and musket fire dissected the redcoats on the bridge and those coming out of the river, but as each British soldier fell, another instantly moved into his place within the ranks, presenting "always a solid column to the mouths of our cannon." British discipline and disregard for their own personal safety inspired the soldiers who followed, creating the appearance that the entire army "moved like clock-work."[11]

The American militia immediately began retreating "in much disorder," or running, as Charles Ball bemoaned, "like sheep chased by dogs," but Barney's naval artillerymen stayed at their guns holding off the British for almost a half hour. Despite the carnage, Ball later claimed that he "could not but admire the handsome manner in which the British officers led on their fatigued and worn out soldiers." They stumbled over their own dead, braved a withering fire as they closed in on Barney's position, and still on they came. Colonel Thornton had rallied his men and slowly led them up the hill to within fifty yards of the American artillery when Barney's 18-pounders again unleashed their fury, driving the British soldiers back down the road. Another round from Barney's cannon crumpled Thornton's gray horse and wounded the colonel in the thigh, forcing him and his men to scurry for cover. General Ross, so striking that Ball later remembered him as "one of the finest-looking men I ever saw on horseback," had his favorite Arabian horse shot out from under him. Once the British appeared in disarray, Barney's black and white marines charged in hot pursuit, waving their cutlasses and reportedly yelling to "board them."

Then it seemed as if the pendulum swung in the opposite direction. British sharpshooters gained the high ground from where they could fire into Barney's artillery positions. The well-directed musket fire drove off the American supply wagons in a panic, carrying with them the artillery ammunition. Then Barney had his horse shot from beneath him and suffered a shot to his thigh, injuring him so badly he could not walk. Barney finally instructed his men to spike the guns and retreat. Ball, who had remained at his gun on Barney's immediate left until the commodore gave the order to retreat, quietly slipped away. The wounded Barney was soon captured and introduced to General Ross and the admiral. The commodore received gracious and courteous treatment from his British captors, who later proclaimed that Barney's flotillamen had "given us the only fighting we have had." Barney's black and white men had stayed at their cannon to the last moment and had "served their guns with quickness and precision," which "astonished their assailants." Had the militia and volunteers not fled, the British might not have been able to sack Washington.[12]

Barney's flotillamen retreated and took cover as the British breeched their lines. Some made their way to Washington while others reformed and harassed the British as the redcoat soldiers marched to the capital city. Many, including Ball, ultimately reached Baltimore, where they would soon have another opportunity to confront the British. Those who made it into Washington found a hysterical city unfolding with chaos and uncertainty.

First Lady Dolley Madison had remained at the President's House until the very last possible moment, before finally loading her carriage with as many valuables—velvet curtains, a small clock, books and papers, and the famed Gilbert Stuart portrait of George Washington—as she could carry. As she hurried out the door, she stuffed a handful of silverware into her reticule. It was all that she could do. The Madisons' teenage slave, Paul Jennings, who remained behind to secure an additional carriage, later saw "a rabble, taking advantage of the confusion." The miscreants, which apparently included a number of slaves, "ran all over to the [President's House], and stole lots of silver and whatever they could lay their hands on" before British troops marched into town.[13]

Cockburn and Ross had pursued the retreating Americans from Bladensburg for about a mile before giving their men a brief rest. When they resumed, leading with fresh troops who had not fought at Bladensburg—including the 21st Regiment, the Colonial Marines who "gained much credit for their services with the regular Army," and the Royal Marines and sailors—they did not encounter an American enemy during their advance, only "a group of negroes, to whom [British] victory gave freedom." Excited, these refugees "manifested their joy in a thousand extravagant ways. 'Ah! Massa, we tink you neber git here, 'Merikan talk so big! One Giniral say, "Come on, ye English cut-throat, red coat rascals, and see how we'll sarve you!" but . . . dat gentleman be the bery fust to run away!'" With refugee slaves following behind, Ross's advance units arrived at the U.S. Capitol that evening. A few minutes after 8:00 P.M., as General Ross approached the Capitol, shots rang from some houses on Second Street, killing a nearby British soldier and the horse on which the general rode, while wounding three other soldiers. British troops immediately entered and searched the dwellings, finding only a few unarmed slaves hiding in the bushes. They torched the structures, which were "in about an hour consumed to ashes."[14]

During the next few hours, the Colonial Marines participated in the incendiarism that destroyed both houses of the U.S. Capitol. Then another blaze suddenly lit up the night sky to the southeast from the direction of the U.S. Navy Yard, where Capt. Thomas Tingey had set fire to the buildings, ships, and stores as he evacuated the city. About a mile to the west of these twin pillars of fire sat the President's House that Dolley Madison had evacuated and the rabble had ransacked only a few hours earlier. As Cockburn sent a force of Colonial Marines and sailors into the darkness down Pennsylvania Avenue, refugee slaves scurried ahead of the two columns of soldiers, spreading the news that the British were coming to burn the President's House. Finding the house empty, Cockburn and his officers partook of some wine and nibbled on the food prepared for dinner that evening; they even took souvenirs before

Slaves Burning Washington. Philanthropie moderne *shows "John Bull" and a Royal Marine Officer offering "Liberty to Negroes." After the late April 1813 American burning of York, Canada, British forces retaliated by burning, raiding, pillaging, and liberating slaves in the Chesapeake region to demoralize Americans and break their will to continue the war. Courtesy of the American Antiquarian Society.*

setting the building afire. British troops had the opportunity to steal a few hours of rest during the night, yet as they did slaves spread rumors of the further destruction to come. Fearful citizens could only wonder what might happen next.[15]

The following morning saw a repeat of the previous night, as black and white British soldiers targeted the offices of the War and State Departments, setting them ablaze. Then soldiers moved on to the Navy Yard, where they torched everything that survived from the previous evening. Lieutenant Scott supervised the destruction of three privately owned ropewalks, which produced a thick, dark, foul smoke that soon covered the city. Other troops moved against the arsenal on Greenleaf's Point, destroying cannon, powder, and shells. In fact, the most devastating carnage of the occupation occurred when the soldiers tossed some 130 barrels of gunpowder into a well and a spark accidentally ignited the powder; the resulting explosion created a crater forty feet wide by twenty feet deep, instantly killed some thirty soldiers, and hideously wounded forty more. The British spared the Post Office and Patent Office because the patents and models were private property and represented the arts and education, and they also left the Marine barracks alone, as the fire could easily spread to nearby private homes. Otherwise, the "punitive expedition" had torched virtually the entire city, and not even a tornado that blew into town on the afternoon of August 25 could make the effect the raid had any worse. Then, almost as suddenly as they had appeared, British forces disappeared. When the sun rose on the following morning, the town was deserted—"thus ended this short and brilliant expedition." In effect, "a handful of British soldiers [had] advanced thro' the heart of their country, and burn[ed] and destroy[ed] the capital of the United States."[16]

For months before the British attack against Washington, rumors of a British-sponsored slave insurrection had percolated throughout the area. Officials in rural Fredericktown, Maryland, had discovered a planned insurrection in early August 1814; surely, a similar uprising near the capital was planned. In fact, locals had increased their patrols, with older and infirm civilians not subject to militia duty prowling the streets of Washington and Georgetown to question any unusual suspects. Still, uncertainty and fear prevailed. Margaret Smith reportedly slept with a loaded pistol under her pillow to protect against "our enemy *at home*." While asserting that the slaves would remain docile or run rather than revolt, she admitted that should the British move against Washington, "our home enemy will . . . assail us." In fact, after the American defeat at

Bladensburg, many militiamen expected such, fleeing home because they believed the slaves "would take advantage of the absence of the men to insult the females, and complete the work of destruction commenced by the enemy." Among the most incredulous stories, one contended that "negroes, drunk with liquor and mad with emancipation, were committing excesses [and] subjecting the whole country to the horrid outrages." Yet that simply was not true.[17]

Instead, white civilians perpetrated far more private property destruction in Washington than did "Cockburn's murders" or "negro conspiracies." Some reports indicated that "the negroes were disposed to be troublesome in the city," but "no houses were half as much *plundered* by the enemy as by the knavish wretches about the town." Margaret Smith recorded that the slaves did not pose any problem at all because they "hid themselves and instead of a mutinous spirit, have never evinced so much attachment to the whites and such dread of the enemy." Smith admitted that they were "spared one evil"—a slave insurrection—and breathed a sigh of relief when slaves "cheerfully" relinquished muskets and ammunition that had fallen into their hands. Slaves did not seize the opportunity of the British invasion to exact revenge, as Admiral Cochrane had hoped, although some "4[00] to 500 blacks" still used the presence of redcoat soldiers as the chance to flee to freedom. In fact, on the return march to the fleet, Lieutenant Gleig witnessed many slaves "who implored us to take them along with us, offering to serve either as soldiers or sailors, if we would give them their liberty." General Ross refused their services and did not offer to provide them with immediate protection, but the slaves still followed from Washington to Benedict anyway. Ross's refusal stemmed from his fear that the noncombatants would slow his army's retreat. Moreover, he no longer needed local guides or knowledge about the area because his army had marched through the region only a few days before. But by not welcoming them, Ross unwittingly created a wall of slaves who shielded his rear guard from a potential American attack. Once they all arrived safely at Benedict, the slaves "were, of course, received on board the fleet."[18]

Cochrane had exercised great caution before and during each operation because he had learned that even though the Napoleonic War had ended in Europe, he would receive few reinforcements. So, Cochrane decided to focus American operations elsewhere. "Negroes south of Virginia are ready to join us in great force—at least they say they will do so." Moreover, some of the New England states needed "very little persuasion to induce them to join the English today." Yet, with strategic responsibility for the entire North American war, by the late summer of 1814 Cochrane concluded to move against New Orleans, increase the raids in New England and along the coasts of Georgia and South Carolina, and launch a major attack against Baltimore.[19]

"WHITE AND BLACK ARE ALL AT WORK TOGETHER": DEFENDING BALTIMORE

Baltimore was the third largest city in the United States, a major port for American privateers and an important shipbuilding center, and, because of the prolonged British blockade in the Chesapeake, the city's warehouses and docks teemed with trade goods waiting to be exported. Baltimore presented a tempting British target. Yet the city had also witnessed the burning of Washington and the humiliating surrender of Alexandria, and local leaders did not want their city to suffer likewise. Soldiers and militia converged on the city from the surrounding areas. The crisis of an impending invasion prompted the city's Committee on Vigilance and Safety to mobilize white and black civilians to work on defensive earthwork fortifications around the perimeter of the city, primarily to the east at Hampstead Hill. Baltimore's "able bodied free men of colour" had been barred from the state militia, but they were expected to "turn out and labour on the Fortifications or other works." Free men of color Abraham Benson, Cato Hughes, Nicholas Kinnard, and Uriah Smith all showed up to work. The city had served as a magnet for unskilled and skilled free black workers who came there because of the flourishing maritime industry; in 1810 a Baltimore city directory listed 220 free men of color, with many of them working in the seafaring trades as shipbuilders, carpenters, caulkers, and sailmakers. The city also had a large population of free blacks and, conversely, a dwindling number of slaves, and city leaders expected this growing body to fulfill their civic responsibilities. During the summer of 1812 an anti-British mob had burned the homes of many free blacks because of an ill-founded rumor that free blacks hoped a British victory in the war would bring freedom to the slaves, as had been promised during the American Revolution. Others believed "all hearts and hands [had] cordially united in the common cause" as everyone rallied to help defend the city. A Baltimore merchant noticed, "they are throwing up trenches all around the city, white and black are all at work together. You'll see a master and his slave digging side by side. There is no distinction whatsoever."[20]

For free blacks and slaves, however, there existed a real distinction that Cochrane hoped an attack against Baltimore might exploit. Whites saw both free blacks and slaves only as a source of manual labor and tried to maintain an ordered society. And while the impending invasion might force whites to partake in physical labor, it certainly did not change the status of black-white relationships. Cochrane's "offering asylum & arms to the oppressed" slaves, former President Thomas Jefferson sensed in August 1814, could radically alter that status and perhaps even hasten "the hour of emancipation." Cochrane anticipated that the prospect of freedom, supported by the appearance of his black soldiers in red uniforms, would undermine southern slave society enough to topple the U.S. government.[21]

Cockburn and Ross landed at North Point, ten miles southeast of Baltimore, on September 12, 1814, with a force of some four thousand men. Cochrane sent his Colonial Marines along with the troops with the expectation that they might win the support of slaves and free blacks in the Baltimore area. And they did influence events, at least in a few instances: British troops, fearing poison, forced a slave boy to taste wine and food left out at a farmhouse; he apparently survived and left with the British. In another, a slave boy deceived a group of three American militiamen who were waiting for a boat at Bear Creek; he led a British patrol to the creek where they captured the unsuspecting Americans. After Ross interrogated the prisoners, he determined that the city defense consisted primarily of militia—some twenty thousand in the city's entrenchments. Delighted to hear such information, especially after the militia's performance at Bladensburg, Ross confidently remarked that he did not "care if it rains militia." "I'll sup in Baltimore tonight," Ross noted, "or in hell." Ross may have been commenting on his providential fortunes or on the "dreadful" heat of that September morning.[22]

Gen. John Striker had marched his 3,200 Maryland militiamen from Baltimore toward the British force on September 12, determined that the British would not stroll into the city as they had done at Washington. Waiting anxiously along the North Point Road, Striker, shortly after noon, sent 250 handpicked men ahead to find and engage the British. When the two groups met unexpectedly a shot struck Ross's right arm and rested itself in his chest. The general fell from his horse, mortally wounded. Col. Arthur Brooke assumed command and positioned his men into a battle formation—with "200 blacks in the British uniform" in a column on the road—and "the whole of the troops advanced rapidly to the charge. In less than fifteen minutes the [American] force being utterly broken & dispersed, fled in every direction over the country, leaving on the field, 2 pieces of cannon with a considerable number of killed, wounded, & prisoners." Brooke did not follow up on the victory.

Instead, he permitted his exhausted men to rest. Then shortly after midnight, a heavy rain began to fall, which dampened the men's powder and spirits. The following morning, the troops resumed their soggy march toward the city, taking almost an entire day to cover the seven miles to the city's entrenchments. There Brooke saw a city prepared and awaiting their arrival.[23]

Militiamen from Pennsylvania, Maryland, and Virginia had fled into Baltimore to man the city's defenses, and many of these soldiers brought their black servants with them. Several regular army units also deployed to the city; among the regular uniformed soldiers of the 38th stationed at Hampstead Hill was twenty-two-year-old William Williams, a runaway slave also known as Frederick Hall. Standing at "5 feet 7 or 8 inches high, with a short chub nose and so fair as to show freckles," the "bright mulatto" Williams had fled from Benjamin Oden's farm in Prince George's County, Maryland, during the spring of 1814. He changed his name, enlisted in the army despite a law that prohibited slaves from making a "valid contract with the government," and received a $50 enlistment bounty and wages of $8 per month. Oden placed an advertisement in a Baltimore newspaper in mid-May, warning that Williams would probably be in the city and use an anonymous name. Apparently the recruiter disregarded the ads in his attempt to meet his quota for enlistments. On September 10, two days before the British landing, the 38th moved into Fort McHenry to defend against a potential British landing near the bastion. Additionally, Charles Ball and many of Barney's flotillamen straggled into the city, finding their way to the entrenchments at Hampstead Hill. Black sailors also took up defensive positions in the city and helped to scuttle ships at the mouth of Baltimore harbor. Ordinary seaman Gabriel Roulson had shipped aboard the U.S. sloop *Ontario* in late November 1813 for $8 per month, yet by September 1814 he found himself land bound in the defenses east of the city. Given what had happened at Washington, it was no surprise to see "white and blacks all at work together."[24]

Shortly after sunrise on the morning of September 13, British ships opened fire on Fort McHenry. Throughout the day and night, cannon and rockets battered the American fort, but the shot did little damage; the barrage wounded twenty-four men and killed four, including Pvt. William Williams, who "had his leg blown off by a cannon ball" and died some months later at the Baltimore Public Hospital. After twenty-five hours of ineffective bombardment, the British withdrew. The next day, Brooke's army returned to the ships and left. During the retreat,

British troops reportedly looted property, burned a farmhouse, and even seized a free black farmhand named Joe Gale, who, although he protested, was taken to Canada, where he remained as a prisoner until after the end of the war.[25]

After failing to capture Baltimore, Cochrane began to focus on increased raids along the coasts of Georgia and South Carolina and an attack on New Orleans. After a spring and summer of constant British operations, the fall seemed somewhat relaxing in comparison. Brooke's troops spent much of the season at Fort Albion on Tangier Island, complaining incessantly about the weather and the "bad water, short allowance of provisions, want of wine or spirits, and dysentery." And while they endured "these difficulties" with "extraordinary patience and good will by every man in the Battalion," the conditions still wore on them. An American rumor charged that sixty of the Colonial Marines, tired of the suffering and deprivation, tried to escape from Tangier Island, yet British records do not confirm the accusation. Instead, more slaves found their way to the island.[26]

Anticipating additional black recruits, Cochrane had ordered the establishment of another marine battalion—designated the 3rd—to be composed of three companies (two hundred men) of the 2nd Battalion and three companies (250 men) of Colonial Marines or Cochrane's "cossacks" who had "behaved wonderfully well in action." They enlisted because of British success during the Washington campaign, the prospect of "perfect freedom—that freedom that the vaunted 'Land of Liberty' denied them," and a $16 bounty, which revealed in them "infinitely more sense and judgment than their late owners gave them credit for." Some men who enlisted in the quasi-military dockyard service received a bounty of $20, as well as the same pay and clothing allowance as the marines, while some who enlisted for naval service received a bounty of only $8. The promise of freedom with gainful employment lured southern slaves from their American bondage, with many enlisting and others taking passage to Bermuda, Nova Scotia, Trinidad, and other British colonies. That staggering numbers of slaves did not flee to the British may seem surprising, but the trepidation and fear of being caught during an escape and the punishment they would suffer weighed more heavily on some than did the potential joy of finding freedom. In the end, British officers commonly acknowledged that those slaves who fled to them did not exhibit even "the smallest disposition . . . to return" to their masters. Most of those who bravely chanced an escape just wanted to get away from their servitude in the United States.[27]

In early December Capt. Robert Barrie led an expedition to Farnham Church near the mouth of the Rappahannock to secure food and supplies with 150 "Virginia & Maryland negroes" "in uniform and apparently well trained, commanded by white officers." Using information he had gained from runaway slaves, Barrie employed Cochrane's black "cossacks" as guides, and once the town had been captured, he sent them to "release a number of slaves" in the woods a few miles away. There the Colonial Marines found some twenty slaves "handcuffed round the trees" and freed them. Within a week, British troops and slaves had begun evacuating Tangier Island. By the beginning of 1815 American reports claimed the British presence on the island was "very inconsiderable." The Colonial Marines had departed for the coast of Georgia in mid-December 1814 to create a diversion for the New Orleans campaign, while the refugee slaves traveled to Bermuda and then on to Halifax.[28]

Cockburn encountered a new problem in Bermuda as his troops and the refugees evacuated the Chesapeake. Having received official instructions to accept "all persons so chusing to avail themselves of our protection," Cockburn and his officers had welcomed men, women, and children of all ages and abilities. Admiral Cochrane's "widely diffused" proclamation "throughout all the counties bordering the American shores" had promised freedom to slaves, and Cockburn soon learned that he had to remind officials in Bermuda of military directives backed by the Ministry. Slaves, "whatever be their number, shall find a ready asylum with all reasonable protection," and Cockburn was determined to reconcile their distribution with Bermuda's colonial laws "respecting People of Colour." Some island officials complained about the "useless numbers" of refugees on Ireland Island, forcing Cochrane to authorize "all the Refugees from America (excepting only workmen of a certain class and description) to be sent in the future to Halifax." This momentarily maintained harmony on Bermuda but left naval commanders in a quandary because communications, supplies, and ships to and from the Chesapeake traveled first through Bermuda; all peoples—slaves or soldiers—evacuated from the Chesapeake also first arrived there. Cockburn reminded naval officers on Ireland Island that the "liberality of the laws at Halifax do not oppose any difficulty on account of Colour to People landing there and endeavoring by honest labor to earn there their own maintenance." He also found gratification in "having relieved so many Fellow Creatures from Slavery" and having established an "efficient and useful corps" of four hundred black soldiers who gave "daily proof of their gallantry and grateful attachment to us."[29]

Though Cochrane did not recruit many slaves for the Royal Navy, some volunteered in Bermuda as royal dock workers at Ireland Island. Many others who were unable to enlist—women, children, and elderly men—helped out on Tangier Island or at Bermuda by picking oakum, finding firewood, doing laundry, or performing general errands; some young boys also became servants to British officers. So, while Cochrane was convinced that thousands of slaves would join British ranks, he had grossly overinflated his estimates, as slaves could not flee unless British forces operated within the area. Slaves could not risk capture and punishment unless they surely knew the British were nearby. As such, only four hundred Chesapeake slaves took up arms; some two thousand men, women, and children chose freedom rather than military service. In the end, however, the British had acquired a smaller than anticipated but tough and loyal auxiliary force.

The mere presence of the British fleet off the Chesapeake coast during 1814 had created a dangerous double-edged problem for American planters because it emboldened slaves to flight and fight while also making the countryside virtually indefensible. Should the militia be called out to confront a British threat, then slaves would have free rein to flee or rise against their masters. In either case, the British benefited, and Cockburn took great pride in noting the degree of alarm among the planters. By the end of the summer of 1814, Cochrane had decided to take this "general and undisguised alarm" to the coasts of other slave-holding areas, primarily South Carolina, Georgia, and the Gulf Coast. Creating havoc in these areas would distract Americans from true British intentions—a campaign against New Orleans.[30]

A "CONSIDERABLE BLACK POPULATION
IN THIS PLACE WHO HAVE A STAKE IN
SOCIETY": THREATENING THE NORTH

Admiral Cochrane had great success harassing the American coastline throughout 1813 and 1814 and had kept blockading squadrons off the coast of New York, New England, and the Delaware Bay. Stories percolated along the entire Atlantic Coast about future British operations, and as soon as a strange sail appeared rumors immediately circulated that the British were coming. Cochrane appreciated the fear that his raids had struck in the American mind and by the late summer of 1814 had considered New Hampshire, Rhode Island, and even New York City to be ideal locations where a partial attack could pay great dividends.

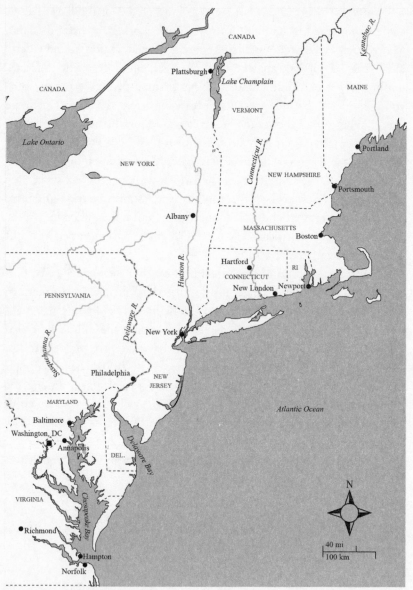

Northern Atlantic Coast, 1813–15. Map by Tracy Ellen Smith.

Although New York's Gradual Manumission Act of 1799 had compelled slaveowners to free any children born to slaves after July 4, 1799 (slaves born before that date would be freed on July 4, 1827), almost 1,500 blacks remained in bondage in the city who might be convinced to join the British cause. Just like in Virginia and Maryland, black British allies could undermine New York City's defenses. In 1810 a publisher had issued the first American edition of Daniel Horsmanden's documentary account of the 1741 "Great Negro Plot," which described how slaves had planned to burn the city. The timely book also revealed the racial nature of the alleged conspiracy and vividly illustrated the potential thievery and treachery among the city's black community. White New Yorkers, who had worked diligently to undermine the expansion of black freedom and circumscribe black rights granted to those who had gained freedom, saw these outrages as real possibilities and after 1811 launched a campaign aimed at racially dividing the black and white communities. The careful monitoring of black culture, leisure activities, and political activity created racial division. It also made whites more cognizant of threats to peace in the city—a division Cochrane could exploit to win the support of all blacks, free and slave.[31]

White New Yorkers feared that the expanding black citizenship would reshape the city's cultural composition. Once slaves secured their freedom, New York law granted them the right to vote on the same terms as whites as long as they paid their taxes. The growing black political power, which even helped determine an 1813 New York City election, combined with black music, dance, and dress that filled the streets of Manhattan's markets, only heightened the tense racial relations in the city. Whites generally distrusted blacks and saw ulterior motives in their assertiveness, autonomy, and lack of deference. White politicians tried to win passage for laws that would disqualify blacks from voting. Some wanted to remove blacks from the city by shipping them out of state to slavery. The prospect of blacks losing their social and political rights and their freedom provided a strong incentive for free blacks to protect all that they had earned. Still, by 1814 free blacks could claim they were advancing under the city's liberal laws. With free blacks flourishing as artisans and proprietors and with black religious and educational opportunities growing, they soon found that war against Britain provided additional options, and they consciously exercised them.[32]

Cochrane's April 1814 proclamation to free American slaves in the Chesapeake also applied to New York slaves, and the Admiral believed some free blacks would side with the British. Many New Yorkers expected that some black servants not yet free would also seize the opportunity to flee to British ships. As the threat of a British attack seemed increasingly likely—especially after the sacking of Washington, DC—New Yorkers suddenly realized they had few defenses and they should prepare for the inevitable. In late August 1814, a black New Yorker, a "Citizen of

Colour" (most likely black educator John Teasman), encouraged his fellow free blacks to work on the city's defensive fortifications. Since they were not slaves, they could freely give their labor and take advantage of an "opportunity of shewing [sic] . . . that we are not traitors or enemies to our country." "Citizen of Colour" also maintained they should show their gratitude toward the state of New York, which had "evinced a disposition to do us justice" and "discard[ed] that illiberal, misguided policy, which makes a difference of complexion a pretext for oppression." Citizen concluded, "Our country is now in danger. . . . Let no man of colour, who is able to go, stay at home." The city's common council heeded the suggestion and issued a call for workers on the city's fortifications. Thousands of free blacks came forward because they believed patriotism and military service would enhance their freedom and equality.[33]

During the next four months free black "patriotic sons of Africa," accompanied by "a delightful band of music and appropriate flags," worked on defenses at Brooklyn and Harlem Heights, while more affluent blacks donated money. Beginning in mid-August black civic groups, such as the New York African Society for Mutual Relief and the Wilberforce Philanthropic Association, competed with one another to demonstrate their patriotism. "As free citizens of the United States," they embraced their obligation and responsibility to the government and to their fellow Americans, contending, "It is our duty to maintain the rights of the land in which we dwell." Religious congregations, such as 150 blacks from the Asbury African Church, also erected fortifications in Brooklyn Heights. Some 850 Manhattan blacks and another thousand black Brooklyn citizens toiled on fortifications in late August, along with nearly one thousand black professionals from the "Patriotic Sons of Erin" society who joined with some three thousand carpenters, cartmen, journeymen, and printers. Throughout September and October, after the immediate crisis had passed, Teasman and other black civic leaders found no problems enlisting free blacks to work on fortifications, and at one point they even advertised for "gentleman employers" to permit their black servants to spare a day for patriotic service. Though black New Yorkers could be denied social and economic mobility, they exercised their political rights and publicly fulfilled their patriotic obligations, with the local press celebrating their contribution in song and verse.[34]

The Patriotic Diggers.
To protect our rights,
  'Gainst your flints and triggers,

See on Brooklyn Heights,
    Our Patriotic Diggers,
Men of every age,
    Color, rank, profession,
Ardently engage,
    Labor in succession.
CHORUS
Pick axe, shovel, spade,
    Crow-bar, hoe and barrow,
Better not invade,
    Yankees have the marrow.
Scholars leave their schools,
    With their patriot Teachers;
Farmers seize their tools,
    Headed by their Preachers,
How they break the soil,
    Brewers, Butchers, Bakers,
Here the Doctors toil,
    There the undertakers.
[CHORUS]
Plumbers, Founders, Dryers,
    Tinmen, Turners, Shavers,
Sweepers, Clerks, and Criers,
    Jewelers and Engravers,
Clothiers, Drapers, Players,
    Gaugers, Sealer, Weighers,
Carpenters and Sailors.
[CHORUS]

The British blockade of New York harbor during the summer of 1814, combined with the raids against Washington and Baltimore and British military operations upstate at Plattsburg, drove black and white citizens to defend their city. The British threat also convinced state leaders to finally relax the military's recruiting restrictions against blacks. New Yorkers proposed that the War Department enlist black citizens because "there is a very considerable black (or colored) population in this place who have a stake in society." Since blacks were vested in society they should be enlisted, one author contended, with white officers and black noncommissioned officers. Yet since the federal government had not developed a uniform citizenship definition, it remained unclear whether blacks could be recruited and enlisted in the federal service. State officials responded by reinstating an old provision of state law allowing blacks to enlist in the state militia. By October legislators had passed a law permitting Gov. Daniel Tompkins to enlist "two regiments [or 2,160 soldiers] of free men of color, for the defence of the State for three years, unless sooner discharged." The law also included provisions for slaves to enlist with the permission of their masters; the master would receive the slave's pay and $25 bounty for his service, and the slave would secure his freedom upon discharge. These black regiments, the legislature maintained, would be transferred to federal service if the U.S. government agreed "to pay and subsist them, and to refund to this State the monies expended by the state in clothing and arming them." In the end, the state made no black enlistments under the provisions of this law. In fact, the war in New York concluded before the provisions of this law could be enacted.[35]

After the British sacked Washington in late August 1814, many believed the City of Brotherly Love would suffer next. Even though the war had been ongoing for more than two years, Philadelphia was "perhaps less prepared to meet such an attack than any important city on the continent." Free black entrepreneur and sailmaker James Forten—respected for his patriotism, benevolence, and civic spirit—joined other citizens on August 26, 1814, in a mass meeting at the Philadelphia State House "to make arrangements for . . . defence of a cause that is common to all without distinction." Organizing a Committee of Defense, they chose four men from each ward "to promote and encourage the immediate formation of volunteer companies, and that every exertion be made to provide arms and accoutrements."[36]

Citizens flocked to the call. French Canadian craftsman Louis M. Merlin, most likely harboring some animosity toward the English enemy, proposed to organize "a legion of people of color, to be called the Black Legion, and to be commanded by white officers." A few weeks earlier Philadelphia printer William Duane, having learned of British operations in the Chesapeake, asked former president Thomas Jefferson about the expediency of using black troops in the war. Contending that "American born blacks . . . feel a sentiment of patriotism and attachment to the U.S," he suggested arming them as soldiers because it "would be to save so many of the whites and if loss to be calculated, to assure a proportional suffering and thereby a proportional Security." Moreover, Duane acknowledged that the British had "corrupted and arrayed the Whites of N. Eng. against the Whites South of them," and that they

had "arrayed the blacks of St. Domingo against the Whites." He concluded that the American government should "counteract them—defeat
them by turning [to] the resources (the blacks) upon which they calculate
against them." Should they not, Duane believed it would "be a fatal
blindness, but perhaps the only mode by which the colored population
can become dangerous or injurious." Though persuasive logic, Jefferson
never responded to his Philadelphia friend, and the city's subcommittee
on defense concluded that with a shortage of weapons and supplies for
"our white citizens," the Black Legion might be better "employed as fatigue [or labor] parties on the works, to act in a manner detached from
the white citizens who may be so employed."[37]

Having castigated state leaders in 1813 for considering legislation
against free blacks, Forten, along with ministers Bishop Richard Allen
and Absalom Jones, solicited "the aid of the people of color in erect-
ing suitable defenses." Forten offered canvas for sandbags and the services of his apprentices and journeymen, even though such contributions
cut into his profit and livelihood. Working with black ministers who
spread the message from the pulpit, Forten and his friend Russell Par-
rott also led a black Committee of Defense that took the message to free
black Philadelphians willing to work for the city's protection. Moreover,
Forten appealed to "those gentlemen that have men of colour in their
employment" to permit "them to join their brethren in this laudable
undertaking." Before sunrise on September 21, brigades of white Irish
and Germans along with more than one thousand Forten-rallied black
Philadelphians gathered at South Sixth Street between Walnut and Pine.
Bringing with them food for the day, they marched out of town to work
on earthen fortifications south of the city along the west bank of the
Schuylkill River. Even the forty-eight-year-old Forten and twenty of his
journeymen worked beneath a scorching sun alongside their "persecuted
and oppressed brethren," laboring primarily at Gray's Ferry, and many
working a second day on September 22.[38]

Many blacks wanted to sacrifice more than their physical labor.
Given the difficulty in raising troops and keeping them in the field to
meet a potential invasion, an anonymous article in *Poulson's American
Daily Advertiser* offered "A Hint to the People of Colour"—since white
men were prepared to march, "free people of colour [should also] form
themselves into parties . . . to take a tour of duty to work at the Batteries." The writer suggested that blacks "would cheerfully give their
aid . . . were they furnished with the means." Although many white citizens recognized the black commitment to liberty, the city's Committee

of Defense had deemed it "improper" to create such regiments. By December 1814, a desperate need for troops combined with a renewed fear of a British invasion convinced the Pennsylvania Senate to consider providing blacks the means to serve. The senate appointed a committee to investigate the value of enlisting black infantry regiments, and within days "a corps of black troops [was] raising in Philadelphia for the government." Yet as in New York, it remains unclear whether any of these steadfast black patriots ever shouldered arms; William Forten, James's youngest son, remembered in 1855 that "a battalion of colored troops was at the same time organized in the city, under an officer of the United States army, and they were on the point of marching to the frontier when peace was proclaimed." Most likely his fleeting memory recalled Col. Richard Dennis's thirty "sober, well-regulated," and prominent black musicians who enlisted during the summer of 1812. Or perhaps he remembered seeing some of the 247 black troops who Capt. William Bezean recruited for the 26th U.S. Infantry Regiment and drilled during the period from August 1814 to February 1815. In any case, the interracial harmony that existed between white and black Philadelphians at the time of crisis quickly passed, and afterward the city entered into a hostile new phase of race relations and limited economic opportunities that continued until the American Civil War.[39]

Without any pressing British threat, New Englanders did not mobilize large armies for coastal defense. Instead federalist leaders convened in Hartford, Connecticut, from December 15, 1814, to January 5, 1815, to debate New England secession and a separate peace with Great Britain. State committees of defense verbally defended their territory while governors prepared to call out thousands of militiamen and provide coastal communities with some surplus artillery pieces. In reality, neither state nor local governments took any real steps to protect against a British invasion. Yet the British offensive campaign for 1814 should have made New Englanders more concerned, as Governor General of Canada Sir George Prevost had developed plans to drive a wedge through the Lake Champlain corridor and down the Hudson River to New York City.[40]

Prevost pleaded that since Admiral Cochrane had the use of southern blacks and the black West Indian Regiments, he should spare troops and officers for Prevost's campaign to occupy a portion of New York. Cochrane's planned South Atlantic and Gulf campaigns, however, prohibited him from sending any troops to Canada. Prevost nonetheless initiated his combined army-naval expedition with eight thousand men moving down Lake Champlain during the summer of 1814, only to find that American naval units under Thomas Macdonough had fortified the lake with hastily constructed ships.

Gen. Alexander Macomb had also cobbled together some 3,400 soldiers, or enough American defenders to protect the city of Plattsburgh on the lake's western shore. A company of black troops who came from Massachusetts with a supply train arrived at Plattsburgh among the many reinforcements. Expecting to serve as infantry under Macomb, they found that the white officers refused to command them. As such, they too refused to serve under the white officers, prompting Macomb to organize them into a segregated labor corps and use them to construct valuable earthen fortifications along the perimeter of the American line. A sprinkling of black soldiers served among the 30th (Vermonter John Alfred), 31st (Massachusetts-born Nathan Gilbert, New Hampshire–born John Moore, and Connecticut-born Jacob Palmer), and 34th (Massachusetts-born George Bolton) U.S. Infantry Regiments manning defenses during the campaign. And contrary to some commanders' claims, the presence of black troops did not result in a spike of white desertions. Yet on occasion black soldiers deserted, including Solomon Sharp, a twenty-nine-year-old Massachusetts farmer who deserted, was captured, and was exchanged as a prisoner of war at the end of the conflict. Not surprisingly, with the appearance of Prevost's army of eleven thousand Peninsula-trained soldiers on the outskirts of Plattsburgh, black and white soldiers alike found themselves digging furiously side by side to complete defensive entrenchments.[41]

Master Commandant Thomas Macdonough had spent months carving a fleet from the New York and Vermont wilderness. Yet despite the speed and skill of his craftsmen building ships, Macdonough lacked sufficient sailors to man the vessels. To compensate, Macdonough gathered enough men to man his fleet primarily from the army, New England naval recruiters, and men transferred from U.S. warships blockaded along the East Coast. Included among his black sailors and seagoing soldiers was Pvt. Cato Williams, who had enlisted in the 11th U.S. Regiment in May 1812. The Massachusetts farmer with black hair, eyes, and complexion had a checkered military career and a record of absence and sickness; officers reported Williams as missing at the time of the battle. The personnel problems that Macdonough received from the army, enhanced by a less than devout chaplain aboard the flagship *Saratoga*, prompted the commander to "call upon a pious colored steward to offer prayers, and especially those said immediately before the Battle of Lake Champlain."[42]

The British campaign for Plattsburgh and Lake Champlain failed with Macdonough's "signal victory" over Capt. George Downie's British boats on September 11, 1814, and Prevost's subsequent decision to break off the attack against the town. Coming during the immediate aftermath of the British burning of Washington, the American victories at Lake Champlain and Baltimore provided significant boosts to American morale and conversely weakened British resolve to continue fighting. Soon the Treaty of Ghent was signed, ending the war. But news that the two governments had agreed to this treaty, with its provisions for *status quo ante bellum* (the state of affairs that existed before the war), concluded on December 24, 1814, did not arrive in the United States until a few weeks later, allowing the war to stretch until mid-February 1815, by which time British forces had wreaked havoc in the South Atlantic and Gulf of Mexico.[43]

DURING THE FALL OF 1814 British operations against Washington and Baltimore left virtually all American coastal cities in a state of panic: no one could predict which city might next feel the full brunt of a British attack. In every city facing this possibility, black and white Americans rallied to work on fortifications that had fallen into disrepair and to man defensive positions that would hopefully discourage a British attack. Their efforts in Washington were in vain as British troops sacked the city with Colonial Marines and liberated slaves during their retreat. The American defeat represented the most demeaning episode of the war. Yet in Baltimore, black and white soldiers and sailors joined together with black and white workers to create a defensive network that prevented the British from capturing the city. In Philadelphia and New York City free blacks also chose to help defend the United States rather than assist the British.

In an attempt to bolster their collective positions within society, free blacks erected defensive fortifications. Knowing that they had something at stake or something to lose—the positions that they had worked so hard to achieve—free blacks supported the regimes under which they were advancing. Should the British invade their cities, a possibility existed that with regime change they would lose their social, economic, and political standing within their communities. The war against Britain provided bargaining power by permitting them to choose sides, and they consciously exercised their options. But in doing so, their unity demonstrated a powerful threat that white Americans acknowledged, ultimately leaving blacks caught between slavery and freedom and between race discrimination and egalitarianism. Their patriotic civic efforts would not reshape white minds about what role they should play in society. In fact, in the aftermath of the war black-white relations would worsen as the collective memory ignored their contributions to the conflict.[44]

CHAPTER 6

WAR ALONG
THE SOUTHERN
COASTS, 1814

*"That pride of distinction, which a
soldier's pursuits so naturally inspire"*

Ned Simmons lived most of his life as a slave on Gen. Nathaniel
Greene's Cumberland Island plantation. Born sometime in 1763,
Simmons recalled late in life a time when he transported Gen. George
Washington through the streets of Savannah during his celebrated visit
of May 1791. The festivities, celebrations, and glorious fireworks dis-
play left a memorable impression on the then-twenty-eight-year-old
Simmons.[1]

Shortly before the War of 1812, Nat Greene, his siblings, and their
mother Catherine began quarreling over the division of the late general's
estate. The question of lands, slaves, ribbons, and medals had bitterly
divided the family since the general's death in 1786, as the items represented the legacy of the famed Revolutionary War hero. In 1810 Simmons and thirty-two other slaves were given to son Nat. Despite not
wanting to be a slaveowner, Nat uneasily held onto the slaves for three
years before giving them back to his mother Catherine. Then, with his
mother's sudden demise during early September 1814, the slaves passed

to his sister Louisa Shaw. Although Simmons and his fellow Cumberland Island slaves' legal status shifted among the Greene family, their monotonous existence on the island changed very little until the waning weeks of the War of 1812.[2]

When Adm. George Cockburn's ships and soldiers invaded Cumberland Island during early 1815, Simmons and other slaves immediately seized the opportunity to decide their own fate. By mid-January, British forces had encamped on the Greene family plantation, offering freedom to any slave who would join the British cause. Although Ned Simmons had belonged to a famed Revolutionary hero, an association that tied Simmons to the narrative of freedom the Revolutionary War represented, he immediately left his enslavement and volunteered for British military service, expecting to find his own freedom. Ned did not hesitate to enlist, taking the surname Simmons that appeared on the Cumberland Island garrison list. He was one of the island's first slaves to volunteer for British service, as he did not see himself burdened by or connected to the white legacy of the Revolution. On January 28 "Ned Simmons" appeared on the muster list of the "Black Company," and a month later he enlisted in the 3rd Battalion of Colonial Marines. Simmons received an old 1808 version of the British red uniform, and soon after he received a weapon and began training to be a marine. Then disaster struck.[3]

Although Simmons had joined the British force, his training had not yet taken him off Cumberland Island. In early March 1815 two American commissioners arrived to inform British officers of the ratification of the peace treaty. They also intended to negotiate for the return of American property, including slaves. After days of contentious bickering between the commissioners and Cockburn, the admiral acquiesced: only property, including slaves, on Cumberland Island at 11:00 P.M. on February 17, 1815, would be returned. Yet even this narrow interpretation of the Treaty of Ghent adversely affected Ned Simmons. He had been one of the first to volunteer, but he had not departed the island. Instead, he fell victim to the diplomatic dispute concerning the return of property. On March 10, 1815, British officers stripped Simmons of his uniform, insignia, and weapon, and he and eighty others were reenslaved on Cumberland Island.[4]

In 1834 Nat Greene and his family sold the Greene plantation to Robert Stafford, and along with it went the seventy-one-year-old Ned. Despite being sold, Simmons remained on Cumberland Island, embraced his Baptist faith, and apparently accepted his fate. When the American

Civil War came to Cumberland some years later, Simmons had another opportunity to flee to freedom, and again he seized his chance. When he crossed the Union lines at Fernandina, Florida, in February 1863, Simmons registered as contraband and gave his age as one hundred years old. Union naval forces provided him with rations because of his age, limited vision, and feeble condition. During the days that followed, the centenarian learned to read. Some months later in 1864 a northern journalist who had often spoken with Simmons reported, "Ned Simmons, an old negro . . . died here last week, at the home of the lady teachers, who have kindly cared for him since their arrival here." Simmons had finally found freedom, according to the reporter, "where no slave-driver will ever follow; where he can sing 'de praises ob de Lord' in freedom and safety."[5]

"TO TREAT NEGROES WITH HUMANITY IS LIKE GIVING PEARLS TO SWINE": SLAVERY, WAR, AND BLACK FREEDOM ALONG THE SOUTH ATLANTIC COAST

Soon after his spring 1814 appointment, Cochrane had proposed to the Ministry bold new American operations conducted by slaves, Indians, Baratarian pirates, and disaffected citizens. These, he suggested, would alter the course of the conflict and "considerably weaken the [American] efforts against Canada." By early August 1814 the Admiralty had approved Cochrane's plans for landing diversionary forces along the coast of the South Atlantic and along the Gulf of Mexico to disguise his primary operation against New Orleans. The Ministry also allotted Cochrane shallow-draft vessels and additional arms for his anticipated black and Indian allies.[6]

Operations in the Chesapeake had heightened American tensions along the entire Atlantic Coast, even in areas that had seen little of the war. North Carolina had not experienced much of the "milito-nautico-guerilla-plundering warfare" that had characterized Cochrane's campaign in the Chesapeake. Then suddenly North Carolinians felt the specter of slave insurrection when Cockburn's forces arrived off Ocracoke in mid-July 1813. British troops quickly swept ashore, meeting no opposition. They requisitioned cattle, sheep, and fowl and paid $1,600 for the provisions they took, even though American customs officer Thomas S. Singleton estimated the payment covered only about half of the items the British took. This operation represented Cockburn's first

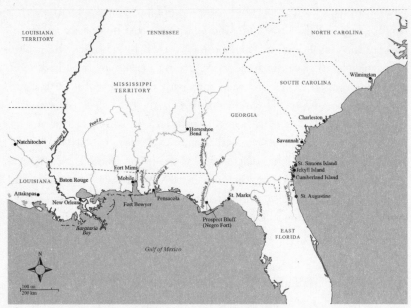

Southern Coasts, 1813–15. Map by Tracy Ellen Smith.

since the June 1813 debacle at Hampton, Virginia, so the admiral had provided strict instructions on personal behavior. Although there were no reports of personal attacks or violations, the continued presence of British ships in the area stifled "the little commerce" that remained after they departed.[7]

Fall 1814 operations along the South Atlantic Coast successfully disguised British ambitions against New Orleans. The state of North Carolina had done little to defend itself, relying instead on natural protection afforded by barrier islands, treacherous waters, and coastal swamps. The Great Dismal Swamp on the border between Virginia and North Carolina provided one safe haven for runaway slaves as well as a refuge for those who defied civil authority. Rumors of slave insurrections had percolated across North Carolina for years; in March and again in May 1810 stories of slave revolts spread across the North Carolina border into Virginia. Once British forces moved into the area in 1813, citizens again felt the doubled-edged blade of war, fearing collaboration between British agents and free blacks and runaway slaves. A slave captured in Beaufort during June 1813 fueled the fear when he shared information that a British-inspired western slave insurrection was imminent. Rumored letters from Virginia Negroes reported a July general massacre, prompting North Carolinians to be even more alert. Local courts increased slave patrols' authority to whip slaves found without a pass and even shoot on sight suspected runaways. In New Bern later in 1814 militia officers needed laborers to work on local defenses, yet they had only a sizable "number of idle negroes . . . doing almost nothing." Local owners refused to permit their slaves to work on an island fort because of the probability that the British would liberate them. In this instance, the fear of losing valuable property trumped civic obligation and the necessity of completing local defenses. The real fear of these possibilities weighed heavily on local citizens. In fact, many citizens chose to flee inland with their property and slaves to prevent loss, greatly increasing the burden on those who remained behind.[8]

North Carolina had passed few laws restricting the movements of free blacks prior to the War of 1812. In 1809 Calvin Jones, the adjutant general of the North Carolina state militia, had requested that the state legislature prohibit free blacks from enlisting. Having "these pests of society" in the service, Jones insisted, lessened "the respectability of a military company" and prevented "many persons from mustering, who would otherwise do so." Instead, he requested that free blacks be formed into segregated labor corps and be "mustered separately, without arms." The legislature did not restrict free blacks from enlisting as soldiers in the militia until 1812, yet they could afterward still serve as musicians. By the fall of 1814, when British operations increased off North Carolina and invasion looked imminent, the legislature suddenly reversed its decision, permitting "free persons of colour" to enlist. Yet only a few free blacks joined local units.[9]

The invasion of North Carolina never occurred. Instead, Admiral Cockburn gathered forces for incursions against Georgia and South Carolina, two southern states with higher concentrations of slaves. Raiding this coastal area would disrupt trade and communications, demoralize Americans, encourage the Red Stick Creeks, and permit Cockburn to recruit more slaves for his units. In late November 1814 Cockburn's vanguard arrived off Jekyll Island, Georgia. After hearing gunfire, marines went ashore and captured Christophe du Bignon's plantation house. There they found and seized silver, cash, jewelry, crops, and livestock. They pillaged the du Bignon home and freed twenty-eight of his slaves. Du Bignon valued his losses at almost $80,000, yet long after his death the British government compensated his heirs only $2,047.50. The British raid had crippled du Bignon's plantation and had also given slaves a chance to escape their brutally hard life on Jekyll Island without regret. St. Simons Island plantation owner John Couper, who lost sixty slaves during the invasion, later visited a British ship to try and convince his slaves to return. As he boarded the frigate *Brune* a former slave cried out, "That is Mr. Couper. I wish my master [du Bignon] was in his place. I should shove him down into the sea." Owners like du Bignon and Couper could not understand why slaves absconded to their freedom; they knew flight was far better than insurrection.[10]

When British ships appeared in force off Georgia in 1814, a new opportunity presented itself to Savannah's slaves and free blacks. British operations gave Low Country slaves a chance to make their way to British freedom. Savannah's city council ordered that all idle slaves be arrested and detained until their owners claimed them. The council also provided money to reimburse planters for slaves to work on the city's defenses, which would keep slaves continually occupied rather than permit their heads to fill with notions of flight and freedom. City leaders greatly limited slaves' social gatherings and did not permit peaceful assembly. For free blacks, the appearance of British forces offered them bargaining power unknown since the War for Independence. Several free black soldiers chose to demonstrate their loyalty to the United States, serving in Savannah's Fort Jackson, three miles downriver. Even so, the council required free blacks to work for two weeks on earthen fortifications surrounding the city. In early 1814 the city marshal also created a detailed list documenting the number of free blacks, their occupations, and where they lived. The city kept track of every aspect of their lives. Facing such restrictions, free blacks turned to the church and to music as their only outlets for worship, self-expression, civic participation, education, and recreation. In fact, black bands often dressed in the uniforms of the city's white militia and were permitted to perform on muster days to publicly display their loyalty. But with increased restrictions placed against them, free black musicians protested in the only way they could—by refusing to play. Their refusal demonstrated their unhappiness with increased limits on their lives, and it also highlighted the paradox of white citizens wanting free, black noncitizens to celebrate liberty and independence, which they did not fully enjoy.[11]

The British did not attack Savannah during the fall of 1814. Instead the nearby barrier islands along Charleston, Savannah, and the St. Johns River of Florida felt the full brunt of British operations. These islands had few defenses, which meant the British could quickly succeed and reap financial rewards. The islands also served as the economic center for American cotton production and were worked by a sizable slave population. Cochrane discovered that each island had "generally 2 to 300 [slaves] . . . with perhaps [only] two or three respectable families to superintend them." This meant that the "whole of this [slave] population might be brought away very easily, and without any difficulty." On January 10, 1815, British forces, including refugee Colonial Marines recruited in the Chesapeake and the black 2nd West Indian Regiment, attacked St. Mary's on Cumberland Island; 1,600 of the 2,500 British troops landed were black, and they apparently "behave better than the white." For the next few days, though the British did not encounter much opposition, they suffered sporadic attacks and ambushes. Capt. Robert Barrie told his mother about an American attack in which he saw his first soldier killed. "A new black soldier was shot through the head standing close alongside me." American army commanders had wanted to fight for the island, but local inhabitants agreed to surrender St. Mary's on January 14, 1815, because they feared the British-supported slave soldiers and Indians far more than they did the destruction associated with battle.[12]

Based on Cumberland Island, Cockburn sent expeditions to the nearby islands as well as into the rivers and creeks, reminiscent of his time in the Chesapeake during the summer of 1814. His black troops "acted with great gallantry. Blacky had *no idea of giving quarter;* and it was with great difficulty the officers prevented their putting *the prisoners to death*." During one American ambush, a slave broke ranks and chased militiamen into the woods. When he caught a disarmed Yankee, the militiaman begged for mercy. The former slave "replied, '*he no come in bush for mercy,*' and immediately shot him dead!" These violent expeditions quickly and easily moved against St. Simons and Jekyll Islands to the north, seizing merchandise and food, capturing ships, and liberating and taking slaves back to Cumberland Island. Cockburn reported that the abundance of merchandise and the "number of refugees who have joined" had convinced him to stay longer so he could "bring the whole away with him." British policy maintained that any slave who made it to British property—a British ship, British territory, or British-occupied lands—would be granted his or her freedom, and Cockburn wanted to liberate as many slaves as he could. Since Cumberland Island represented British-captured territory, it meant that any slave who made it to the island would be freed. Cockburn also thought many would willingly take up arms against their former masters, and he was extremely pleased to learn that the Americans perceived that "all or nearly all the negroes on Cumberland Island are in training." Zephaniah Kingsley was amazed by the "magical transformation of his own negroes . . . into regular soldiers, of good discipline and appearance."[13]

On St. Simons Island, observer George Baillie claimed that British naval officers seduced the slaves. They were shameless, he recalled, in their attempts to woo the slaves, even telling some refugees that the Queen of England was a black woman. British black West Indian troops also explained how they were freemen and how they chose to serve in British ranks. Their genuine, heartfelt assertions offered hope, and their stories enticed so many refugees to leave their bondage for the uncertainty of British freedom that Cockburn barely had enough ships to transport them to Bermuda.[14]

Maj. Pierce Butler had represented South Carolina in the Continental Congress and at the Constitutional Convention. He had fought as a soldier during the 1780 British southern campaign, and he had lost a considerable fortune during the fighting, as many of his ships and plantations suffered the depredations of war. By the fall of 1814 Butler had rebuilt his fortune by investing in Georgia sea island plantations when again war threatened his financial security. Butler angrily demanded that his manager Roswell King protect his cotton and slaves from British seizure. Underestimating the extent of this conflict, King calmly yet naively assured Butler that he had taken precautions, promising that "your Negroes truly behave well." King had taken cotton far up the Altamaha River and driven oxen deep into the woods, but he had done little to protect Butler's most valuable slave assets.

As soon as British forces arrived, Butler's greatest fear came true. The British immediately imprisoned King for thirteen days, and during that time he despondently reported that "the Negroes are all declared free that will go off with them." Apparently, most of Butler's slaves "wish to try their New Master." That Butler's slaves departed with the British crushed King's psyche, leaving him "in too much pain." I "can never git over the Baseness of your ungrateful Negroes," King claimed. "I cannot write nor do I know fairly what is best to be done." For twelve years, King asserted, he had tried "to make these ungrateful retches comfortable but it is all nonsense and folly. To treat Negroes with humanity is like giving Pearls to Swine, it is throwing away Value and gifting insult and ingratitude in return." King could not fathom why the slaves might leave with the British, but he intended to find them and persuade them to return. Once he did, King insisted that he would rule "those animals . . . with a rod of iron." No wonder Butler's slaves seized freedom as soon as it was within their grasp.[15]

A few months earlier the British had ravaged nearby Jekyll Island. The news permeated through the barrier islands, and John Couper took notice. As soon as the British landed on St. Simons Island, Couper approached British officers to ask if private property would be respected if the inhabitants offered no opposition. Initially informed that property would be respected, a British officer later confidentially told Couper that the opposite was true. This officer advised "him by all means to move off his property, particularly his negroes, and tell his friends to do so" as well. Since British forces had already landed, Couper had no alternative but to implore his driver Big Tom to try to persuade slaves to remain on his plantation. Tom, a devout Muslim, had been a slave in the British West Indies after his initial capture from an African village on the Niger River. Experiencing life in British bondage, Tom warned his fellow slaves that conditions on St. Simons were far better than anything the British could promise. Known as a particularly kind master, Tom's appeal apparently persuaded half of Couper's slaves to return to their life of bondage, with some sixty choosing to remain with the British. Couper later visited them aboard British ships and tried again to convince them to return. On nearby Sapelo Island, just beyond the extent of active British operations, Thomas Spalding armed his slaves as a last recourse, and he was surprised that once armed some of his slaves "exhibited signs of rebellion." British operations had thrown the Low Country into a state of panic, with "every one moving their negroes that can, and many leaving everything behind." Ultimately, this three-pronged assault—slaves, British-sponsored Indians, and redcoat soldiers—successfully and completely diverted attention from the British invasion of New Orleans.[16]

Once the British seized Cumberland Island, refugee slaves also found their way from Spanish Florida. Cochrane's proclamation offered them the same promise of freedom as it did to American slaves, leaving the Spanish facing a quandary. The Spanish governor of East Florida at St. Augustine, Sebastián Kindelán, accused Cockburn's officers of helping Spanish slaves escape, promising them freedom, and then enlisting them in British ranks. Though Cockburn did not deny that British officers provided assistance when slaves approached them, offered them freedom, and gave them the opportunity to serve the British government, he insisted that no royal officer helped slaves escape. Spanish authorities, Cockburn retorted, should prevent slaves from escaping rather than begging the British to assist in their return. In fact, Cockburn had no objection to Spaniards visiting Cumberland Island and trying to encourage slaves to come back, but he informed Kindelán that he would not force any slave to leave or prevent any slave from returning to Spanish Florida. The former slaves ultimately had the freedom to choose.[17]

In late February 1815, sixty-six slaves stole a boat on the Spanish St. Johns River and fled toward Cumberland Island. Most of the "Florida Refugees" belonged to British merchant and Indian trader John Forbes, and he pursued after realizing they had fled. By the time Forbes caught up with the group, they had already secured their freedom aboard a British frigate. Forbes was given the opportunity to address the refugees and try to convince them to return to his plantation, but the slaves refused. He then immediately petitioned Admiral Cockburn, attesting to his British citizenship and his thirty-year residence in Spanish Florida, to no avail. Lastly, Forbes maintained that the detention of the slaves contradicted Spanish law, and again Cockburn ignored his argument. Just as the admiral had previously told the Spanish governor, slaves would not be forced to return to servitude, yet Cockburn did offer to return the stolen boat, provided Forbes could prove ownership.[18]

Cockburn's operations along the South Atlantic Coast greatly exceeded expectations. He had ravaged the economy, he terrorized the population, and, by early February 1815, he was overwhelmed by refugees, who strained his resources. He tried to enlist every able-bodied male as a sailor or soldier, but not all slaves would enlist. Cockburn had those who did not enlist immediately transferred to vessels, where they would await departure to Bermuda. Spreading the refugees throughout the fleet also lessened the material demands on individual ships. Even so, he needed more supplies, food, and clothing, as well as additional ships to take them away. Once a vessel arrived with supplies, it was quickly unloaded to provision the troops and refugees. The vessel soon refilled with anxious men, women, and children for the voyage to Bermuda. This routine moved so methodically that by the end of March 1815, some 1,483 refugees had been whisked away. Yet many of those who arrived at Cumberland Island were already sick and weakened, succumbing to disease. More than 280 people died during the occupation, or about four people each day. Ultimately, the total number of refugees who found their way to the island during the two-month period totaled more than 1,700, representing one of the greatest short-term black diasporas in antebellum American history.[19]

Cockburn had staked out a position supporting the slaves' bid for freedom. By mid-February 1815 Cochrane knew the results of the Battle of New Orleans and that the United States and Great Britain had signed the Treaty of Ghent. This complicated matters greatly because the treaty's first article called for the restitution of "any Slaves or other private property" immediately on the ratification of the treaty. Cockburn sent a note with evidence to Admiral Cochrane at Bermuda detailing his position on the subject of slaves and asking how he should deal with Spanish and American slave property who had escaped to freedom in British territory. Until his instructions arrived, Cockburn shipped as many slaves away from Cumberland Island as he could.[20]

On March 6, 1815, Thomas Spalding and Capt. Thomas M. Newall arrived on Cumberland Island at the behest of American generals Thomas Pinckney and John Floyd. They had instructions to meet with Cockburn, inform him of the ratification of the peace agreement, and negotiate for the return of American public and private property. The Americans brought with them a copy of the newspaper *National Intelligencer,* which had printed in it a copy of the February 17, 1815, ratified Treaty of Ghent. Cockburn refused to accept the legitimacy of the publication, instead asking the commissioners to draft a copy of the publication and sign a statement certifying that it was a true copy. Cockburn would then accept their statement. The formalities greatly angered the Americans, and they pushed Cockburn on the question of slave property. Cockburn responded that he had no public property on Cumberland Island; the guns had been removed, the powder destroyed, and the slaves distributed to the fleet. As such, they were on British soil at the time of the treaty ratification. Before he could make any final determination regarding property, Cockburn insisted that he needed to await orders from Admiral Cochrane.[21]

Hard rain and fog inundated Cumberland Island for four days—March 7–10—preventing the American commissioners from returning to meet with Cockburn. During this tempest Cochrane's flagship arrived and a flurry of British activity ensued. Boats zoomed between ships and from ship to shore, and warships weighed anchor and suddenly departed. Watching from the mainland the American commissioners could not determine what was happening. By the time the weather cleared, Cochrane had departed again for Bermuda, leaving Cockburn with instructions for handling the property question. Cockburn finally responded to the American commissioners, with Cochrane having initialed the dispatch, that the British would evacuate Cumberland Island without destroying property. As for slaves, Cockburn indicated that captured slaves on Cumberland Island on January 10, 1815, represented spoils of war. Narrowly interpreting the Treaty of Ghent, Cockburn insisted that only slave property on Cumberland Island at 11:00 P.M. on February

17, 1815, would be returned. If they had been removed previously, they were technically free. Slaves moved from other points of origin before February 17, 1815, were on British property and also technically free. To support his view, Cockburn developed extensive lists to determine the date slaves joined the British and from where they came, and these documents ultimately formed the basis of the British argument regarding American slave emancipation for decades afterward. All told, Cockburn did leave behind eighty-one slaves, including Ned Simmons, some cotton bales, horses, and cattle. Cockburn's flagship departed on March 18, 1815, leaving behind a wake of destruction in its path.[22]

British ships slipped off the South Atlantic Coast in mid-March 1815 after receiving news that the war had come to an end. Undoubtedly, for southerners the most pressing issue was the British evacuation of so many slaves. Cockburn's operations in the Chesapeake and along the South Atlantic Coast provided the means for slaves to embrace their new life of freedom, and between four and five thousand slaves seized the opportunity to relocate to British colonies. They did not know exactly what to expect, but they unquestionably understood that the freedom accompanying their departure offered opportunities that they would never experience while in American bondage. While the decision to leave family and friends behind must have been heart-wrenching, encouraging British officers permitted slaves to make choices about their own destiny. Never before had they been allowed to make such important decisions regarding their own future. Thereafter, they alone would make those decisions.

"[P]UTTING ARMS IN THE HANDS OF MEN OF COLOR, WE ONLY ADD TO THE FORCE OF THE ENEMY": STRUGGLE FOR THE GULF

Knowing only that a sizable number of Indians were still fighting the Americans, in the spring of 1814 Cochrane sent naval Capt. Hugh Pigot to the Gulf with arms and supplies for his potential black and Indian allies. Pigot arrived at the mouth of the Apalachicola River in May 1814, and Bvt. Capt. George Woodbine went ashore with a small complement of men to establish a British presence some two miles south of the confluence of the Chattahoochee and Flint Rivers. Pigot remained among the southern Indians throughout the summer and fall of 1814, training and drilling, supplying and feeding, as well as trying to recruit additional slaves and warriors. Cochrane had also sent Marine major Edward Nicolls to the Gulf to encourage slaves to join the British war effort. If they would enlist in the "Corps of Negroes," Nicolls promised them freedom and land in the British West Indies. With proxies along the Gulf, throughout the summer and early fall of 1814 Cochrane received reports about the growing number of former slaves and Indians who represented potentially powerful allies who could be counted on during a campaign against Louisiana.[23]

Cochrane had experienced considerable success encouraging slaves to run away and arming many against their former masters during the Chesapeake campaign, and he anticipated similar results along the slaveholding Gulf. Besides, early reports from Florida and Louisiana already indicated that there was "a strong and irresistible party in the free people of colour, and the slaves who to a man will join." The British War Office had also instructed commanders to use black troops to occupy New Orleans once it had been conquered unless locals objected. While commanders received authority to encourage slaves to join their ranks, "[b]y no means" could they "excite the Black Population to rise against their masters." Navigating this fine line challenged British officers. Even so, the Americans did not know the dilemma that British officers faced. Publicly Americans learned that Cochrane had instructed Nicolls to "raise a regiment of Colonial Marines from the American Blacks" and that the major even brought blank lieutenant commissions to offer to selected men. To Americans, these British devils were unleashing Satan's agents.[24]

Nicolls traveled across the Gulf region encouraging former slaves with a bold proclamation similar to Cochrane's. "Unrivet the Chains of Thousands of your Colour now lingering in Bonds," he said, and he promised they would receive land, "the comforts of enjoying rational liberty," and the "rights of a British Man." By joining with His Majesty's forces, he promised that never again would these "Men of Colour" see their spouses or children dragged away by a cruel oppressor. Nicolls simultaneously encouraged restraint. "Show yourselves to be Christians by your deeds-mercy" because, as he reminded them, others would be watching and waiting for depredations. "Do them no other harm or violence than is necessary" and do not "inflict an unnecessary wound, when they ask for quarter." Nicolls reminded them, "It is only the coward that will take revenge on a fallen enemy." Should they have faith in God and remain loyal and true to their king and country (Britain), the major assured them they would succeed. Their reward would be "Industry,

Plenty and Happiness" for them and their progeny, which represented grand future rewards for only a brief military life.[25]

Nicolls's instructions had called for him to aid the Indians, recruit a slave army, and lay the groundwork for a British invasion along the Gulf. He found willing slaves and Indians; provided them with uniforms (slaves received red caps), arms, food, and supplies; and organized and drilled them under white officers. Woodbine reported that "negroes are flocking in from the states" because of the availability of food and the promises contained in British proclamations. Yet Nicolls knew that idle hands became troublesome, so he wanted black troops from the 2nd West Indian Regiment to come to Prospect Bluff. Seeing "men of their own color in a state of discipline" would "have a good affect [sic]" on them he believed. Until the West Indians arrived Nicolls enticed the former slaves to use the abundance of wood in the area to build a fort and houses for their own protection and construct small boats for communication and transportation. He also purchased slaves who belonged to the Indians to prevent them from "sacrificing their all without compensation." By treating them justly, Nicolls gained the support of the "trusty black and mulatto men" and "useful" Indians.[26]

Nicolls immediately proceeded some 150 miles west to Pensacola, where he found more than two thousand Red Stick Creeks and Seminole Indians waiting for clothing, food, and weapons to continue their struggle against the United States. Not surprisingly, the Spanish lacked supplies in Pensacola for their own troops, much less to outfit the growing slave and Indian army gathering around the city. He immediately requested food and spirits from London because American raiding parties looted outlying settlements, killed cattle, and destroyed crops as they encroached on the Spanish city, greatly reducing the available food stocks. The rising fear that Andrew Jackson's army would soon descend on Pensacola convinced West Florida governor Mateo González Manrique to request British assistance, and within days the entire British Gulf force occupied Pensacola. Nicolls hoisted the Union Jack over the city in mid-August 1814 and declared himself the military commander of the city. He established a strict passport system to limit movement into and around the city and used his black force to patrol the city streets.[27]

Nicolls recruited about one hundred black Colonial Marines in Pensacola, in addition to some five hundred Indian warriors. Captain Woodbine also apparently went to great lengths to encourage any slave to join the British cause. He often spoke to slaves personally, offering freedom, liberty, and protection under the British flag. When his personal appeal did not work, Woodbine offered monetary bribes for their defection. The British captain also frequently hired "all sorts of Negroes" and Indians to encourage and assist slaves with their flight to the British. He promised a slave named Prince, who had gained Woodbine's confidence and later became one of the maroon leaders at Prospect Bluff, monetary wages and an officer's commission for his recruitment of other slaves in Pensacola. On several occasions Woodbine's black troops reportedly guarded a ferry that provided the means to evacuate slaves to British forces.[28]

A number of Spanish slaves from the city calling themselves Americans had also enlisted in the black unit, drawing howling protests from Governor Manrique. Cochrane had instructed Nicolls not to recruit Spanish slaves because Britain and Spain were then allies. Yet the prospect of freedom was too much to resist. Cochrane sheepishly conveyed to Manrique that the slaves had not joined the British ranks but instead had "gone over to the opposite side of Pensacola" with the growing contingent of Britain's allies.[29]

Nicolls believed that his combined force of redcoat soldiers and marines, Colonial Marines and Indians, and Spanish forces and local townspeople could protect Pensacola from American threats. Unfortunately, Spaniards, fearing the slave soldiers and renegade Indians who looted and terrorized the town, refused to cooperate or assist with his preparations to defend the town at all. In fact, Nicolls became hypersensitive to the anti-British attitude, especially after learning that a group of Spanish officers and townspeople had developed a plan to surrender Pensacola to Andrew Jackson. The British officer responded by threatening to destroy the town rather than to permit it to fall into Jackson's hands.[30]

British naval captain Sir William H. Percy believed that the conquest of Fort Bowyer on Mobile Point, a sandy peninsula that commands the narrow entrance to the bay and the approach to the city of Mobile, represented the next step in capturing New Orleans. Although hesitant, Nicolls agreed to participate in a joint attack, believing that a victory over this bastion would embolden his black and native warriors and encourage even more to flock to his ranks. On September 14–15, 1814, the British expedition, led by Percy and Nicolls, moved against Fort Bowyer. The two-day attack accomplished virtually nothing militarily, except the devastating loss of the frigate *Hermes,* the strongest British ship on the station. Afterward, Nicolls and his black soldiers slinked back to Pensacola, dejected but still convinced that the Gulf leaned toward the British.[31]

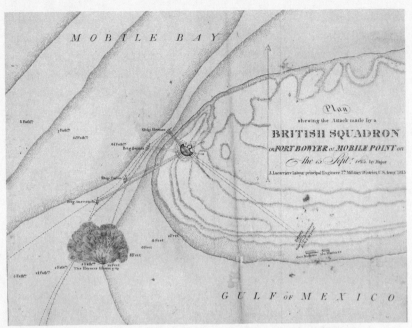

British Attack on Fort Bowyer. British attack on Fort Bowyer by Arsène Lacarrière Latour, 1815. Latour misidentifies the date of the attack, as it occurred in September 1814. During the operation American cannon fire sank HMS Hermes, forcing Edward Nicolls's black troops to break off their landward attack. Image from Arsène Lacarrière Latour, Historical Memoir of the War in West Florida and Louisiana in 1814–15: With an Atlas *(Philadelphia: John Conrad and Co., 1816).*

On November 7, 1814, Andrew Jackson's troops swept into and captured Pensacola. Taking Spanish slaves with them, British forces evacuated the city, sailing under cover of darkness to Apalachicola. Jackson had momentarily secured a military advantage at Pensacola, then he made sure that Spanish citizens were treated fairly, which both surprised and pleased them, especially considering their treatment under the British. News of the American and British occupations and of the treatment of Spanish citizens found its way across the Gulf to New Orleans, helping to create enmity and suspicion, driving the multiracial and ethnic Louisianans more firmly into the American fold, and depriving Cochrane of a potential source of support.[32]

The possibility of British-sponsored racial uprisings along the Gulf Coast had troubled Jackson for months. In mid-August Indian agent Benjamin Hawkins had reported to Secretary of War John Armstrong that the British had clothed, armed, and trained black forces at Prospect

Bluff and Pensacola. Two weeks later, he informed Jackson that the British planned "to free and prepare for war all of the Blacks in this quarter." Suspecting that "spies and traitors" swarmed the country, Jackson warned Louisiana governor William C. C. Claiborne of British intentions to move against New Orleans and to excite "the black population to insurrection & massacre." He also railed that "they must be for, or against us." Though the "people of Louisiana are disaffected," Claiborne reassured Jackson that the free black Louisiana militia—re-created by a September 1812 act that organized propertied free blacks into four companies of sixty-four men each to be commanded by white officers—had served Louisiana under the Spanish regime with the "greatest firmness & courage." And while the state legislature had expressed misgivings about reconstituting the black unit, Claiborne promised Jackson that these men were loyal to Louisiana and the United States. More importantly, they had "good characters," "extensive connections and much property to defend." They represented men of status and class and should the United States not embrace these "men of Colour," Claiborne warned that "the enemy will be encouraged to entrigue & to corrupt them." The governor also warned local militia leaders to examine closely "all negro cabins and other places where arms are most likely to be concealed."[33]

Ultimately Cochrane failed to gain the extensive support he expected from the slaves and Indians, forcing him to modify his operational plans. Initially, he had wanted to land troops at Pensacola or Mobile and march overland against New Orleans. The failed September 1814 attack against Fort Bowyer combined with the November evacuation of Pensacola left Cochrane with reduced options. British activities along the Gulf—especially Nicolls's recruiting of slaves and Indians and the fortification of Prospect Bluff on the Apalachicola River—had also frightened Americans in the region to action. Despite the setbacks, British agents along the Gulf continued offering rosy forecasts for the campaign, promising Cochrane, as he reported, "jam tomorrow, but never jam today."[34]

Confident that New Orleans and the Gulf region would be subdued before the end of the year or shortly thereafter, Cochrane had sent Admiral Cockburn and six thousand troops to the coast of Georgia and South Carolina to seize islands, harass coastal towns, and recruit slaves and Indians into his ranks during the fall of 1814. "Satisfied that these two states will be at our Mercy," he insisted that he could raise additional companies of Colonial Marines during the winter and by April 1815 "recommence our operations in the Chesapeake." As such, Cockburn's aggressive strike-and-retreat warfare stimulated and supported Cochrane's operations in the Gulf while also satisfying larger objectives. The New Orleans campaign, in effect, represented but one more operation within his broader strategy of harassing the Americans until they begged for peace.[35]

By mid-December 1814 Jackson desperately needed more time and additional troops. On December 16 he declared martial law, and two days later in the square at the cathedral he reviewed troops, including two battalions of freemen of color. Edward Livingston read Jackson's call to arms: "I invited you to share in the perils and to divide the glory of your white countrymen." With emotion, Livingston told them he expected much, knowing they "could endure hunger and thirst, and all the hardships of war." Believing that they loved their land, he extolled them "to defend all that is most dear to man." This ceremony showed Jackson's desperation, as he later even accepted an offer to use Jean Lafitte's "hellish banditti" (pirates/privateers), along with their important cache of powder, shot, and flints. The general initially refused to seek help from the black troops or Lafitte's pirates, but given the critical state of affairs he could not refuse their assistance any longer.[36]

Jackson reacted to the British advances, attempting to engage the freemen "by every dear and honorable tie to the interest of the country who extends to them equal rights and privileges with white men." In an address to Louisiana's white citizens, Jackson had warned against "negro assassins" who would become slaves to Britain. Yet, in a separate address to the "free coloured inhabitants of Louisiana" he pleaded for their assistance, desperately calling them "sons of freedom," "brave fellow citizens," and even "adopted children" who had been deprived the chance to defend their country. The slaveowning Jackson begged them "to defend our most inestimable blessing . . . to defend all which is dear in existence." Those who did, he promised, would "be paid the same bounty in money and lands" as white soldiers—$124 in cash and 160 acres of land. Additionally, those who followed the "path of glory" would "receive the applause and gratitude" of their country.[37]

Claiborne delayed publishing Jackson's appeal to the freemen until late October 1814 because of the distrust that existed "against this Class of people." Many "excellent citizens," Claiborne reported, condemned the plan, supposing that by "putting arms in the hands of men of color, we only add to the force of the enemy." The white New Orleans Committee of Defense surprisingly endorsed Jackson's proposal, "provided there could be a guaranty, against the return of the regiment" when

> ## TO THE MEN OF COLOR.
>
> Soldiers—From the Shores of Mobile I collected you to arms—I invited you to share in the perils and to divide the glory of your white countrymen. I expected much from you, for I was not uninformed of those qualities which must render you so formidable to an invading foe—I knew that you could endure hunger and thirst, and all the hardships of war—I knew that you loved the land of your nativity, and that, like ourselves, you had to defend all that is most dear to man—but you surpass my hopes; I have found in you, united to those qualities, that noble enthusiasm which impels to great deeds.
>
> Soldiers—the President of the United States shall be informed of your conduct on the present occasion, and the voice of the representatives of the American nation shall applaud your valor, as your general now praises your ardor. The enemy is near; his 'sails cover the lakes,' but the brave are united; and if he finds us contending among ourselves, it will be for the prize of valor and fame its noblest reward.
>
> By command,
>
> THOS. L. BUTLER,
> Aid de Camp.

General Andrew Jackson's Plea. General Andrew Jackson's December 1814 plea to the "Men of Color" revealed his desperate need for soldiers prior to the Battle for New Orleans. Ultimately, Jackson accepted free blacks and even slaves to man his defensive line at Chalmette. Image from the National Intelligencer (Washington, DC), January 21, 1815.

the war ended. If "the individuals were to settle in to Louisiana, with Knowledge of the use of arms, & that pride of Distinction, which a soldiers pursuits so naturally inspires, they would prove dangerous," the committee concluded. In effect, what white citizens really wanted was to hire black soldiers, pay them after the crisis, and then send them off far away.[38]

Jackson's appeal to the freemen of color did not pay immediate dividends. Many Louisianans decried the objectionable proclamation that put blacks on par with white citizens and that called them "fellow citizens" and "countrymen." Despite the complaints, Jackson, Claiborne, and the freemen saw advantages to joining with the Americans. Governor Claiborne reported that a Frenchman, a Mr. A. M. Bourgeois (likely Antoine Bourgeau), agreed to raise a company of one hundred freemen of color as long as he received a captain's commission. Bourgeois also indicated that other gentlemen planned to raise colored companies. Claiborne commissioned a free black named Ferdinand Lioteau as a captain and sent him south with a detachment of thirty freemen of color to Fort St. Philip on the Mississippi River. White planter and merchant Col. Michel Fortier Sr. provided funds to arm and outfit the first battalion of freemen of color; by mid-December Maj. Pierre LaCoste led these men to the Chef Menteur to prevent the British from taking that road to the city. Fortier also provided arms and equipment for a second battalion of black refugees from St. Domingue. These men were raised, organized, and drilled by Capt. Joseph Savary, a mulatto who had seen considerable action in the wars on St. Domingue. Mustered into service on December 19, they immediately proceeded to Chalmette where they played a conspicuous role during the campaign in the middle of Jackson's defensive line. In addition, Capt. Alexandre Lemelle commanded the fifty-man 15th Louisiana Regiment of freemen of color while Capt. Charles Forneret commanded a thirty-one-soldier company. Other individual free blacks fought with different regular and militia units, including a fourteen-year-old mulatto drummer boy named Jordan B. Noble, who gained recognition for continuing his beat during fierce night fighting on December 23 and during the chaotic main British attack on January 8, 1815.[39]

The first Battalion of Free Men of Color consisted of 353 men, staff officers, and an eleven-piece band headed by shopkeeper and musician Barthelemy Campanel. The battalion elected shoemaker Vincent Populous as second major in early December 1814, and thereafter he commanded the unit in the field. The six companies had black officers, and many of the men had long histories of military service to Louisiana. Joiners Baltazare Demozeillier, Jean Louis Dolliole, and Louis Daunoy, cabinetmaker Charles Porée, and auctioneer Pierre Bailly had all signed the 1804 free men of color petition to Governor Claiborne and had served previously in the Spanish militia. Cabinetmaker Louis Simon had fought against the Chickasaw during the 1790s, while Noel Carrière had served with Bernardo Gálvez during the American Revolution. Others represented traditional skilled occupations: Charles Chapron was a carter (someone who literally carted things around); Pvt. Celestin Danneville a carpenter; shoemaker Peter Dolliole resided at 65 St. Philippe; Francois

Ford was a drayman (someone who hauled things around in a cart without sides); Jean Foucher a bricklayer; Celeste Jourdan was a gardener; Joseph Lavigne a baker; Antoine Raby a tailor; and James Thomas a grocer. This group of "chosen men of color" represented an important element of lower-middle-class professional society and property owners who anticipated that performing their civic obligations would win for them broader rights as citizens.[40]

Newly promoted Maj. Joseph Savary's second battalion had far different roots. Comprised of 256 free black émigrés from St. Domingue, most of these men had fought as French loyalists against L'Ouverture during the slave revolt in Haiti. Mustering into service on December 19, they had the distinction of having a black staff officer (Savary) appointed by Jackson, yet white company commanders. Moreover, the black soldiers selected the white baker Maj. Louis Daquin to command them in the field. Jackson had established this arrangement in his first proclamation to the freemen of color in September 1814, and having black soldiers commanded by white officers remained in effect throughout the nineteenth and well into the twentieth century. The four companies, varying in strength from fifty-three to sixty-seven, had a rank and file that quickly volunteered to fight the British even though they did not have long-standing ties to Louisiana. Many did have long-standing ties to one another, and they saw service as a way to elevate themselves in society. The four brothers Bonseigneur—Paul, Caesar, Detterville, and Jean—who had come to New Orleans from Haiti answered the call. Shopkeeper Richard Gautier and baker Jean Pierre Michel both resided on Toulouse, while milliner Joseph Augustin, shoemaker John Davis, broker Ament Morin, and merchant Esope Oliver all lived close to one another. They represented the same lower-middle-class property owners as the first battalion and agreed to fight to protect their material possessions. Some patriotic members volunteered without the shoes and blankets needed for a cold-weather campaign, which further demonstrated their willingness to sacrifice in order to gain recognition and acceptance.[41]

In addition to the two battalions, an older group of freemen of color who were not liable for military service also answered Jackson's call for assistance. Seventy-nine of these men served in the home guard, a police unit that maintained order and conducted nightly patrols, and served "as a police among the slaves" in order to discourage insurrections. Commanded by the well-respected and elderly black man Gabriel Gerome, the home guard had only twenty-seven weapons to fulfill its mission. Once Jackson declared martial law, most of these volunteers patrolled the city, extinguished street lamps, and apprehended violators. A group of eleven commanded by black Cpl. John Pierre Labau served at Fort St. John, near the mouth of Bayou St. John and Lake Pontchartrain. Additionally, several black women worked in the local hospital, tending to the injured without any expectation of compensation, yet fulfilling their civic obligations.[42]

Jackson's willingness to co-opt slaves into his ranks worked to eliminate the specter of a servile insurrection. Because of previous incidents, including the January 1811 uprising when five hundred armed slaves dressed in military uniforms revolted near New Orleans, there was a persistent fear. This feeling was further exacerbated when Louisianans received news that British forces landing along the Gulf would rally slaves to their standard as they marched on New Orleans. Jackson prevented such a possibility by recruiting slaves to join the American cause. A slave named James Roberts recalled some years later that General Jackson came to his Natchez area plantation "to enlist five hundred negroes." Jackson promised, "If the battle is fought and the victory gained . . . you shall be free." This prospect of freedom motivated Roberts and other slaves, who traveled to New Orleans where the general again promised them freedom. Jackson "had obtained from the masters . . . their word of honour, that they would grant them a full and entire pardon" once a victory had been secured. This promise helped Roberts and other slaves to overcome their "fears and dread" and fight with ferocity, completely insensitive to death and pain; Roberts himself lost his left forefinger and suffered a severe head wound. And although Jackson later acknowledged the bravery of these men, once the campaign had been determined and the crisis averted he refused to grant the slaves their freedom, claiming that he could not "take another man's property and set it free." Instead, Jackson told them to "go home and mind their masters," denying them a chance to secure the opportunity that other combatants had won.[43]

The slaveholding Gen. Andrew Jackson understood well the dichotomy Louisianans faced, but he needed men to counter the British invasion. Jackson did not co-opt slaves into his ranks because he had acknowledged their equality. Instead, he saw slave men as much-needed troops who could protect New Orleans from a British attack. By promising slaves their freedom, Jackson committed them to his cause rather than permitting them to assist the British, and this tied them to the United States. Moreover, Jackson's promise resembled what slaves had experienced in earlier wars and what they collectively anticipated during this conflict: brave military service could open the door to freedom and keep them close to family and friends. Yet Jackson had no intention of freeing slaves because doing so would undermine the social and economic order of Louisiana and the South, and a slaveholder understood that danger. Once Jackson had secured victory, he denied slaves their promised freedom while he had white armed troops to enforce his decision. White Louisianans would not feel deceived by his betrayal, nor would the freemen of color. In effect, Jackson had made a calculated decision, and the slaves would remain in bondage.

The political stability and future of the Gulf Coast rested on slaves and their masters, who transformed the frontiers into arable and productive farmlands. In doing so, they strengthened and expanded slavery in the region, incorporating Louisiana into the American republic. Admiral Cochrane's proclamation to free slaves and evacuate them to other colonies would undermine the Louisiana economy, threaten the tenuous social fabric of this recently incorporated region, and potentially destabilize American control of the Gulf. In fact, the British offer had the potential to foster a racial divide in the region and threaten the livelihood and lives of Louisianans—French, Spanish, and Americans alike. Once the war came to the Gulf, the multiethnic Louisianans, like those in the Chesapeake, had to watch for a British invasion while also anticipating a British-inspired slave revolt.

While Jackson rallied soldiers to his cause, Governor Claiborne pleaded with Louisiana's white citizens to send their slaves to help construct fortifications for the city. Planters "furnished thousands of their slaves, and sent them to every particular place where their labour was thought necessary." They dug trenches, raised parapets, strengthened breastworks, and eased "the labour of the soldiery and preserve[d] their health and activity for more important service." Given the number of projects that Jackson needed to complete, he had no choice but to enlist slaves in large-scale work projects immediately, regardless of the season or weather. In one instance, Fort St. Leon's commander impressed two hundred slaves to work on that bastion during early January, including clearing timber from the Bayou St. John. A "negro man" named Arche, owned by Jacob Purkill in Eddyville, Kentucky, and hired out to a barge descending the Mississippi River, fell victim to U.S. forces, who impressed him and worked him for twenty-seven straight days in cold water and mud; Arche ultimately became sick and died. Jackson's engineer Arsène Lacarrière Latour took "one hundred negroes" for "ten days" to construct a battery on the west side of the Mississippi River, south from New Orleans across from Fort St. Philip. Benjamin Latrobe's son, Henry, supervised 150 slaves who constructed a defensive line at the rear of the American position at Chalmette. Engineer Charles Lefevre gathered another "one hundred fifty negroes," who for six days built an earthen rampart on the west side of the Mississippi River on the Bois-gervais Canal. Reportedly, a black laborer named Pompey working for Latour offered the idea of using cotton bales to reinforce Jackson's artillery emplacements at Chalmette. Perhaps apocryphal, the story nonetheless illustrates the centrality of slaves and free blacks to the New Orleans defense story.[44]

During the British campaign against New Orleans—a series of engagements lasting from December 23, 1814, until January 8, 1815—Jackson cobbled together a heterogeneous army that embodied the first genuine American fighting force, consisting of U.S. regular soldiers, Spanish and French Louisiana creoles, Tennessee and Kentucky frontiersmen, Baratarian pirates, freemen of color, slaves, and some Choctaw Indians. This polyglot, cosmopolitan group chose for a variety of reasons to join Jackson's defense of the city, and their services helped ensure the American victory.

During Jackson's first engagement on the night of December 23, 1814, Savary's battalion of freemen of color from St. Domingue, along with Maj. Jean Plauché's French Creoles, attacked surprised British troops some ten miles south of New Orleans along the Mississippi River. Savary and Plauché ordered their men in French *"En Main! En Main!"* ["Charge! Charge!"], and the commands undoubtedly shocked British soldiers fresh from European battlefields. Those familiar words proved that the French population had chosen to support the Americans rather than remain neutral. Despite the gun and cannon smoke, and the fog and encroaching darkness, the two sides moved within a few feet of one another. It became a general melee in the darkness, when suddenly many of the guns provided to the freemen of color failed, forcing the soldiers to use them as clubs in hand-to-hand fighting. "Savary's volunteers manifested great bravery" while suffering only seven wounded. After two-plus hours of fighting, Jackson withdrew his troops to a defensive position at the Laronde plantation. His surprise attack had forced the British to delay and be more cautious, buying Jackson enough time to prepare his defenses on the Rodriguez Canal at Chalmette.[45]

On December 24, 1814, the same day that British and American ministers signed the Treaty of Ghent concluding the war, Jackson moved his army north along the Mississippi River to Chalmette. He ordered engineers Latour and Barthelmy Lafon to cut the river levee and flood the ground in front and behind the British position. Within a few days the temporary swell of the river had subsided, but the water saturated the ground, creating a sticky morass. Meanwhile Latour's defensive preparations had continued at Chalmette, as slaves dug a deeper canal ditch, using the earth to strengthen the parapet wall. The first battalion of free-men of color arrived and took up a position next to Savary's battalion, and Captains Lemelle and Forneret's free black Louisiana companies also joined the Chalmette line. Their timely arrival helped to repel a British frontal attack on December 28, which was attempting to determine the strength of Jackson's position. Three days later, on January 1, 1815, the British began an unsuccessful two-hour artillery barrage, designed to demolish the American position.[46]

Finally, British general Sir Edward Michael Pakenham made a fatal frontal attack en force against Jackson's line. The climactic battle of the New Orleans campaign occurred on January 8, 1815. The American lines contained the largest collection of armed black combatants before the American Civil War, and they suffered through the most intense fighting of the day. It was also reported that the "mulatto corps" even engaged in an unauthorized sortie against the British, "advancing over . . . breast works and exposing themselves." In particular, the three Savary brothers—Joseph, Belton, and their father Charles—deserved praise when they crossed the line and engaged the British; Belton Savary suffered severe wounds, dying a few days later. In fact, of the thirty-nine men wounded during the day's fighting, thirteen of them were black.[47]

Black soldiers from the British 1st and 5th West Indian Regiments, who had suffered greatly from the bitterly cold winter weather, led the charge against Jackson. Some fellow redcoats complained that the black units "had not been employed in sieges," and as such they should not have the honor to lead the attack. Others claimed that they had been "useless, [and] absolutely in the way." Regardless, the West Indian Regiments bravely marched shoulders abreast toward the sparsely guarded eastern portion of the American line that petered out in a thick cypress swamp. As they moved closer, they took a withering fire from John Coffee's Tennesseans, who jumped from log to log and scurried behind stumps and bushes only to fire again. One West Indian troop had the lower portion of his face shot away: "His eyes were gone, and the bones of his brow all jagged, and dripping blood." Some of the black soldiers succeeded in getting close to the Americans before they bogged down in the cold sticky mud. Some soldiers drowned and some remained immobilized from the "stormy and frosty" weather, while others were captured by the Tennesseans. Several of the "poor devils" refused to advance or retreat. When approached, one black soldier screamed that he had "rader stay here and get kill at once; neber see de day go back to Jamaica, so me di now, tank you." Given the butchery and death continually surrounding them, such a fatalistic expression seemed perfectly natural.[48]

Despite the less-than-flattering accounts of black participation, their casualties totaled only five killed, twenty-four wounded, and one missing. This was an extremely low number when considering that total British losses numbered more than two thousand killed and wounded, and especially since the black troops led part of the British attack. Four West Indian troops (George Byng, Robert Corbet, William Pattin, and Robert Pegan) killed were African "Eboe" men, who had all served in British ranks for more than a decade. The fifth, upholsterer James Augustine, had been born in St. Domingue and had served in the 5th West Indian Regiment since May 1801. Taller than most of his fellow soldiers, the five-feet-ten-inch Augustine would have received an increase in pay by May 1815 had he not been killed on December 28, 1814. Though not in combat, another 160 West Indians succumbed to disease in camp or aboard ship during the campaign. These warm-blooded Caribbean soldiers did not weather the frigid Louisiana winter temperatures and swampy morass very well.[49]

British forces had traveled almost seventy miles to land soldiers at the Bienvenu Canal south of New Orleans. Then engineers and some unarmed black laborers hacked their way through the cane fields, clearing paths for the army. Having spent "their livelong service in a warm climate," many of these black laborers went "to the hospital, and most likely to their graves." While excavating a canal the "poor wretches . . . worked awkwardly and groaned incessantly, under an occupation which inflicted deadly suffering." Once they had dug the canals, they had to drag barges and launches through the "insufficient passage" to the shore of the Mississippi River. Throughout their tiring work, they had little food and could not light a fire at night, lest they reveal to American spies the progress they had achieved. So they huddled together each frigid evening, "a little afraid that some stray alligator" might make a meal of them. Even once they reached the British encampment, their job did not stop. When Jackson's forces cut the river levee on December 26, these men immediately stepped into the river's cold waters to fill the gap. They then helped build and rebuild batteries. These laborers could never find a moment to rest, as they constantly received instructions to move guns and supplies, dig entrenchments, and repair the damage incurred during the various engagements. When they did have a moment, a stray cannon shot or a burst of gunfire frequently disrupted their rest. This continued until January 8, when the laborers began the reverse trip to ships at anchor off the Louisiana Coast.[50]

With Pakenham's death on January 8, new British commander Maj. Gen. John Lambert tested other American defenses downriver before choosing to retreat. His successful evacuation had to be conducted discreetly without providing Jackson and the Americans a sense of British weakness. For ten days and nights, British troops trickled out of their Mississippi River encampment, and by January 18, 1815, virtually the entire British army had disappeared; the West Indian regiments departed on January 13 and 14. They left behind considerable equipment, wounded soldiers, and two surgeons. "A vast number of these wretched creatures" (slaves) had descended on the British encampment expecting to be evacuated, but Lambert had promised Jackson that slaveowners could visit under a flag of truce and try to reclaim "their stray sheep." One young slave wandered into camp with a collar of spikes around his neck. The intelligent, multilingual slave explained that his master had attached this device when he first tried to escape to British lines. Being in great pain and unable to lie down, he stalked through the woods for days, finally finding the British camp. After securing his freedom from the spikes, the boy joined with other refugees who made their way to British ships in the Gulf of Mexico. Another slave named George learned of the impending arrival of the white owners, and he adopted a prudent policy of invisibility. "All the Negroes who had enlivened our camp" were coaxed to return to their previous condition of servitude except for George, who had cautiously kept himself hidden; George's deception permitted him to leave with the British army.

During the evacuation of the army and refugees from New Orleans, fleet captain Edward Codrington gave strict instructions to enlist ten slaves on each of the gun vessels under his command. This would permit him to draw rations from the fleet, making more provisions available for receiving "as many other black slaves . . . as may wish to be brought away." He also instructed his captains to distribute the refugees "among the ships that have black regiments on board, in order to induce them to enlist which will be a means of providing for their wives and families" during the next campaign against Mobile.[51]

British officers accepted the American surrender of Fort Bowyer off Mobile on February 11, 1815, only two days before news of the Treaty of Ghent reached the Gulf Coast. During the following weeks, British troops remained on Mobile Point while Cochrane and Lambert sorted out the provisions of the treaty; the return of prisoners obviously dominated early discussions. Cochrane offered to transport American prisoners to the mouth of the Mississippi River, where they could be exchanged for British soldiers. Then Jackson raised the question of "negroe slaves belonging to" Americans, explicitly questioning whether the property was "intended to be restored." Initially ignoring Jackson's query, Cochrane used silence as a way to ensure protection of his black and Indian allies. Lambert conveyed that he could not force the slaves to go back, but he would happily permit slaveowners to visit and try to persuade the refugees to return. Within days a number of white Creoles arrived to reclaim their slaves, and some owners succeeded in enticing them.

Then American officials informed British commanders that they were prepared to receive all captured property, including "such slaves as may be in your control, belonging to any inhabitant or citizen of the United States." Lambert detailed how slaves had not been taken; instead, they had voluntarily joined or followed as refugees or deserters. The commander acknowledged that if Britain had in fact forcefully absconded with the slaves, the treaty would compel their return. After consulting with Admirals Malcolm and Cochrane, Lambert contended that the slaves had made free choices to follow, and he promised to make every effort to persuade them to return. Yet Lambert also maintained that he could not abandon them or force them back into servitude. Had he intended to flee with the slaves, Lambert asked Jackson, why would his refugee transports have remained in American waters until March 30, 1815, weeks after the battle? British ships remained off Mobile, and Lambert reportedly "used every persuasion that the [slaves] should return to their masters, and many have done so." The British decision to provide safe haven for refugees gave the slaves an opportunity to make their own decisions, and ultimately more than 160 fled from the shores of the Mississippi.[52]

During a public thanksgiving at New Orleans' St. Louis Cathedral on January 21, 1815, Jackson praised the service of his soldiers, including the freemen of color, some 10 percent of his total forces at Chalmette. "The two corps of coloured volunteers have not disappointed the hopes that were formed of their courage and perseverance in the performance of their duty." They had made conscious choices to side with the Americans because they had much to lose if the British succeeded. British promises of liberating slaves would have greatly diluted the influence of the free black community, which in the end would lessen their collective status within Louisiana society. These men represented a prominent social group of skilled artisans and small businessmen, and serving in the militia had been a way to express publicly their status. Likewise, joining with Jackson and the Americans fulfilled their civic obligations to Louisiana and the United States, and Jackson's promises of land and money served as icing on the cake. Yet military service did not ultimately elevate their status but rather created renewed suspicion and distrust.[53]

The expected demobilization of soldiers occurred slowly. After the celebration Jackson ordered the black troops to return to the city, remain alert, and drill daily. Martial law remained in effect until Jackson knew conclusively that the war was over. By mid-February, Jackson learned that many of the soldiers refused to return to their units or had simply deserted their posts, including many from the black corps. Though the war had ended, the possibility of contracting disease in camp proved too dangerous to endure. The black soldiers' general dissatisfaction intensified when Jackson assigned them to travel to the Chef Menteur to perform military labor. Not wanting to be treated as slaves, Major Daquin reported that the black soldiers would willingly die in combat for their country, but they would not perform manual labor. Such discord within Jackson's ranks spelled trouble, especially with the British enemy still in the neighborhood. If the British were sowing discontent within his ranks, they could also be planting the seeds of slave insurrection within an area where the racial harmony seemed precariously unbalanced. When Jackson received news of reported slave insurrections in Attakapas, Opelousas, and St. Martin, as well as information that seventeen men had been jailed, he saw further proof that the British were still meddling with racial relations. As long as militiamen remained in the field and focused on the British enemy, slaves had a perfect opportunity to secure their freedom, whether by boldly fleeing or slinking away under cover of darkness to British lines. As long as the Union Jack flew in the area, slaves could hope for and still find an opportunity to steal away to freedom.[54]

ALONG THE SOUTH ATLANTIC COAST AND GULF OF MEXICO, British forces had found little opposition until they approached New Orleans. Admiral Cockburn's operations off Georgia and South Carolina wreaked havoc: the British seized contraband, destroyed commerce, and evacuated some 1,500 slaves from the United States. Much like operations in the Chesapeake, British activities along the coasts of Georgia

and South Carolina left isolated American plantation owners caught between the dual-edged threat of British liberation and slave insurrection.
Many owners tried to move their slaves inland to prevent them from
easily fleeing to British lines. Others even armed their slaves to keep
the British away; not surprisingly, these owners felt threatened when
their armed slaves revealed signs of insurrection. Coastal owners who
did not take precautions quickly realized that the presence of British
forces emboldened their slaves to flee, especially as officers and soldiers
encouraged them. Slaves such as Ned Simmons decided immediately to
flee when given the chance to leave bondage. Simmons put on a British
uniform, accepted a weapon, and began training to become a Colonial
Marine. Many others chose to be evacuated, leaving slavery with the
promise of freedom in an unknown British colony. Their choice revealed
uncertainties, but they accepted that they would be free, and freedom
would provide future opportunities. Unfortunately, Simmons and some
other slaves fell between the cracks of evacuation and the Treaty of
Ghent and were thus returned to a life of bondage.

Admiral Cochrane anticipated that the black population along the
Gulf would give the British an easy victory at New Orleans. Major
Nicolls and Captain Woodbine laid the foundation for slave and Indian
support, establishing a British base at Prospect Bluff on the Apalachicola
River. This concerned the Spanish, who, although allied with Britain
against Napoleon, feared that British operatives would unravel the social fabric of the area. Cochrane also tried unsuccessfully to gain the
support of the Jean Lafitte and the Baratarian pirates and the disaffected
Spanish and French populations in Louisiana, as well as the numerous
free blacks and slaves of the region.[55]

True, slaves fled from Georgia and the Mississippi Territory to the
British base on the Apalachicola River in Spanish Florida, but never in
enough numbers to undermine American morale or alter the outcome of
the New Orleans campaign. They did congregate on the Gulf in sufficient
numbers to create fear and apprehension. Only a few of the Louisiana
slaves who Cochrane anticipated would don red coats actually assisted
the British, and fewer still participated in the Louisiana campaign. Instead, Andrew Jackson guaranteed "a full and entire pardon" to slaves
who helped defend New Orleans, and he promised a monetary and
land bounty to those free blacks, or "sons of freedom," who supported
the American cause. Louisiana free blacks believed that supporting the
Americans in this struggle would broaden their own social, economic,
and political rights and help to undermine British attempts to free slaves,

which, if successful, would dilute their position in the eyes of white society. In fact, if slaves won their freedom, it would result in a much greater number of free blacks, collectively reducing the hard-won status of those who had already secured their freedom. In the end, Jackson's proclamations and promises denied to Cochrane an important source of much-needed manpower for British operations while maintaining the social status quo within the region. Ultimately, Jackson never fulfilled his promises to the slaves and only slowly fulfilled his obligations to the free blacks, further diminishing the status of both groups as the South moved toward a southern slave society based on cotton plantation agriculture.[56]

CHAPTER 7

DIFFERENT PLACES, SAME RESULTS, 1815 AND AFTER

*"They were in every sense of
the word Free Men"*

Ninety-year-old Jordan Bankston Noble died at his children's New Orleans home in the early hours of June 20, 1890. The following day, the New Orleans *Daily Picayune* sadly reported the "death of 'the Drummer Boy of Chalmette,'" ran a woodcut picture of the "Colored Veteran of Four Wars," and encouraged family and friends to attend his Saturday-afternoon funeral so they could look on the white hair and "familiar face of 'Old Jordan'" one last time. The announcement stressed his patriotic service and that "army veterans are also invited to attend." Finally, it stated that Noble "ha[d] gone to join his comrades of many campaigns," being buried in the city's St. Louis Cemetery No. 2, Square 3.[1]

Born a mulatto slave in Augusta, Georgia, on October 14, 1800, to African and European parents, Noble arrived in New Orleans in 1812. By 1813, the then-teenage Noble had joined the U.S. Army as a drummer in the 7th U.S. Regiment. Whether he had secured his freedom or remained a slave is unclear. Though only a teenager, Noble nonetheless handled his drum like a veteran during the New Orleans campaign of

December 1814–January 1815. He kept a steady beat and led Major Daquin's company to meet the British for the fierce night fighting of December 23, 1814. On January 8, 1815, "the rattle of his drum was heard [even] amidst the din of battle," "in the hottest hell of fire" during the chaotic main British attack at Chalmette. After the war Noble reportedly remained in New Orleans, participating in the Seminole War in Florida and the Mexican War and marrying into the free black community.[2]

On January 8, 1851, thirty-six years after the glorious victory at Chalmette, ninety free veterans of color finally marched for the first time in the annual January 8 parade. During the procession "Old Jordan" provided the same beat that he had on the Plains of Chalmette years earlier. Marching in the center of the parade, the freemen of color had finally achieved community recognition, an honor long overdue. The *Daily Picayune* rhetorically asked, who had "endured the hardships of the camp, or faced with greater courage the perils of the fight?" "Who more than they deserve the thanks of the country and the gratitude of the

Jordan Noble. Drummer boy Jordan Noble, shown later in life, served with the Americans at the Battle of New Orleans. He later participated in the Seminole, Mexican, and Civil Wars. By the late nineteenth century Noble's drum represented the memory of the Battle of New Orleans and black participation in the victory. Courtesy of The Historic New Orleans Collection, MSS 216, Creole Historic Exhibit Collection.

succeeding generations?" Finally, they had made "an impression on every observer" present that day, even as they passed in a slow and steady cadence that reflected their age.[3]

Noble became a *de facto* leader of this aging group as his drumbeat reminded all of the sacrifice they had endured and the victory they had helped secure; he also organized or participated in a number of events celebrating their wartime efforts. On January 8, 1860, the black soldiers participated in another parade, the largest and most festive held during the pre–Civil War era, even though the number of aging veterans had greatly declined. The freemen of color still held a prominent place in the center of the parade, but they now rode in carriages, as their marching days were over. At Maj. Gen. Winfield Scott's request, Jordan Noble was honored with a medal for his contributions at the Battle of New Orleans, and the aging crowd became rowdy, cheering and applauding their fellow soldier. When called on to offer remarks, Noble had to wait for the cheering to stop before he boldly announced that he was ready to serve his country again as he had done in New Orleans, Florida, and Mexico. Within a few years Noble's wish would be fulfilled.[4]

In April 1861, as the United States descended into Civil War, Noble and approximately 1,500 Louisiana freemen of color offered their services to the Confederacy to defend the city of New Orleans until federal troops occupied the city during the spring of 1862. With the city under federal control, Noble patriotically volunteered for the Union Army, organizing a company of free blacks known as the "Native Guards" who remained active from July to August 1863. His immediate switch of sides reflected his long-standing service as a federal soldier and his desire to be an American. Although he served only a short time, Noble's Union participation won him a post–Civil War state pension of $100 for his activity during the War of 1812.[5]

Jordan Noble's life spanned the early republic until near the end of the nineteenth century. He participated in four wars and gained distinction. After his fighting days had passed, he also contributed to the civic life of the community. His activities bridged the civic and military divide, winning respect from members of both communities. During the 1881 funeral ceremonies in New Orleans for President James Garfield, one journalist commented that "Old Jordan, strong and portly, is still about and despite his eighty one years, walks the streets as a sedate looker-on, reads the paper, writes letters, chats with old acquaintances, watches the military parades with interest, and stoutly maintains his ability still to rub-a-dub-dub all its music out of a drum." Although too old to work, during the New Orleans Exposition of 1884–1885 Noble and his "well-worn drum" entertained audiences. The music provided him an entree into respectability, yet he held on tightly to his position within the New Orleans free black community and his military legacy as the drummer boy of the Battle of New Orleans. His distinction and talent, combined with an intense patriotism to Louisiana and the United States, also permitted Noble to navigate the perils associated with pre– and post–Civil War race relations. His drum represented the memory of the Battle of New Orleans, and by playing it he transcended southern racial stereotypes. So, when discrimination and persecution came his way, Noble simply took out his drum and beat it away. Too many of Noble's contemporaries did not enjoy the same advantages for orchestrating the perils of life.[6]

"A RECEPTACLE FOR RUNAWAY SLAVES": NEGRO FORT AND THE BLACK FUTURE ALONG THE GULF OF MEXICO

During November 1814 British major Edward Nicolls's slave soldiers and Indian allies built, under George Woodbine's supervision, a strong earthen fort, 120 feet in diameter. Sitting on a cliff commanding the Apalachicola River, the bastion at Prospect Bluff had walls fifteen feet high and eighteen feet thick, as well as a moat and another wall made out of a double row of pine logs. Within the middle of the structure stood a thirty-foot octagon-shaped powder magazine constructed of earth and logs. With the river in front, a swamp to the rear, a large stream to the north, and a small creek to the south, the stronghold was virtually invincible to any landward approach.[7]

Nicolls had raised a fighting force of four to five hundred soldiers, including both runaways and free African Americans, and many had settled with their families near Prospect Bluff. Those slaves who had found their way to Negro Fort (a common name for Nicolls's fort) had come from near and far. They had traveled from Spanish East Florida (Fernandina and St. Augustine), from the Seminole territory of Alachua, from Spanish West Florida, from Louisiana, Mississippi Territory, and Georgia, and from Virginia. Settling in the fertile Apalachicola River Valley, the black population in the area most likely hovered around six hundred to seven hundred, with the surrounding pastures and fields extending for more than fifty miles north and south along the river.[8]

Although British forces began departing Negro Fort in late February 1815, Nicolls left behind at least three thousand stands of muskets, a tremendous quantity of ammunition, and an assortment of other weapons. He had also provided the fort with several cannon, leaving it a strong, secure position that commanded transportation and communication routes into southern Georgia and the Mississippi Territory. The British had either stored or distributed at least six thousand stands of muskets, rifles, and carbines to their Indian allies in the area, which made those who manned the fort a potent force along the southern frontier. Such a heavily armed maroon settlement so near the American border gravely threatened concerned plantation owners along it.[9]

Officials in Madrid had tried to convince the English to destroy the settlement and return the slaves to Spanish control, but British Ministry and military officers along the Gulf Coast had ignored those pleas. Spanish government officials in East and West Florida had also expressed interest in eliminating Negro Fort, and Spanish Florida citizens wanted British commanders to return the slaves to their former masters. Throughout, the British had responded in a unified tone—they would permit any person to go back unmolested to his or her master, but they would not force anyone to return against his or her will. Despite a barrage of Spanish protests, the British refused to modify this basic position, and local military officers refused to give way. The British Ministry did agree to return black Spanish Florida soldiers who had deserted because they were not considered refugees. The British government's responsibility to slaveowners emerged as a thorny diplomatic issue even before the war ended. When the matter was finally settled in 1826, the British government agreed to pay some claims in Spanish Florida for damages, including $20,000 (approximately $360,000 in today's dollars) to Forbes and Company, which likely lost the greatest number of slaves.[10]

The U.S. government had tried to persuade Spanish officials to deal with Florida, or what Secretary of State John Quincy Adams called a "receptacle for runaway slaves." Spain's inability to maintain order in Florida had become even more evident after the British evacuated Prospect Bluff, as the former slaves who remained behind took complete control over this visible symbol of black insurrection. The presence of the heavily armed Negro Fort offered three contradictory images. For the Spanish it revealed the near collapse of authority in Florida. For the blacks and Indians it represented a British promise to return and assist their allies. For the Americans it embodied the embers of a renewed racial war along the Gulf frontier, and American brigadier general Edmund Pendleton Gaines—commander of the southern sector of the southern military district—began planning an expedition against it.[11]

General Jackson sent a military representative to Pensacola during the spring of 1816 to demand that Spain take action against Negro Fort. Baiting new governor Mauricio de Zúñiga in hopes that the Spanish official would make a misstep, Jackson asserted that should Spain not take action the United States would have to destroy the fort. Zúñiga informed Jackson that he, too, wanted the bastion eliminated, but that he had not yet received approval from Madrid. He would neither approve nor forbid action against Negro Fort.[12]

With this tacit Spanish approval, in April 1816 General Gaines sent Col. Duncan Clinch to establish Fort Scott near the confluence of the Flint and Chattahoochee Rivers, about 120 miles north of Prospect Bluff. This position would serve as the operational base for the joint army-navy American expedition against the slave bastion. Clinch then advanced to a position near Prospect Bluff to await supplies coming by navy gunboats from New Orleans. Since the Apalachicola River flowed through Spanish territory, Gaines needed Governor Zúñiga's permission to transport supplies north to Fort Scott. The governor agreed, but he also warned Gaines that Negro Fort physically controlled the river, rendering passage difficult.[13]

The first shipment of American provisions arrived at the mouth of the Apalachicola in early July. Yet Sailing Master Jairus Loomis had instructions to wait until army forces could escort the convoy north. As they waited, a boat suddenly tried to exit the river, prompting Loomis to send a small vessel to intercept the craft and determine its intentions. But as the U.S. vessel approached, the boat fired—harmlessly—on the Americans. American gunboats anchored nearby quickly returned fire, forcing the boat to turn back. The following day, July 16, 1816, Loomis ordered Midshipman Luffborough, "a young Gentleman of fair promise," to replenish the vessel's fresh water supply. During his search for water, Luffborough apparently encountered a black man standing along the riverbank. The young midshipman ordered his crew to proceed cautiously, hoping that a captured fugitive could provide information about the fortress upstream. But as the American boat landed, a volley of musket fire blazed from the undergrowth, instantly killing Luffborough and two seamen. Dazed by the onslaught, American sailor Edward Daniels surrendered in the confusion, and the Indians and slaves scurried him into the woods. Meanwhile, Indians stripped the clothing from the dead sailors and scalped them. This brazen attack made sailors much more cautious as they waited for army forces to arrive.[14]

The joint army-navy-Indian force had done little more than harass Negro Fort prior to the arrival of Loomis's naval vessels and their much-needed artillery pieces. During the evening of July 23, Clinch's Indian leaders entered the fort under a flag of truce to demand its surrender.

Once inside, the black chieftain, a man named Garçon, treated the Creeks contemptuously. Heaping "much abuse on the Americans," he refused to surrender, instead proclaiming that he would "sink any American vessel that should attempt to pass, and would blow up the fort if he could not defend it." As Clinch's Indians departed, they noticed that Garçon and the "negroes had hoisted the red flag of 'no surrender'" and above it the Union Jack, an ominous sign indeed.[15]

The three leaders of the Negro Fort community, Garçon, Prince, and Cyrus, had all come from Spanish Pensacola with Nicolls. The British major had selected the three because of their intelligence, skills, and leadership qualities. Garçon, a thirty-year-old carpenter, had been the property of Don Antonio Montero and was valued at seven hundred pesos, and he commanded the respect of all within the fort and the surrounding community. Prince was twenty-six years old and a master carpenter, and he held the distinction of being one of the most valuable slaves in all of Pensacola—valued at 1,500 pesos. Woodbine had encouraged him to recruit Pensacola slaves to join the British, and his construction skills proved valuable as the slaves reinforced Negro Fort after the British departure. Cyrus was a twenty-six-year-old carpenter and literate, once owned by the mayor of Pensacola, and thus he likely understood the ebb and flow of political machinations and how quickly fortunes could change. None of these skilled slaves had experienced the brutal hardships of bondage, but their choice to join with the British finally provided them with the opportunity to make their own decisions. As they faced an American military force surrounding the fort, they probably did not understand the extent to which this ever-expanding slave plantation nation would reach, but they undoubtedly knew what the consequences might be if they lost this engagement.[16]

For the attack, Loomis agreed to bring his gunboats forward under cover of darkness. By sunrise on July 27, the Americans prepared to target the fort without land support. Shortly after 6:00 A.M., the defenders of Negro Fort responded by firing their 32-pound cannon as a warning to the sailors. Gunboat *No. 154* immediately returned four consecutive volleys, using each to determine the fort's range. The fifth discharge, a hot shot heated in the gunboat's galley, rolled into the fort's powder magazine, causing a sudden explosion that was heard as far as Pensacola some sixty miles away. The blast instantly destroyed Negro Fort and killed 270 of the 334 defenders inside. After only five shots, "the largest and most heavily armed Maroon community ever to appear in the Southeast" and the threat it represented had been eliminated.[17]

The hot shot from the gunboat ended in a few minutes what otherwise might have been a lengthy prolonged siege. The explosion was "awful, and the scene horrible beyond description." "The fort," Clinch insisted, "contained about one hundred effective men (including twenty-five Choctaws), and about two hundred women and children, not more than one-sixth . . . saved." The "war yells of the Indians, the cries and lamentations of the wounded, compelled" even the most experienced soldiers to grimace at the carnage. Arrogantly, Clinch prophesied that the "great Ruler of the Universe must have used [them] as his instrument in chastising the blood-thirsty and murderous wretches that defended the fort." In the end, only three enemy Indians escaped without serious injury. American troops rounded up another twenty-five wounded runaway slaves as prisoners. Despite the relatively small number of survivors, the Americans captured alive both the chief of the Choctaws and Garçon. Once Clinch and his Indian allies discovered that Garçon and his soldiers had tarred and burned alive captured seaman Edward Daniels, the Creeks brutally executed both captives. William Hambly, acting as an agent for Forbes and Company, assumed custody of most of the surviving slaves, since most had once belonged to Spanish residents. The army transferred the American blacks to Fort Scott, where they remained for a time before being returned to their owners. Not surprisingly, most slaves had fled long before the attack, escaping into the woods or joining the Seminole Indians.[18]

The Seminole Wars that followed are intertwined with the War of 1812 because the Treaty of Ghent did not settle affairs along the Gulf frontier. Indians hostile to the United States fled into Spanish territory, and blacks tried to relocate to out-of-the-way places they thought land-hungry Americans would ignore. "The destruction of [Negro] fort, and the band of negroes who held it," according to New Orleans naval commander Daniel Todd Patterson, "is of great and manifest importance to the United States." The fort had "become the greatest rendezvous for runaway slaves and disaffected Indians; an asylum where they found arms and ammunition to protect themselves against their owners and the Government." With the destruction of the fort, slaves and Indians "have no longer a place to fly to, and will not be so liable to abscond." In fact, the destruction of Negro Fort, combined with the Seminole Wars, removed the obstacles to American southwestward settlement and to the development of a slave society across the cotton lands of the Gulf frontier. Armed black soldiers and their Indian allies could not be permitted to hold an entrenched position along the Gulf, if for no other reason than that such a fortress posed a continued threat to southern American society and set a dangerous precedent that could potentially disrupt the fragile developing slave economy. Ultimately, Manifest Destiny needed powerless neighbors in order to succeed.[19]

"FREE TRADE AND SAILORS' RIGHTS":
DARTMOOR PRISON AND FREEDOM

Being captured during wartime was a traumatic experience, especially for black mariners taken in slaveholding territory. There was always a possibility that black British soldiers and sailors could be taken further inland, stripped of their British connections, enslaved, and never again get an opportunity to escape to freedom. White British prisoners could fare better because officers were generally entertained as gentlemen, and ordinary soldiers and sailors were given the opportunity to desert to the American cause.

Yet American prisoners were marched off to one of several ill-provisioned prison camps. Army officers would often be exchanged quickly or even paroled while soldiers languished. When the British captured seagoing privateers, they gave the American sailors, known as "tars," the opportunity to join the British navy. Sometimes the British forced unwilling Americans below decks to serve aboard their warships. Those who refused to fight their fellow Americans would be transported to Dartmoor Prison in Devon, outside of Plymouth, England, and to other prisons used by the British—Stapleton in England, Melville Island at Halifax, Nova Scotia, and prison ships in England, eastern Canada, Bermuda, and the West Indies. During the war the British incarcerated more than 6,550 Americans at Dartmoor Prison, and 14.5 percent, or 955, were not white.[20]

More than half of the black prisoners at Dartmoor came from New York, Maryland, Pennsylvania, and Massachusetts, with another 10 percent coming from slave states Virginia and Louisiana. Fourteen prisoners claimed Africa as their birthplace, suggesting that they had, in fact, escaped slavery. Regardless of birthplace, members of this heterogeneous group had one thing in common—they were prisoners in the most bleak, barren, and remote prison camp in England, and they remain incarcerated there until months after the war ended.

Although blacks were not segregated on board the ships they served, once they landed in England, their sense of maritime equality began to crumble. In early April 1813, some twenty-four black sailors began the

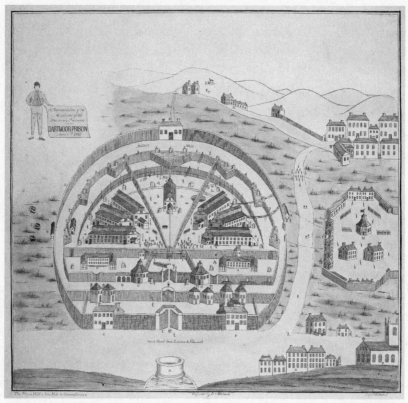

Dartmoor Prison, England. DeWitt C. Hitchcock's "Massacre of American Prisoners" shows the notorious Dartmoor Prison built on England's remote southwestern moor. Originally housing only French prisoners, American sailors were transferred there during the War of 1812. By 1814 black American sailors occupied Block Number Four, located in the top middle of the image. Courtesy of The Lilly Library, Indiana University, Bloomington.

seventeen-mile uphill march from Plymouth inland toward Dartmoor, perched atop the desolate Devonshire moor. For nine days British soldiers prodded the black sailors with bayonets, forcing them along a rutted, muddy track to the prison's stone walls. It was a godforsaken place with three concentric walls and a natural moat surrounding it, making escape almost impossible. As one prisoner recalled, "The moor affords nothing for subsistence or pleasure. Rabbits cannot live on it. Birds fly from it, and it is inhabited . . . by troubled ghosts. . . . This unhallowed spot was believed, by common superstition, to belong to the Devil." Once they entered, British soldiers channeled these sailors into Prison Number Four, a self-contained unit and yard that held the most undesirable prisoners. First they were taken to the bathhouse, stripped of their filthy rags, scrubbed from head to toe, and clothed. Prison Number Four was separated from the others by its own yard, and black prisoners initially lived in squalor because food and the other essentials remained in short supply. They endured racial taunts, threats, and punishments designed to keep them subservient to white sailors—a system that lasted until the number of black sailors increased.[21]

By September 1813 the number of black prisoners in Dartmoor had grown to sixty-two, and by the following spring the number had increased to seventy-six. Once the number of black sailors increased, white sailors began making complaints about their behavior. They suggested the blacks were stealing from the whites, even though white sailors frequently pickpocketed and swindled their shipmates. Both black and white tars were guilty of petty crimes, but the accusations against black sailors appear rife with racial stereotypes of blacks as thieves. Even so, the complaints resulted in the black sailors being moved or segregated during February 1814 to the third level of Number Four. In a reversal of fortune for the black prisoners, the third level represented the smallest, yet warmest, airiest, and lightest quarters in the building and soon became the center for prison culture and order.[22]

In the spring of 1814 the British opened Number Four's gates to permit inmates access to the prison market developed by French prisoners years earlier. In this closed economic world, sailors could purchase food, clothing, and essentials from Devonshire farmers and merchants for consumption and for bartering around the prison. Prisoner merchants began selling items such as apples, potatoes, and other vegetables when in season. Many sailors began crafting their own products made from wood, bone, straw, and other seemingly useless or discarded items. Sailors could buy shoes, clothing, and blankets. Schools of various types offered to educate sailors in writing, reading, dance, theater, and other skills. Sailors could also find gaming opportunities, including dice, cards, or roulette, if they desired. Some stands and shops sold tobacco, coffee, beer, or ardent spirits. Others began selling prepared foods, such as butter or milk porridge, stew, plumgudgeon (boiled and mashed potatoes flavored with codfish), and fritters. One black fritter-seller gained a reputation for preparing the biggest and best-tasting fritters in the prison. This extensive economic system kept inmates occupied and content, lessened the financial burden of their British captors, and did not discriminate based on race but rather on the ability of sailors to pay for the products they desired.[23]

By the early fall of 1814 the number of black inmates had grown to almost five hundred, threatening the racial balance of the prison; before the end of the year the numbers had swollen to almost one thousand. Fortunately the French soldiers received their freedom after the defeat of Napoleon, permitting black sailors to assume complete control over Number Four. These living arrangements, following a plan ordered by the British, permitted each block to choose which inmates controlled activity in the unit, and these men comprised the ruling entities or the elected "governments." Yet Number Four developed a new, more vigorous economic life, social organization, and stable hierarchal government, and a "stout black" privateersman named Richard Craftus (called "King Dick"), wearing a bearskin grenadier's cap and carrying a long staff, soon ruled the prison by strength and magnitude. Arriving at Dartmoor in October 1814, the charismatic and imposing six-feet-three-inch Craftus possessed "strength far greater than both height and proportion together." He also used physical intimidation to cajole others into line. Should they not heed his warning, King Dick felt no compunction in using his staff to enforce authority. Through strength and force of personality, Craftus commanded gambling, the sale of goods, and the distribution of beer. He ran a well-disciplined building that virtually all considered orderly and the cleanest in the compound, even to the point that some whites chose to live there because they considered it cleaner and safer than all the others. King Dick not only maintained good order, but he managed to improve prison life with the proceeds of his business interests as well as the small allowance, often called "tobacco money," afforded all American prisoners of war.[24]

Block Four became a flourishing center of entertainment business for prison social life. White sailors admitted that they spent considerable time in the black prison, learning boxing, fencing, dancing, drawing, and other skills. Some enjoyed the twice-weekly theater performances, which even included production of Shakespearean plays. Others found themselves drawn to the unusual sounds of lively music and black singing. An impassioned Methodist minister named Simon also catered to the spiritual needs of prisoners, and his evangelical style attracted large numbers of both blacks and whites; a more subdued Reverend Jones of Plymouth preached to Number Four on Thursdays. While many whites saw King Dick's power as dictatorial and antidemocratic, his leadership brought stability to the cell block and established order and safety. He made daily rounds to ensure that each sailor behaved appropriately. When they violated individual norms, King Dick brought them back into order through a trial and punishment dictated by a judge and jury. The political structure certainly did not resemble a dictatorship; rather, it mirrored the unofficial black governments that worked alongside the formal white systems in the New England cities from which many of the black prisoners originated.[25]

On December 29, 1814, sailors at Dartmoor learned that the United States and Great Britain had signed the Treaty of Ghent, officially ending the war. Two days later, black sailors hoisted "saucy flags" emblazoned with "Free Trade and Sailors Rights." That same afternoon some British officers "came up to see the prisoners & the [black] band of No 4 played up Yankee Doodle dandy. O it galls them." Each prison began flying the Stars and Stripes to show their patriotism and to antagonize their British captors. Musicians from all the prisons formed a marching band that processed with a large following around the guards while playing "Hail Columbia" and "Yankee Doodle." The prison's public space became a venue to express American honor and pride as well as black solidarity, collective rights, and displeasure at being kept under British confinement for the remainder of the following winter.[26]

Throughout the early months of 1815, Capt. Thomas G. Shortland, the British commandant at Dartmoor, fought a war of will with the American prisoners, especially the black ones. While the Treaty of Ghent had ended the war with the Americans and the prisoners clamored to be released, Shortland did not yet have the authority to set them free. During this standoff, Shortland closed the market on several occasions when the prisoners refused to abide by his will. Finally, in early April, Shortland returned from a trip to learn of a near riot the previous day. On April 5, Shortland sent two hundred additional soldiers into Dartmoor, determined to finally break the prisoners' control. But not even the additional soldiers could dampen the American sailors' attitude, as they had heard that seven cartel ships would be arriving shortly at Plymouth to take them home. The news "inspired [them] with high spirits and good humor." It lightened some of their hearts while emboldening others.[27]

Near 7:00 the following evening, the time for rambunctious prisoners to retire to their quarters, Shortland rang the alarm "and the drums of the garrison in every direction beat to arms." The early ringing bell attracted a press of American sailors who wanted to see the commotion. Hordes of sailors drew closer and closer to the gate, giving the appearance that they would force themselves through. Then some sailors began yelling "Keeno! Keeno!," which meant a prison free-for-all. Shortland appeared with soldiers while others redcoats secured positions on the wall above. With bayonets mounted, the soldiers slowly pushed the agitated crowd back into the yard. Meanwhile sailors began "howling, hooting and daring the [British] soldiers to fight." Reportedly,

Americans began throwing stones, and one British soldier claimed that his hat was knocked off. "Suddenly someone shouted the word 'Fire!' and a number of muskets were discharged over the head of the prisoners. Slugs and buckshot rattled on the roofing-slates of the buildings." Since no sailors fell wounded, the emboldened prisoners pushed harder toward the soldiers, threatening the British to load their guns. This time the British soldiers aimed their weapons into the crowd, and actually fired, and then thrust their bayonets into any nearby American. The prisoners scattered, fleeing back into their yard and scurrying into their barracks with guards in pursuit. Within three minutes, the whole affair was over as seven died, six sustained wounds requiring amputation (of whom two later died), and fifty more suffered wounds from the buckshot and slugs. The Dartmoor Massacre became part and parcel of the American mythology of brave tars being sacrificed on the altar of despotism with freedom just out of reach.[28]

During the following weeks prison artists painted and drew pictures and sculpted mementos of the massacre that they sold to fellow sailors. By April 19, the first cartel ship arrived in Plymouth, and 249 prisoners marched out of Dartmoor for the coast. With them they carried "a large white banner on which was painted a tomb with the Goddess of Liberty weeping over it and a murdered sailor at her feet." The expression "Columbia weeps and we remember" served as a poignant reminder of what they had endured. A week later, another 350 departed, and prisoners continued trickling out until the last American sailor left Dartmoor in July 1815. Those who survived embraced an American patriotism fueled by their black and white brotherhood of sailors. In their expression of life, black sailors embraced black culture but incorporated white culture, all the while insisting they were Americans. They created mementos that reinforced their status as free black seamen struggling to uphold their belief in "Free Trade and Sailors Rights," which applied to black as well as white tars.[29]

"AN INDELIBLE CONFIDENCE IN THE INVIOLABILITY OF BRITISH FAITH": IRELAND ISLAND, BERMUDA, AND THE PROMISE OF FREEDOM

The naval base at Bermuda had represented an important winter anchorage for the British North American fleet during the War of 1812. Located some 640 miles from the coast of North Carolina, the island

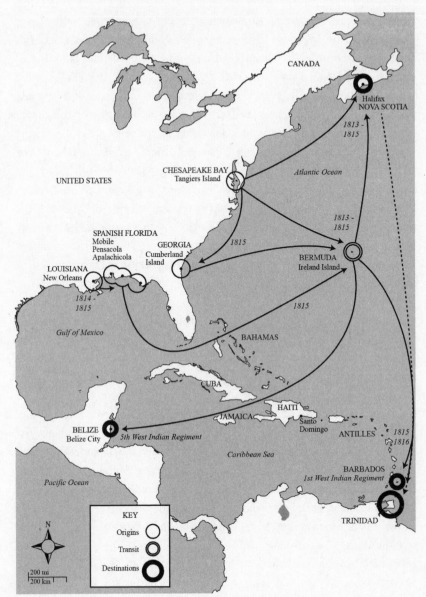

Refugee Evacuation. Map by Tracy Ellen Smith based on drawings by John McNish Weiss.

had a mild climate and other benefits that Halifax, Canada, did not possess. It was far removed from the United States, and that distance protected it from American naval or privateer assaults. The distance also made it a safe place for the refugees who were evacuated from the United States.[30]

Slaves started fleeing to British protection beginning with Adm. George Cockburn's raids in the Chesapeake during 1813. Cockburn's superiors, initially John Borlase Warren and then Alexander F. I. Cochrane, instructed British officers to remove slaves as quickly as possible from the coast of America. They loaded slaves aboard empty supply ships and troop transports and sent the vessels to the British naval base at Ireland Island, Bermuda. Throughout the summer of 1813, the number of refugees flooding into Bermuda increased daily. And as the number began to grow, naval officers and government officials faced the problem of clothing and provisioning the refugees. Adm. Henry Hotham, commanding at Bermuda, instructed officers to employ "the American Negroes . . . on the public works" and to pay them "at the rate of two shillings per diem." Such an arrangement would allow inexpensive completion of naval installations without importing more unskilled labor and provide the British something in return for the provisions they doled out to the refugees. Members of the Bermuda Legislative Council worried less about naval expenditures and much more about the "pernicious effects" the "considerable number of Negroes" would have on the colony. The council had previously passed measures "to restrain the importation of slaves" because they feared "an unlimited importation of negroes (probably of the worst class)" might undermine the social and economic stability of the island community. Could naval officers, they pleaded, not transport them "to Nova Scotia, or to some other British Colony, into which their importation may not be detrimental to the public"? Much to the council's chagrin, dispatches from London arrived soon thereafter, indicating that the refugees would remain on the island as long as the naval officers deemed necessary.[31]

Admiral Hotham found clothing, food, and work for the refugees, but the demand soon taxed the naval base's food supply. So, Hotham instructed ship commanders to list the refugees as "supernumeraries" aboard vessels, meaning that ships' pursers disbursed rations drawn from the ship until the refugees could be enlisted in the army or navy or relocated to another British colony. Cochrane further directed Hotham to list the refugees as supernumeraries on the troopship *Ruby* and to give the men only one ration per day. Cochrane insisted that all working men should be paid only one shilling per day, yet he still insisted that all British-supplied clothing should be deducted from their pay. Earlier Cochrane had pleaded with Warren to construct temporary wooden barracks on the island to house the new black soldiers, along with their wives and families, just as the government did for other British soldiers.

Cochrane intended that women and children should receive food (women a half ration, children a quarter ration), yet they should also be expected to work. Cochrane even intended for boys older than thirteen to receive a full ration and four pence sterling per day for "light work," but he prohibited them from receiving any grog or alcohol.

Abiding by British "Laws of Naval discipline," Cochrane demanded that the "Articles of War" be read to the refugees one Sunday each month. Should any of them not fulfill their duty, he ordered that they be punished with deductions of pay or reductions of spirits. Finally, Cochrane also requested agents from the West India regiments be sent to Bermuda to recruit and train refugees. According to Cochrane, he faced two immediate problems: Bermuda law prohibited "the introduction of colored persons into this island," and locals did not want to give arms to the former slaves because they already had a "Volunteer Corp of Free Blacks," meaning they had no need for slave soldiers or for the West Indian regiments. Cochrane knew this would be a lost opportunity if he could not secure a temporary suspension of the acts. If he could, he anticipated that the strict discipline and high expectations would create productive British subjects.[32]

Then, during the spring of 1814, the refugees created new problems for the British. The influx of slaves had apparently frightened some Bermudan officials, who complained about "the inconvenience likely to arrive from accumulating useless numbers" of refugees on Ireland Island. Their constant complaints forced Cochrane's hand, compelling him to send all men with families, as well as women and children, to Halifax. "American Negro men . . . who have neither women nor children" remained on Bermuda as laborers or potentially as army or naval recruits. The splitting apart of refugees from the same communities produced intense anxiety and discontent, especially among those men who remained behind on Ireland Island. In protest, they refused to work, which prompted Cochrane to offer concessions. As soon as space became available on ships bound for Canada, those men remaining at Bermuda would be sent to Halifax. Until that time, they had to return to work in order to receive their pay and provisions. But even this promise did not settle the discontent among the refugees, forcing Cochrane to threaten, "they shall have no provisions until they return to their work, and that for each day they continue disobedient, they will be kept a month longer on the Island." Should these former slaves not acquiesce at all, Cochrane promised "they will be sent back and landed in Virginia." Freedom in Bermuda did not mean complete freedom from work.[33]

Cochrane's decision to send all future "refugees from America (excepting only workmen of a certain class and description) . . . to Halifax" brought momentary harmony to Bermuda, even if it created new hardships for the navy and for Canada. All communications, supplies, and ships to and from the Chesapeake traveled first through Bermuda, which meant that everyone evacuated from the Chesapeake followed that same route. Afterward, the refugees boarded British ships for Canada or other British colonies. While Halifax laws did not forbid blacks from "landing there and endeavoring by honest labor to earn there their own maintenance," getting them there, providing them with food, and settling them in that rocky, barren Canadian landscape became Cochrane's newest dilemma. Troop transports and supply ships received instructions to make room for American slaves; they should provision refugee men at two-thirds pound of beef per day, while women received a half pound and children a quarter pound. By the end of spring Cochrane reconsidered providing beef because of the growing expense. He instead suggested giving the refugees a "sufficient quantity of . . . their usual food," meaning rice, vegetables, and other staples. This reduced costs until the refugees could be passed on to other administrative units.[34]

Cochrane also faced a serious administrative issue concerning the Colonial Marines. If they did not join the West Indian Regiments, where would they be attached? Apparently the Colonial Marine displayed a "strong and determined prejudice . . . against the West Indian Corps, & the high idea of superiority which they attach to themselves over the African negroes." This strong-mindedness led Cochrane to believe he could not combine the two units as he had done during the Chesapeake campaign. If he acknowledged their "prejudice," they could be kept on Ireland Island and assist with navy yard construction projects. Should Cochrane disregard their "prejudice" and appoint them to the West Indian Regiments, these men would not be available for navy yard work, and the white Bermudans would want them removed as quickly as possible. Nor did Cochrane think he could transfer the "American Negroes" from their current commanders "to whom they look up with implicit confidence" because they believed they had a promise not to be separated. "They are tenacious to excess of every stipulation directed or implied, which they believe to have been made with them." As such Cochrane acknowledged he could not "reason them out of belief once firmly adopted." Even after weighing these different possibilities, Cochrane concluded that he could incorporate them successfully into the West Indian Regiments since they had contributed to the campaign and naval works on Ireland Island. Moreover, he knew his own officers and soldiers had impressed the Colonial Marines "with an indelible confidence in the inviolability of British faith."[35]

Throughout 1813 and 1814, American refugee slaves fled to British units operating along the coast of the United States, and by doing so they secured their liberation from slavery. Yet freedom did not appear immediately in the form that most American blacks anticipated or expected. When they were herded into temporary quarters on Ireland Island, they did not expect to trade American slavery for British peonage. Nor did they expect to be separated from family and friends or anticipate having to work for another. Most undoubtedly believed they would be whisked away to freedom—an idyllic concept at best. They had no real understanding of what the expression meant, other than thinking it meant they did not have to work. Yet such was not the case. When British officers began separating communities and shipping them away, the refugees' greatest fears seemed to materialize because it appeared to them that they were being reenslaved in another land, but without their networks of family and friends.

And the Bermudans did everything they could to prevent the situation that occurred during 1813 and 1814, even levying a £30 tax on all "Negroes returning to Bermuda." Prejudice and racism remained on the island—one naval officer even derisively referred to the "Negroes" as a "lazy set." By the end of 1815 the many blacks who remained on Bermuda worked on Ireland Island's fortifications and naval installations and were segregated there. While the British boldly proclaimed they would free the American slaves, neither individual Britons nor British colonies were prepared for what this possibility truly meant.[36]

NOT "INCLINED TO RETURN TO THEIR MASTERS OR TO AMERICA": CANADA AND THE REALITY OF FREEDOM

The British began shipping American refugees to Nova Scotia in 1813, and by the end of the war some two thousand had found their way to the rocky, barren Canadian landscape. Yet this 1813–15 black exodus represented a far different type of refugee than had previously fled to Canada. During the American War for Independence, black Loyalists, including several thousand former slaves from New York, had arrived after the British defeat at Yorktown. Accustomed to a colder climate and intermixing with a white population, they adjusted well until other

opportunities presented themselves. In 1796 a group of Jamaican maroons arrived, having been exiled after a failed struggle against white
settlers on the Caribbean island; once in Canada they resumed their agi-
tation against a different regime in a different British colony. Through
their own perseverance, both of these groups ultimately made the most
of their Canadian opportunity, finding a way to immigrate to freedom in
Sierra Leone, Africa, rather than remaining in the frigid clime of Nova
Scotia.[37]

The first wave of 133 Chesapeake slaves landed at Halifax in September 1813 without naval officers notifying the local government. Surprised Lt. Gov. Sir John Coape Sherbrooke of Nova Scotia immediately
administered an oath of allegiance to the refugees. He then sent the sick
to the Halifax Poor House and the healthy into the interior to "support themselves by their labour and industry." Since the refugee men
consisted of laborers and farmers, with some shoemakers, sawyers, and
wheelwrights, Sherbrooke maintained they could provide for themselves.
Yet the governor also understood that others would be forthcoming, so
he asked the Colonial Office to provide clothing and rations for the future arrivals. Unfortunately, these items did not arrive in Nova Scotia
in time for the winter of 1813–14 or even 1814–15 because, as Sherbrooke learned, every item that landed in Halifax shipped first through
Bermuda. As a result many of these former slaves died during the cold
winter of 1814–15.[38]

Admiral Cochrane's proclamation freeing American slaves during
the spring of 1814 fulfilled Sherbrooke's prophesy, as hundreds of slaves
began appearing at Halifax during May, June, and July. The fall brought
additional refugees, including many who Cochrane claimed were in
"great distress" or desperately needed food, clothing, and shelter. By
the end of the year, Sherbrooke counted some "1200 Negroes . . . [who]
have been brought into this province." Granted, most of them were docile and simply relieved to be in Canada, but another group "conducted
themselves in a most disorderly manner." Even so, all of them had to be
provisioned, and this ultimately made the "Negroes and Mulattoes . . .
burthensome [sic.] to the public." Sherbrooke pleaded with the House
of Assembly for funds to continue feeding the refugees through the winter, and they begrudgingly fulfilled his request. Yet the legislators also
warned Sherbrooke that this "separate and marked class of people, [are]
unfitted by nature to this climate, or to association with the rest of His
Majesty's Colonists." Sherbrooke understood the Assembly's sentiments
and sent their address to the Colonial Office. Just as he did so, he received

information from Admiral Cochrane, warning that an additional 1,500 to 2,000 refugees would be arriving shortly from Bermuda.[39]

The influx of so many more refugees, essentially doubling the number who had previously arrived, created a host of new problems. Sherbrooke had previously found ways to provision the refugees and then witnessed "the greatest part of these people . . . [becoming] able to support themselves." With so many more coming, he knew they would "experience some difficulty in finding employment on their arrival." Then, as expected, winter weather took its toll. They suffered terribly from hunger and cold with little relief. Also, two hungry, destitute refugees participated in a robbery at Cole Harbor because they needed food and money. Thereafter locals complained of their presence and constant begging. People such as these, many locals reasoned, were simply one step removed from a life of crime against the community. Then, compounding their misery, smallpox swept through the refugee community, forcing Sherbrooke to quarantine those affected on Halifax's Melville Island—a three-acre former prison located on the Northwest Arm—and to provide mandatory inoculations. Still, more than eighty succumbed to the disease because of their weakened condition and the lack of food. By

Melville Island, Halifax, Canada. Melville Island, Halifax, Canada, had originally been used to hold French and American prisoners. By the spring of 1815 the three-acre former prison had been transformed into a holding depot for American refugees, who remained there until they could take care of themselves. The British closed the depot at the end of June 1816. Image taken from William Little, London Illustrated News, *27 (July–Dec. 1855).*

the spring of 1815 the disease had abated, and Melville Island could be transformed to an entrance depot for refugees entering Canada.[40]

Once the weather improved, Sherbrooke suggested that the refugees should relocate to the hills outside of Halifax. Settlers who took this offer would receive "small grants of land" and two years of provisions, which would sustain them until they brought in their first crop. Forests covering the area there would provide timber for construction lumber and firewood. Sherbrooke truly believed that the relocation of the refugees acquainting them "with the capability of the soil" would create the type of productive citizen whom the Crown expected. Unfortunately, unknown to those who accepted or made the offer, the next two years would prove calamitous. During 1815, or the "Year of the Mice," entire fields of grain were devoured by the rodents within days; they also burrowed into the ground and consumed the entire potato crop. The following year, the "Year without a Summer," brought cold weather, frost, and even ten inches of snow during June, greatly shortening the growing season in an already unproductive soil. The refugees soon "expressed an aversion to settle at any great distance from Halifax."[41]

With the financial backing of the British Treasury, Customs Collector Thomas Nicholson Jeffrey took active control over Melville Island and contracted with Halifax merchant Lewis de Molitor to supply the refugees until they could take care of themselves. Paying for the refugees proved an expensive proposition. Additionally, Jeffrey had to pay for medicine, coffins, and hired help, the latter of which included a medical attendant, a clerk, and a steward. The bill for the first three months totaled a staggering £2,036, but even so the Ministry approved the high expenses. Yet as the number of refugees began declining during the following months, the expenditures correspondingly decreased. By the end of June 1816 only eight refugees remained on Melville Island, and they were old, were sick, or required medical attention. Given the numbers, Sherbrooke removed the eight to the Halifax Poor House and closed the depot.[42]

Sherbrooke had distributed the refugees as broadly as he could, but they also chose where they would relocate. More than nine hundred blacks relocated to Preston, some five hundred to Hammonds Plains, another seventy-six to Refugee Hill (Beechville), and some seventy-two on the Halifax-Windsor Road, while a reported 115 remained in Halifax proper. Chesapeake slaves frequently clustered together in Preston, while the Sea Island refugees of South Carolina and Georgia moved to Hammonds Plains. They consciously chose to join others like them so they could preserve their traditions and culture. Once they had settled, the refugees received licenses of occupation rather than freehold grants, which meant the refugees could not sell their land to raise money for a move to another part of Canada or another British colony. This was because colonial officials did not envision them becoming anything other than a perpetual laboring class, tied to the land they tilled and working for others. With the small plots, ten acres each, Surveyor General Charles Morris hoped that they could furnish vegetables, berries, and poultry to feed themselves and to supplement the Halifax market, yet most were poor farmers on barren land who did not fish or raise chickens very well. Some picked berries, while others created brooms and tubs or burned charcoal. Most, however, were relegated to day labor to eke out a survival. Some indentured themselves to farmers in the hopes of surviving and perhaps learning how to cultivate the barren, rocky land. Virtually all found themselves in bondage to an utterly unproductive and small quantity of land, meaning that their survival and prosperity remained tenuous at best. Even though the Canadian government treated the refugees as second-class citizens for the next thirty years, the refugees had chosen to come to Canada, and they were not enslaved.[43]

Sherbrooke's successor, the Earl of Dalhousie, arrived in the fall of 1816, and he immediately began slashing expenditures. Soon he realized that many refugees could not take care of themselves. He prejudicially thought "slaves by habit and education, no longer working under the threat of the lash, their idea of freedom is idleness, and they are altogether incapable of industry." Although he believed many resented "having left their masters" or had been coerced by sailors and marines, none of them wanted "to return to their masters or to America." Even as winter again approached, the governor had "no doubt . . . many men will desire" to return to America, yet he was mistaken.[44]

Dalhousie wanted the refugees to be sent to the West Indies, but the government lacked the funds in 1817. He also learned that the possibility of finding an asylum for them in Trinidad produced "certain alarms and prejudices entertained by several of these People that they would prefer remaining where they are . . . to being sent to any part of the West Indies." By October 1818 the last of the rations had been distributed, and soon the refugees again faced starvation. This time the House of Assembly refused to allocate any additional funds for them, forcing Governor Dalhousie to provide rations a little at a time at his own expense. He could not let these people starve, but Dalhousie acknowledged that "the habits of [their] life and constitutional laziness will continue and these miserable creatures will for years be a burden upon the Government." Fortunately, Dalhousie's burden ended, as Sir James Kempt replaced him as governor in 1820.[45]

The new governor quickly renewed plans to send refugees to Trinidad. Kempt sent representatives to each of the "several settlements of Black Refugees to determine if any would wish to relocate." He also advertised in local papers, requesting bids for ships to transport and feed them during the voyage. Some ninety-five refugees—eighty-one adults and fourteen children—agreed to relocate. Of the group, almost two-thirds were Georgia and South Carolina Sea Island refugees from Hammonds Plains. A majority of them were young, married, without children, and illiterate, so once they arrived in Trinidad, they had no way to pass news back to family and friends in Nova Scotia. They chose to leave because there were few jobs, a frigid climate, and sterile soil. Government rations had also run out, meaning that their future prospects looked bleak indeed. With seemingly no other choice, they decided to chance reenslavement in Trinidad rather than remain in economic peonage in Canada.[46]

On January 6, 1821, the small group set sail. Upon landing on the island in August, the refugees began making a life for themselves, and within eighteen months they had become self-sufficient. During the years that followed, successive Canadian governors and assemblies periodically attempted to encourage refugees to relocate to Trinidad. Since no information had reached Nova Scotia regarding the first group that had departed, the refugees there were convinced that those who left for Trinidad had fallen again into slavery. So, regardless of who asked or the promises made, the Canadian refugees "entertain so great a fear of slavery that no persuasions can induce them to remove to any place where slavery exists." During the next decade the question of relocation came before the Canadian refugees repeatedly, without anyone choosing to leave. Finally, in 1839 a representative from Trinidad visited the black settlements for one last attempt to encourage the refugees to move to the island. Again, they refused.[47]

By the 1830s some of the refugees living in Canada had begun to prosper, and the majority saw no reason to leave the sense of security they had finally developed. They had created a life, albeit a difficult one, but they had freedom, family, and friends around them. They had cleared land, built homes, created gardens, learned to endure the frigid temperatures, and found jobs to survive. Some abided by their Baptist preachers' suggestions to stay. Many chose to remain because they controlled their own destiny, even earning a living from their own labor. As an "old tidy wench" Mrs. Deer described it, "de difference is, dat when I work here, I work for myself, and when I was working at home [in Maryland], I was working for other people." Though they had freedom and a sense of security, they were never welcomed or embraced by white Canadians, and the colonial government did not help them secure a prosperous future. Though free, the refugees remained indentured on government-owned land, barely surviving year to year because their farms were too small and the land poor. In 1841 a hundred refugees petitioned the assembly for free land because at that time they were "tied to the land without being able to live upon it." In 1842, some twenty-seven years after their arrival, the Canadian government finally granted the refugees ownership of 1,800 acres of land. Not surprisingly many sold their land and chose to move on. Even so, they were free, and it was their choice to make.[48]

The refugees who remained in Nova Scotia faced discrimination and racial prejudice as intense as what their free black brethren faced in the northern United States. Over the years, they slowly moved on to other settlements, such as Africville, Beaverbank, Dartmouth, Five Mile Plains, Truro, Liverpool, Shubenacadie, Tracadie, and even Cape Breton Island. Some 371 others still, with many from Maj. Pierce Butler's Cumberland Island Georgia plantation, moved to Willow Grove near a black Loyalist community on Loch Lomond. A group of freed Virginia slaves occupied a site on the north side of Otnabog Lake, and the government granted them the land in 1830. Another group moved to Fredericton and lived near the Indians. They had dispersed across the landscape, but for the most part they remained together, unassimilated with the white Canadians. Even so, they all had chosen to stay with the freedom they knew rather than chance the uncertainty of a distant land. In staying they created a new class consciousness that emphasized their identity within Canada rather than their previous connection with slavery and the United States. For better or for worse, the refugees were now Canadians.[49]

"[V]ERY HIGH SPIRITED MEN WHO LOOK UPON THEMSELVES AS QUITE ON A FOOTING WITH OTHERS": FREEDOM IN THE CARIBBEAN WORLD

As the Napoleonic Wars and the struggle with the United States came to an end, Great Britain no longer had a need for a large military establishment or the thousands of West Indians and North American slaves recruited to supplement their manpower needs. Many of these black recruits, like their white brethren, fell victim to the postwar demobilization. But in their case, where would the government send them? Would they be free or reenslaved? If free, how would they be incorporated into productive society? Could they adjust to a new life of freedom without military trappings? These questions were troubling because the men knew how to handle weapons, had experienced the horrors of battle, and provided a vivid living example that black men could successfully fight like white men, setting a dangerous precedent for white slaveowners who feared armed blacks could upset the precarious balance of racial power.[50]

The Admiralty Office sent the 1st West Indian Regiment to Barbados after the war, and that proved providential for the British government because a slave insurrection soon erupted. The end of the wars had depressed the sugar market on Barbados. Plantation owners had responded by driving slaves to increase production while reducing their rations, threatening slave autonomy and culture. The Barbadian Assembly, or legislature, which a few years earlier had welcomed the prospect of slave emancipation, now pleaded with the British government for relief and the authority to decide issues of slavery themselves.

Then, shortly before the revolt began, the assembly denounced an imperial plan to emancipate slaves, sealing the fate of those in bondage. Slaves had already anticipated their freedom, and when it was denied to them they took matters into their own hands. On Easter Sunday, April 14, 1816, they assembled, gathered weapons, and began setting fires. Within hours the insurgents had overrun a third of the island. Col. Edward Codd, the island's senior military officer, declared martial law, and the militia joined with regular troops to suppress the revolt. During the following night the 1st West Indian Regiment, also known as the "Bourbon Regiment" because of their French-speaking black soldiers, confronted four hundred rebellious slaves armed with "firelocks, bills, pikes, hatchets, who gave three cheers, and [who] dared him to come on . . . under an impression the black Troops would not fight against them." Instead, the black soldiers loaded their muskets, prompting the rebels to fire first, killing a black private and wounding a sergeant. The soldiers calmly returned fire, mounted their bayonets, and aggressively charged, killing forty of the insurgents and capturing seventy more. The next morning, the soldiers again fought the slaves, and again the insurgents doubted whether the soldiers "would fight against black men, but thank God [they were] deceived. . . . The conduct of [the] Bourbon Blacks . . .

has been the admiration of every body & deservedly." Seven years later, other black soldiers from the 1st West Indian Regiment helped suppress the slave uprising in Demerara (British Guyana). In both instances the decisive fighting that suppressed the uprisings occurred because black soldiers followed orders and fired on men disturbing community order. Though written from Jamaica in April 1817, one observer understood completely why black soldiers would fire on slaves. Black soldiers "are very high spirited men who look upon themselves as quite on a footing with others in His Majesty's Service." Just like their white compatriots, these men followed orders and defeated their enemy.[51]

The British understood that postwar demobilization meant a reduced need for troops in the Caribbean and that West Indian Regiments could be used as settlers to expand the footprint of the empire. They began using black American refugees and discharged troops to expand British control over Trinidad and Tobago. During the fall of 1814 Trinidad governor Sir Ralph Woodford learned that the Royal Navy would soon bring American refugees to his island. Admiral Cochrane had instructed his officers to take slaves to Trinidad because the governor "could grant them lands." While Woodford had instructions to provide for the refugees, he was stunned when in late May 1815 the frigate *Levant* arrived with eighty-six refugees. The governor gave the group, predominantly Virginians from the Chesapeake and "Creoles, intelligent and apparently well disposed, particularly those from New Orleans," a choice between being apprenticed as servants or receiving a small grant of land. As expected, nearly all the former slaves wanted land. Spring monsoons unfortunately delayed land distribution for months, and before it could be completed fifty-eight more Gulf Coast refugees arrived.[52]

Woodford initially dispersed these early groups within easy distance of the Port of Spain on the island's northwestern coast, where colonial officials could supervise them. In November 1815, when the *Caron* arrived with another group of refugees from Bermuda, Woodford sent them to Naparima, "where two large sheds had been prepared for their reception and some ground cleared." Located some fifteen miles inland from San Fernando and more than forty miles south of the Port of Spain, Woodford believed that no other place would provide "so much advantage to themselves or security to the public." Woodford soon realized their talents and took "advantage of the intelligence of some of the American Refugees to establish some carts for the government." Carts were always needed, and Woodford knew this would save the government money. In fact, he wanted to expand these operations quickly and even agreed to allocate food, clothing, and medical attention and pay carters or laborers $10 per month for their services. Their success in Naparima could provide a vivid example for future refugees and "encourage others to settle there."[53]

The Corps of Colonial Marines, recruited along the coast of America and stationed for more than a year on Ireland Island, landed in mid-August 1816 with 574 people. Since they represented the largest group ever to land in Trinidad, their appearance created apprehension and mistrust among the local population. On August 17 they began a rain-soaked march inland toward Savanna Grande, a location near the south coast and in the neighborhood of a large river, which afforded the refugees plenty of fish and turtles. Woodford hoped the former soldiers would clear land and form a separate community under their own control. When they made it inland, the "Merikens" (as they became known in Trinidad) received their farming tools and displayed "a strong desire to be immediately employed in the cultivation of their grounds." Woodford wanted their former officers to "impress upon them the necessity of conducting themselves with obedience and regularity," so Maj. Andrew Kinsman reminded "them that idleness and dissipation in any station of life is the certain parent of poverty and wretchedness."[54]

Kinsman established a semi-military hierarchy for settlements consisting of fifty or sixty people, based on the company organization of the battalion, to calm the fears of local whites. The sergeants, who took an "oath of fidelity . . . as constables, in the church, and in the presence of the whole of the people," were "responsible for the behavior of those placed under their guidance," and they dispersed discipline as needed. The free settlers' first task included building one large house in each village to provide immediate shelter; once individual accommodations had been constructed, the large house became public space. Each settler received a cutlass, a hoe, a hatchet or an axe, and an iron pot, and each was expected to work "sixteen acres of land" between six and eight hours a day. The settlers did not own the land outright but instead paid an annual quit rent for each allotment. Once they had conquered their own plots, each soldier could "receive paper with liberty to work out[side]" the village to earn extra money. In fact, 150 of the Merikens became accomplished lumberjacks, felling trees as skillfully as any freeman. Otherwise, they could not leave their settlements without a pass, could not conduct business with slaves, and were expected to apprehend runaway slaves.[55]

Woodford's method had proved a successful example for settling black soldiers on Trinidad. They had easily adjusted to peace and embraced their obligations as free citizens. Rather than fomenting slave insurrection or trouble, they had created social and economic stability. Within two years they had harvested crops of potatoes, corn, pumpkins, and plantains, and they had begun to raise chickens and pigs. By the mid-1820s they produced enough—as much as two thousand barrels of corn and more than four hundred barrels of rice in 1825—to market their surplus crops and livestock in San Fernando and Port of Spain. Except for a few "trivial" cases of disorder and theft, the Merikens were model citizens.[56]

In the spring of 1821 the ninety-five illiterate refugees from Nova Scotia, Canada, arrived at Naparima. Upon seeing them, Woodford worried that they appeared "to have been of a description inferior to those already established." Knowing that the Canadians had "an absurd fear of being reduced to slavery," Woodford did not realize that the illiteracy of this first group and their inability to communicate with those left behind in Canada jeopardized his plans completely. He had wanted to lay the foundation "for establishing a free Colored English Population very superior to any . . . yet seen in this part of the World," and the unwillingness of the Canadians to relocate threatened his aspirations. Fortunately, Woodford's initial assessment of the refugees proved incorrect as the Canadian refugees quickly assimilated with the other Merikens and soon shared in the community's general prosperity. By the 1830s some of the more prosperous refugees moved on to other districts, and by 1847 those who still resided on plots recognized by the government qualified for gaining full ownership and absolute title to the property.[57]

The plight of the 5th West Indian Regiment mirrored the experiences of the Colonial Marines who had relocated to Trinidad. Once the era of warfare had ended, the 5th was transferred to Belize (Honduras) and then disbanded. Once troopships docked at Belize City in late July 1817 soldiers were allotted land in the interior, given tools to clear the brush, and provided rations until they could harvest a crop. Unhappy with their situation, many refused to work on the property allotted to them. Instead they "engaged in quarrels and disputes with the inhabitants," engaged in robbery, and "much mischief . . . ensue[d]." They created a "great deal of trouble in the country," and many troublemakers found their way back to the coast. These former soldiers, who had suffered through the disastrous British attack at New Orleans on January 8, 1815, appeared unready to transition to nonmilitary life, leaving Gov. George Arthur with a crisis on his hands. Finally, Arthur devised an ingenious solution, playing on the men's sense of responsibility and loyalty. He incorporated the former soldiers "into the Prince Regent's Royal Honduras Militia," which convinced them to return peaceably to their plantations and works. After explaining to them the expectations of the militia, the former soldiers acknowledged "they were in every sense of the word Free Men and had Property to protect." They would fulfill their obligations as citizens, and not a single soldier refused to accept appointment to the militia. During the following months, Arthur remarked on the immediate transformation of the formerly "very bad characters." He reported that the colony could support another 1,000 to 1,500 settlers, as long as they behaved like the 5th West Indian Regiment. Arthur had unintentionally discovered what the soldiers wanted—they desired to be accepted for who they were, to contribute to the betterment of society, and to be considered equal and free.[58]

The men of the 5th transitioned to a nonmilitary life and embraced their duties as subjects of the British crown. The refugees sent to Bermuda and Canada had wanted the same opportunity, yet they feared that being sent to the Caribbean would result in being reenslaved. Rumors abounded and newspaper accounts even seemed to confirm stories that British troops had liberated American slaves so that they could profit on their sale in the West Indies. American planters and soldiers parroted these stories in an attempt to keep the slaves from leaving the American coast aboard British ships. In one reported June 1813 episode, the British liberated a slave carpenter from Norfolk, Virginia, and transported him to Nassau, Bahamas, where he was sold to a Mr. James Wood for $1,000. This brazen fabrication appeared in the London *Times* on November 21, 1814, and in Secretary of State James Monroe's letter to the American peace delegation at Ghent. Incensed, Admiral Cochrane immediately began gathering evidence and soon disproved it. The story, according to Cochrane, was but "malicious intentions" designed to disparage Great Britain and Cochrane, as well as undermine British efforts to liberate slaves.[59]

Another more troubling story suggested that Admiral Cochrane had personally sent refugees to his plantation in Trinidad. Although Cochrane did indeed own a plantation there, he vociferously maintained that he was not guilty of this "false and malicious" rumor. He claimed that he "would be happy to get rid of [the plantation] at a considerable loss" and that he had not been "dipping deeper into that species of property." "The founder of this falsehood," Cochrane posited, did not completely understand the regulations for importing slaves into the various British West Indian colonies. "Sending of Negroes from one Colony to another is subject to very particular restrictions," Cochrane reminded his superiors at the War Office. Moreover, by the end of 1814 all refugees evacuated from the coast of the United States had been sent only to Bermuda and Halifax. After much consternation, Cochrane could only conclude that the Americans obviously "trumped up" the story to prevent their Negroes from fleeing to his ships.[60]

There is no evidence that the British ever sold refugees back into slavery. In fact, Admirals Cockburn and Cochrane both felt a strong sense of duty to liberate as many slaves as they could and to send them on to freedom in a British colony; they sent the refugees to Bermuda, Halifax, and by the summer of 1815 to Trinidad. Many British officials in London were trying to dismantle the slave-based Old Colonial system and replace it with a modern free market empire where British commerce dominated the world. Those same officials ultimately saw the choices made by refugees as a method for taming harsh and remote British colonial lands, creating British consumers and producers, and expanding the reach of the growing British Empire. Freedom meant many things to many different people, but to the American refugees who eventually ended up in Bermuda, the frigid landscape of Canada, or the hot jungles of Trinidad or Belize, freedom simply meant that they were no longer slaves.[61]

"THEIR GOOD DEEDS HAVE BEEN CONSECRATED ONLY IN THEIR MEMORIES": FREEDOM AND EQUALITY—UNFULFILLED

The American victory at the Battle of New Orleans and the British evacuation of the Gulf Coast marked the last major engagement of the War of 1812. Great Britain had tried to mobilize the black population to assist them in the Gulf campaign, yet they did not materialize in the numbers that could have determined the outcome. In effect, Andrew Jackson and the Americans had co-opted black support by giving the appearance that white society would accept broadened rights for free blacks in New Orleans.[62]

After the conflict had ended, the two battalions of freemen of color, as Jackson promised, received the same pay as their white brethren. Alexis Andre, a private in Captain Demozeillier's company who had been blinded during the battle at Chalmette on January 8, 1815, received a federal pension for his service. The Louisiana General Assembly also awarded relief pensions to persons wounded and to the widows and legitimate minor children of those soldiers killed in action, including the children of Morne Jesse, Fraise Colomnie, and Joachim—all colored soldiers in Daquin's battalion—who received pensions as a result of their fathers' deaths. Charles Savary received a pension of $8 per month because of his son Belton's death. Peter Valery and Jousin Reynier, whose sons also died, received a similar sum. In 1819 the Louisiana legislature voted to award Maj. Joseph Savary, who had raised the second battalion of freemen of color and who had gained distinction during the campaign, a pension of $30 per month for a period of five years; when the pension expired, the legislature extended it for another four years, making it the highest pension paid to any Louisiana soldier after the War of 1812.[63]

Between 1830 and 1850 many of the aging black soldiers or their heirs applied for and received pensions. The Louisiana legislature awarded pensions of $8 per month to Vincent Populus (1831), the widow of Capt. Louis Simon (1835), militia captain Jean Baptiste Hardy (1836), Lt. Isidore McCarthy Honoré (1847), Sgt. Pierre Dupart (1848), and senior musician Louis Hazeur (1850). Eighty-year-old Captain Hardy's pension increased to $25 in 1845, making him the second-highest pensioner from the Battle of New Orleans. By the early 1850s the state legislature tightened pension applications to include only those who had been exposed to battle. The two battalions of freemen of color who served at Chalmette remained eligible for pensions, and the "Association of Colored Veterans of 1814 and 1815 of New Orleans"—a group chartered in 1853 by thirty-one living freemen of color who had fought at Chalmette, including Jordan Noble and Barthelemy Populus—worked to help claimants and their survivors qualify for benefits. Additionally, the Association also provided for the veterans in sickness and death and tried to keep alive the memory of free black participation during the battle.[64]

The land bounties promised by the state of Louisiana and the federal government to veterans who served during the War of 1812 were not immediately forthcoming. Not until 1850 did the federal government finally make provisions for land bounties for War of 1812 veterans; veterans who served one month of service qualified for 140 acres, extended in 1855 to 160 acres. Most of the freemen of color or their descendants sold their holdings to settlers from the east rather than settling on them. Unfortunately, many of the freemen of color had died before the federal government finally lived up to Old Hickory's promise.[65]

At noon on January 8, 1816, the two freemen of color battalions assembled in full uniform on the square in front of St. Louis Cathedral and fired blanks as part of the anniversary ceremony honoring the Battle of New Orleans. These men returned afterward to their lives and assembled as militiamen only during the required twice-monthly muster.

The general postwar prosperity created unparalleled business opportunities that military service could not equal, and many militiamen quit attending muster. While money and general economic advancement could not further their desire for rights and equality, it certainly made their lives easier and more comfortable. Cultivating and improving business opportunities took far too much time, with militia service suffering as a result.[66]

The free colored militia, which had been a mainstay of inculcating free blacks into Louisiana society, began to decrease in numbers in the years following the battle. Militias nationwide fell into decline after the War of 1812 because Americans were not enthusiastic about military service during peacetime. In Louisiana, the free black militia's membership aged and died, and the number of those connected to the events at Chalmette declined. Younger members also lacked a noteworthy bond of contribution to the war. But perhaps more problematic, black militiamen became caught in the national struggle between slavery and freedom, and they found it increasingly difficult to maintain their personal freedom, much less their status as free colored militiamen. By 1834 the Louisiana state legislature revised its militia law, eliminating the "Battalion of Chosen Men of Color." Refusing to reconstitute the freemen of color battalion, the state legislature officially disbanded an institution that had existed since the colonial era. With old leaders and members of their ranks passing from the scene, the free black militia's contributions would slowly be forgotten.[67]

Although no longer a legally recognized and constituted body, on January 8, 1851, thirty-six years after the victory at Chalmette, ninety aging free men of color were finally invited to march in the annual January 8 parade. Previously, pension legislation had been the only acknowledgment for the veterans. The parade finally recognized publicly in New Orleans their service to the city, the state, and the nation. As Jordan Noble's drum provided the same beat he had as a fourteen-year-old on the Plains of Chalmette, the battalion gained notice and recognition. The Daily Picayune sheepishly acknowledged that "their good deeds have been consecrated only in their memories." The paper conceded that "the respectability of their appearance, and the modesty of their demeanor, made an impression on every observer and elicited unqualified approbation." Perhaps the graying of hair and the slow steadiness of movement finally made this group acceptable to the public rather than threatening or intimidating.[68]

When Jordan Bankston Noble died on June 20, 1890, American racial relations had evolved from the slave-based southern plantation system into which Noble had been born to a two-tiered segregated world. He and his fellow black compatriots had sacrificed in the hopes that they would gain freedom. They and other free black Louisianans had hoped that the war with Great Britain would permit them to solidify and expand the rights they possessed. They had made conscious choices to side with the Americans because they had much to lose if the British succeeded. British promises of freeing the slaves would create a greatly expanded free black community, which in the end would demote their collective status in Louisiana's tri-cornered society. Those who sided with the Americans also represented a prominent social group of skilled artisans and small businessmen, and serving in the free black militia had been a way to publicly express their status. Unfortunately, military service did not elevate the status of free blacks, creating instead renewed suspicion and distrust. Nor did their service win for them the immediate pensions, land warrants, and bounties promised by Jackson. In fact, a generation passed before black soldiers began receiving pensions, and many had to be renewed periodically by the state legislature. The promises of land were not fulfilled until the 1850s, and even then most of the survivors or their descendants sold their holdings for cash. The promises that Jackson made were eventually fulfilled, but not in time for those who sacrificed to benefit from them. Those like Jordan Noble would suffer through the slavery controversy, the American Civil War, and emancipation, and by the late nineteenth century they would find themselves living in a segregated society. Whether they were slaves or freemen, they remained objects of scorn.[69]

THE SEARCH FOR FREEDOM FORCED BOTH slaves and free blacks to make difficult choices without any sense of what the future could bring. Whether it was along the Gulf Coast, in Canada, Bermuda, or Dartmoor, or on Trinidad, former slaves saw the chaos of war as an opportunity to build a new life of freedom. The slaves at Negro Fort believed that force of arms and a well-defended bastion provided them the security to fend off white expansionist-minded Americans. Instead, Negro Fort experienced the full brunt of American fear when a combined army-navy expedition attacked and destroyed it. During the aftermath, surviving blacks were rounded up and reenslaved. Hostile Native Americans also felt the fury of American fear when Andrew Jackson's forces swept across the Gulf region during the First Seminole War. The misplaced confidence in Prospect Bluff established a forceful tone for what happened along the Gulf Coast during the next three decades as white Anglos expanded across the region, entrenching a slave plantation system that destroyed black hopes for freedom.

Those refugee slaves who fled with the British found varying degrees of comfort in their continued quest for freedom. In Bermuda, refugees became the focus of white antagonism, and those who remained there had but one alternative: working as freemen in economic peonage for the British military on Ireland Island. Technically, they remained free, but their economic liberty was encased in a white prejudice that limited their advancement and kept them as second-class citizens. Much the same occurred for those who relocated to Halifax, Canada. Initially welcomed, the refugees occupied a barren, rocky land inadequate for agriculture. They scratched out a living and most survived, yet they did not prosper. They were free, but they did not control their destiny until decades later when the British government finally gave them the land they farmed. Those who remained created a segregated life for themselves with their own jobs, friends, and community circles. In doing so, they created a new sense of identity that discarded their status as slaves and embraced a sense of freedom and dignity.

Those who chose to relocate to Trinidad took the greatest chance of all. Slavery on the island was still legal, and many feared that they would be reenslaved. Instead, the British co-opted the refugees, playing on their fears, and settled them in a remote portion of the island. This isolation satisfied refugees who saw conspiracy in every British action, yet it also permitted Colonial officials to begin developing areas of the island that showed promise. Initially the refugees held the land as tenants, but in time they too gained possession of the property they worked. But in coming to Trinidad, the refugees did not realize they would face a never-ending battle against nature. Each year the jungles reclaimed lands that were not continually worked and demoralized those looking for some relief. But as long as they continued to work their jungle lands, the refugees remained free and had the opportunity for advancement.

Blacks who sided with the Americans faced an uncertain future after the war. Those who had chosen to join Andrew Jackson during the New Orleans campaign found an uneven fulfillment of promises. The "Sons of Freedom" received pay equal to that of their white counterparts, but the state pensions, federal land warrants, and bounties promised by Jackson did not arrive immediately. The slaves who had joined Jackson fared far worse. Jackson promised them freedom, yet returned them to their previous condition of servitude. American victory earned at the Battle of New Orleans did not mean freedom to slaves.

The American sailors at Dartmoor Prison endured hardships equal to those of the refugees who fled to the British. They were housed in a bleak, barren, and cold facility that offered little comfort. In this environment the black tars created a community that bound them together as sailors, black men, and American patriots. They had games, enjoyed opportunities for education and betterment, and, through the leadership of King Dick, built a clean, orderly, and stable society. Although captured, they consciously chose to remain there. They could choose, and a few did, to join the British navy and escape the deplorable conditions at Dartmoor. Yet their patriotism trumped their perceived sense of racial opportunities for black Americans. These black tars collectively created a culture that defined themselves and placed them on par with their white counterparts. They embraced the slogan "Free Trade and Sailors' Rights" despite having few rights when they stepped onto land. During the years following the War of 1812, "Free Trade and Sailors' Rights" became a white expression of maritime patriotism as blacks jostled to define their place in an ever-changing American culture.

The War of 1812 did not completely fulfill promises and dreams in the United States, Canada, Bermuda, or other British colonies. Black dreams for freedom and equality virtually disappeared for years after the war. Those who had sacrificed did so because they believed military participation would smooth their path to freedom and equality. Moreover, being free and not having to worry about the sale of their loved ones provided a powerful motivation for those who fled to the British; those who remained behind suffered the whims of white American slaveholders. For those who fled, if they fulfilled their civic obligation to society, would they not be accepted as equals? The 5th West Indian Regiment certainly thought so when they were disbanded in Belize. They proclaimed such, forcing Gov. George Arthur to appeal to their basic instincts about the responsibilities of "citizens." By doing so Arthur co-opted the black ex-soldiers, allying them to white British society and all of its responsibilities. Thereafter they would fulfill their obligations as citizens: pay taxes, remain peaceful and law-abiding, protect their property as well as the government's, and expect to be treated as equals—no more, no less. Yet not all black combatant allies received the fair treatment they expected. Yes, some achieved their freedom. Others advanced economically. Some later received land. Others, still, gained an elevated place in their local society. But all refugees could take solace in knowing that they had seized their opportunity for freedom during the war. And regardless of what happened to them, they remained *free*.[70]

EPILOGUE

How many slaves ultimately fled to British freedom during the war? The exact number unfortunately remains unknowable because of poor record-keeping. Moreover, it is unclear whether British officers kept faulty records or whether American planters later submitted inflated or unsubstantiated claims. During the months following the War of 1812, British officers and local American officials verbally jousted over the meaning of the Treaty of Ghent's Article One, which required the return of private property. As such, both sides gathered data to defend their positions, including lists, reports, correspondence, and depositions. Even though both British and American diplomats were assured of the accuracy of their own interpretations of the treaty, they soon found the other side uncompromising. Though the war had ended, it quickly became apparent that outstanding issues could not be settled by the two powers. Finally, in 1818 both governments agreed to accept the arbitration of Russian Czar Alexander I to adjudicate the question of slave compensation, and in 1823 he ruled that Great Britain should pay a "just indemnification for all private property [including slaves] which the British forces may have carried away."[1]

After three years of examining claims and evidence and haggling over the value of those claims, on November 13, 1826, the two governments agreed that Britain would pay a settlement of $1,204,960 to the United States. This sum was based on paying owners either $280, $390, or $580 for each slave (depending on where they were taken from) and that a total of 3,582 slaves had been taken from the American coast—1,721 from Virginia; 714 from Maryland; 833 from Georgia; 259 from Louisiana; twenty-two from Mississippi; eighteen from Alabama; ten from South Carolina; three from Washington, DC; and two from Delaware.[2]

Not surprisingly, these official numbers reveal some discrepancies with British naval accounts and Colonial Office records. Although commissioners claimed that the British liberated 269 slaves from Georgia and South Carolina during the conflict, British naval officers acknowledged evacuating 1,483 slaves by the end of March 1815, not including 280 who died during the occupation of Cumberland Island, for a total of 1,763. Substituting a number of 1,763, based on naval claims for the commissioners' number of 269, increased the total slaves to almost 4,500. Conversely, the governor of Canada reported that more than 1,200 refugees had arrived in Halifax by the end of 1814, and another 812 arrived the following year, amounting to more than two thousand. When combined with the more than eight hundred refugees who resettled in Trinidad from 1813 to 1816, the six hundred who donned British uniforms, and the few hundred who remained on Bermuda after the war, the total number of slaves evacuated to British colonies appears to be more than 4,800 slaves. Undoubtedly, the true number lies somewhere among British claims of some three thousand, the commissioners' claim of 3,582, and the Americans' claims of five thousand plus.[3]

Perhaps an even more important number to acknowledge is that the United States had more than 1.1 million slaves by the time the British interjected a racial component to the war. The British Ministry and naval commanders had believed that the preponderance of slaves in the Chesapeake region (four hundred thousand plus slaves), the South Atlantic Low Country (three hundred thousand plus), and along the Gulf of Mexico (one hundred thousand plus) could provide enough men for a slave army that would topple the American government. And while that possibility theoretically existed, in reality fewer than five thousand individuals absconded to freedom, and six hundred more joined the British military and took up arms. That means slaves rose or fled mainly when British forces were in an area. When slaves knew of British operations, they bravely made their way to the redcoats and the prospects of freedom. If British troops were not operating in an area, slaves logically calculated the risk and most remained in bondage, fearing that a failed escape could result in punishment or death. In reality, the war threatened slavery little in the southern United States and only where British troops concentrated and conducted operations. Perhaps even more importantly, the slaves' inability to flee to freedom reveals the peculiar institution's enduring stability, strengthening American slavery for the postwar period.[4]

For Americans the war had intensified their apprehensions about insurrections and slave flight even though their faith in the institution had remained firm. In areas where the British had actively raided, neither

federal, state, nor local authorities had provided much assistance to protect property holders, which frustrated southerners and left them questioning the government's role in defending its citizens. Without federal
support, southerners saw no alternative other than tightening the bonds
of slavery themselves, beginning at the local and state levels. After 1806
any freed Virginia slave had to leave the state within one year, and en-
forcement became strict during the postwar period. In 1811 Delaware
also denied entry to free blacks, making Pennsylvania the closest safe haven. The Georgia state legislature prohibited the manumission of slaves
altogether, while South Carolina forbade free blacks from entering the
state. It appeared that the liberation rhetoric that flowed from the Revolution into the War of 1812 era had lost its influence on southerners who
retained their property, but had to worry about holding onto it during
and after the war.[5]

Free blacks learned throughout the postwar period that their contributions to the conflict would be minimized and their quest for equality
and citizenship would be undermined. In New York City free blacks who
had worked on fortifications during the fall of 1814 found themselves
subject to increasing discrimination, prejudice, and economic disloca-
tion. Free blacks in Baltimore experienced increased intolerance combined with new competition from Irish laborers, who relegated blacks
into a position where they could only get unskilled jobs as common
laborers at the lowest wages. Likewise, Philadelphia free blacks did not
find abundant opportunities in the city's declining maritime industry and
faced prejudice and adversity at the bottom of a biracial occupational
hierarchy as the city moved into an industrial era. Black unity that had
been valued during the war thereafter became viewed as a threat; less
than a year after the Philadelphia crisis, whites in the city's Northern
Liberties destroyed a black house of worship because they claimed to
have been bothered by the emotionally vocal services. No longer would
free blacks be embraced as civic contributors and continue their march
toward equality. Instead, they would find themselves wedged between
slavery and freedom, between race discrimination and egalitarianism.
Their patriotic efforts had not reshaped white minds about what role
they should play in society. New prejudicial racial distinctions replaced
class differences among blacks and destroyed once and for all the optimism of the Revolutionary era.[6]

The six hundred slaves who enlisted in the British Colonial Marines
created other problems for southerners, despite the musings of one edi-
torialist who insisted that slaves "perform their daily" labor not because

of fear but rather because it was "their duty." Their willingness to take up arms and lead redcoats into American neighborhoods was voluntary, yet it also demonstrated that these soldiers wanted to punish and exact revenge on their former masters. They had the intelligence, bravery, and fortitude to serve, and they seized that opportunity during the war. More importantly, their assertiveness demonstrated an unquestioned antagonism toward a country that professed equality for all and yet permitted bondage of some. The British successfully harnessed that animosity and instilled great fear and trepidation in American southerners. And while the British did not enlist as many slaves as they anticipated, their black soldiers provided the tip of a double-edged threat: when slave soldiers landed, American militiamen had to be especially alert, patrolling for oncoming British forces while glancing over their shoulder for signs of a potential slave insurrection or for slaves fleeing to the British. Granted, the Ministry gave strongly worded orders to officers not to foment a slave insurrection, yet American slaveholders did not know the extent of those British directives. Most Americans realized only that the monarchial British made large-scale use of slaves as soldiers, and the American republic relied on free white men instead. Using slaves as soldiers came to represent a dichotomy that did not bode well for blacks in the United States, and they would not be permitted to participate on such a big stage again until the American Civil War.[7]

The results of the War of 1812 were undeniable for slavery. The opening of lands in the Old Southwest brought three new cotton areas into production: Natchez, Mississippi, and Baton Rouge, Louisiana; areas along the Mississippi River; and the Tombigbee and Alabama River valleys. These three regions had witnessed racial unrest during the War of 1812, and American leaders had cautiously negotiated with Indians and blacks, promising favorable conditions for their assistance. Once the British war ended, whites removed the Indians from the area and then relegated free blacks and slaves to subservient positions. By 1819, Alabama had joined Mississippi (1817) and Louisiana (1812) as slaveholding states, and cotton soon became the staple that ensured the region's economic success, with productivity increasing by some 300 percent during the next forty years. Before the war slavery had also been concentrated in the Atlantic states, from the Chesapeake Bay south to the St. Johns River. By defeating the British and the Indians in the South and emasculating the Spanish in Florida, Americans spread their reinvigorated slave system southward and westward across the Gulf, giving them access to these new fertile lands for cotton cultivation.[8]

AFTER THE WAR OF 1812, privateer and sailor George Roberts spent the rest of his life basking in the glow of his martial exploits, much like New Orleans drummer Jordan Noble. Each Defenders' Day, Roberts put on his uniform and marched with other veteran defenders of Baltimore, even though their ranks continued to shrink. Thousands of free blacks and slaves had thrown up defenses, others had shouldered arms in the army or militia in support of the United States, while others still had sat confined in prisons or aboard British ships because they maintained their American citizenship. They, too, could take pride in the contributions they had made to the American cause. Francis Scott Key, who had witnessed the attack against Fort McHenry from aboard a British ship, memorialized the bombardment with the poem "Defence of Fort McHenry," soon thereafter known as "The Star-Spangled Banner," and within weeks of the battle it appeared in American newspapers around the country. The first well-known verse still makes Americans swell with pride as they sing of the rockets' red glare and the bombs bursting in air. Yet it is the third verse that recalls a darker side of this conflict:

> And where is that band who so vauntingly swore
> That the havoc of war and the battle's confusion
> A home and a country should leave us no more?
> Their blood has wiped out their foul footstep's pollution.
> No refuge could save the hireling and slave
> From the terror of flight, or the gloom of the grave:
>
> > And the star-spangled banner in triumph doth wave
> > O'er the land of the free and the home of the brave.

The reference to "hireling and slave" alludes to the black Colonial Marines who had joined British ranks because they had been promised freedom and wanted to exact some revenge against their former masters. Those who had fled American slavery by evacuating to other British colonies did not warrant mention by Key, yet they too found their own "land of the free," be it in Canada, Bermuda, Belize, or Trinidad. George Roberts, Charles Ball, or Jordan Noble could have just as easily been one of those hirelings or slaves that the British mobilized or one of the many who fled the coast of America. Peter Denison found his freedom in Canada. Ned Simmons definitely tried to enlist as a British marine, while Prince Witten cast his lot with the Spanish to find his own freedom and security. In the end, the free blacks and slaves who Andrew Jackson had mobilized and called "Sons of Freedom," like those who had joined with the British, wanted only one thing—their land of the *free*. The War of 1812 provided the last opportunity for blacks as a group to secure that freedom through force of arms until the American Civil War finally ended slavery once and for all.[9]

NOTES

INTRODUCTION

1. Spencer C. Tucker and Frank T. Reuter, *Injured Honor: The* Chesapeake-Leopard *Affair, June 22, 1807* (Annapolis, MD: Naval Institute Press, 1996), 1–13.
2. Tucker and Reuter, *Injured Honor*, 14–16.
3. Robert E. Cray, Jr., "Remember the USS *Chesapeake*: The Politics of Maritime Death and Impressment," *Journal of the Early Republic* 25 (Fall 2005): 464–66.
4. E. Wilder Spaulding, *His Excellency George Clinton* (Port Washington, NY: Ira Friedman, Inc., 1964), 286; Samuel Smith to James Madison, June 30, 1807, Jefferson MSS, Library of Congress; Frank A. Cassell, *Merchant Congressman in the Young Republic: Samuel Smith of Maryland* (Madison: University of Wisconsin Press, 1971), 136–37; Cray, "Remember the USS *Chesapeake*," 446–49, 467–68.

CHAPTER 1: BLACK SOLDIERS IN NORTH AMERICA

1. Richard White, *The Middle Ground: Indians, Empires, and Republics in the Great Lakes Region, 1650–1815* (Cambridge, UK: Cambridge University Press, 1991), ix–x.
2. Lorenzo J. Greene, "The Negro in the Armed Forces of the United States, 1619–1783," *Negro History Bulletin* 14 (1951): 123; Jesse J. Johnson, ed., *A Pictorial History of Black Servicemen* (Hampton, VA: Jesse J. Johnson, 1970), 58; George Washington Williams, *History of the Negro Race in America, 1619–1880* (New York: G. P. Putnam's Sons, 1883), 1:121–23, 128–29; Winthrop Jordan, *White over Black: American Attitudes toward the Negro, 1550–1872* (Chapel Hill: University of North Carolina Press, 1968), 125–26.
3. Jesse J. Johnson, *The Black Soldier: Missing Pages in United States History* (Hampton, VA: Jesse J. Johnson, 1969), 68–69, 71–72, 131–35; Williams, *History of the Negro Race in America*, 300–301.
4. Johnson, *A Pictorial History of Black Servicemen*, 58; Johnson, *The Black Soldier*, 45–46, 49–50, 68–69, 71–72; Greene, "The Negro in the Armed Forces of the United States," 123.
5. Greene, "The Negro in the Armed Forces of the United States," 123–24.
6. John Ferling, *Struggle for a Continent: The Wars of Early America* (Arlington Heights, IL: Harlan Davidson Inc., 1993), 107; Ian K. Steele, *Warpaths: Invasions of America* (New York: Oxford University Press, 1994), 165–66; Bernard C. Nalty, *Strength for the Fight: A History of Black Americans in the Military* (New York: Free Press, 1986), 5–6; Agent for Carolina and Merchants Trading Thither to the Right Honorable Lords Commissioners of Trade, July 18, 1715, in *Blacks in the United States Armed Forces: Basic Documents*, ed. Morris J. MacGregor and Bernard C. Nalty, (Wilmington, DE: Scholarly Resources, 1977), 1:16–18; Kenneth Wiggins Porter, "Negroes on the Southern Frontier, 1670–1763," *Journal of Negro History* 33 (1948): 56–57.
7. William S. Willis, Jr., "Divide and Rule: Red, White, and Black in the Southeast," *Journal of Negro History* 48 (1963): 165; Gary B. Nash, *Red, White and Black:*

The Peoples of Early North America, 3rd. ed. (Englewood Cliffs, NJ: Prentice Hall, 1992), 292–93; Tom Hatley, *The Dividing Path: Cherokee and South Carolinians through the Revolutionary Age* (New York: Oxford University Press, 1995), 70.

8.   Jane Landers, *Black Society in Spanish Florida* (Urbana: University of Illinois Press, 1999), 35–39; [Edward Kimber], *A Relation or Journal of a Late Expedition,* facsimile reproduction of the 1744 edition, ed. John Jay TePaske (Gainesville: University of Florida Press, 1976), 30; Nash, *Red, White and Black,* 182.

9.   Ferling, *Struggle for a Continent,* 132–41; Greene, "The Negro in the Armed Forces of the United States," 124; Nalty, *Strength for the Fight,* 8–9.

10. Greene, "The Negro in the Armed Forces of the United States," 124; Nalty, *Strength for the Fight,* 8–9; Williams, *History of the Negro Race in America,* 287–88.

11. Lorenzo Johnston Greene, *The Negro in Colonial New England* (New York: Atheneum, 1974), 98, 126–28, 187–90, 303; Scott A. Padeni, "Forgotten Soldiers: The Role of Blacks in New York's Northern Campaign of the Seven Years' War," *The Bulletin of the Fort Ticonderoga Museum* 16 (1999): 167; Leon F. Litwack, *North of Slavery: The Negro in the Free States* (Chicago: University of Chicago Press, 1961), 3.

12. Benjamin Quarles, *The Negro in the American Revolution* (Chapel Hill: University of North Carolina Press, 1961), 8–9.

13. Quarles, *The Negro in the American Revolution,* 4–7, 10–11; Greene, "The Negro in the Armed Forces of the United States," 124–25; Nalty, *Strength for the Fight,* 8–9; William Lloyd Garrison, *The Loyalty and Devotion of Colored Americans in the Revolution and War of 1812* (Boston: R. F. Wallcut, 1861), 14.

14. Quarles, *The Negro in the American Revolution,* 4–7, 10–11; Greene, "The Negro in the Armed Forces of the United States," 124–25; Nalty, *Strength for the Fight,* 8–9; Gen. John Thomas to John Adams, October 24, 1775, in *Papers of John Adams,* ed. Robert J. Taylor, (Cambridge, MA: Belknap Press of Harvard University Press, 1977), 3:240–41.

15. Quarles, *Negro in the American Revolution,* 14–15; Resolution of the Massachusetts Committee of Safety, May 20, 1775, item 20; Instructions for Recruiting Officers, July 10, 1775, in *American Archives,* series IV, ed. Peter Force, (Washington, DC: M. St. Clair and Peter Force, 1839), 2:1385.

16. Quarles, *Negro in the American Revolution,* 16–18; Greene, "The Negro in the Armed Forces of the United States," 125; Nalty, *Strength for the Fight,* 12–13.

17. Lord Stirling to the President of Congress, March 14, 1776, Force, *American Archives,* series IV, 5:217–19; Minutes of the South Carolina Council of Safety, January 22, 1776, in William Bell Clark, ed., *Naval Documents of the American Revolution* (Washington, DC: Naval History Division, Department of the Navy, 1968), 3:929; Quarles, *Negro in the American Revolution,* 99–100.

18. George Livermore, *An Historical Research Respecting the Opinions of the Founders of the Republic on Negroes as Slaves, as Citizens, as Soldiers* (Boston: A. Williams, 1862), 113–16; Nalty, *Strength for the Fight,* 14–15; Robert J. Gough, "Black Men and the Early New Jersey Militia," *New Jersey History* 88 (1970): 228.

19. Garrison, *The Loyalty and Devotion of Colored Americans in the Revolution and War of 1812,* 14–15; Gough, "Black Men and the Early New Jersey Militia," 229; George H. Boker, *Washington and Jackson on Negro Soldiers; Gen. Banks on the Bravery of Negro Troops; Poem—the Second Louisiana* (Philadelphia: privately printed, 1863), 3; Williams, *History of the Negro Race in America,* 368–69; Nalty, *Strength for the Fight,* 17; Greene, "The Negro in the Armed Forces of the United States," 127.

20. Greene, "The Negro in the Armed Forces of the United States," 126–27; Robert Middlekauff, *The Glorious Cause: The American Revolution* (New York: Oxford University Press, 1982), 556–57; Alan Taylor, *The Divided Ground: Indians, Settlers, and the Northern Borderland of the American Revolution* (New York: Alfred A. Knopf, 2006), 172–73.

21. Jordan, *White over Black,* 345–46; James Kirby Martin and Mark Edward Lender, *A Respectable Army: The Military Origins of the Republic, 1763–1789* (Wheeling, Illinois: Harlan Davidson, Inc., 1982); Quarles, *Negro in the American Revolution,* 193–95; Donald R. Wright, *African Americans in the Early Republic, 1789–1831* (Arlington Heights, IL: Harland Davidson, Inc., 1993), 13–14.

22. Quarles, *Negro in the American Revolution*, 196; Matthew Mason, *Slavery and Politics in the Early American Republic* (Chapel Hill: University of North Carolina Press, 2006), 33–35; Gough, "Black Men and the Early New Jersey Militia," 230; Williams, *History of the Negro Race in America*, 287–88.

23. Wright, *African Americans in the Early Republic*, 3; William H. Riker, *Soldiers of the States: The Role of the National Guard in American Democracy* (Washington, DC: GPO, 1957), 18; Litwack, *North of Slavery*, 30–35; John K. Mahon, *The American Militia: Decade of Decision, 1789–1800* (Gainesville: University of Florida Press, 1960), 22; Jordan, *White over Black*, 412; Jack D. Foner, *Blacks and the Military in American History* (New York, Praeger, 1974), 21; Johnson, *The Black Soldier*, 135–36; Gough, "Black Men and the Early New Jersey Militia," 232–33; Benjamin Stoddert to Henry Kenyon, August 8, 1798, in Dudley Knox, ed., *Naval Documents Related to the Quasi War between the United States and France* (Washington, DC: GPO, 1935), 1:281; Col. William Ward Burrows to John Hall, September 8, 1798, Commandant's Letter Books, National Archives, RG 127; Richard H. Kohn, *Eagle and Sword: The Beginnings of the Military Establishment in America* (New York: The Free Press, 1975), 290.

24. Thomas Paine, *Common Sense*, Project Gutenberg, http://www.gutenberg.org/files/147/147-h/147-h.htm, accessed July 17, 2012.

25. Quarles, *The Negro in the American Revolution*, 20, 23; Sylvia R. Frey, "The British and the Black: A New Perspective," *The Historian* 38 (1976): 226–27; Douglas R. Edgerton, *Death or Liberty: African Americans and Revolutionary America* (New York: Oxford University Press, 2009), 68–73.

26. Galloway to Dartmouth, January 23, 1778, Stevens, ed., Benjamin F. Stevens, ed., *Facsimiles of Manuscripts in European Archives Relating to America* (London: Malby and Sons, 1889–95), Nos. 2079, 2098; Quarles, *Negro in the American Revolution*, 32, 112.

27. Roger Norman Buckley, *Slaves in Red Coats: The British West India Regiments, 1795–1818* (New Haven, CT: Yale University Press, 1979), 2–3.

28. Jonathan Boucher to George Germain, November 21, 1775, and Archibald Campbell to George Germain, January 16, 1776, William L. Clements Library (hereafter cited as WLCL), University of Michigan, Ann Arbor; George Germain, 1st Viscount Sackville Paper; Tonyn to George Germain, October 30, 1776, Edgar L. Pennington, "East Florida in the American Revolution, 1775–1778," *Florida Historical Quarterly* 9 (1930): 30; Sylvia R. Frey, *Water from the Rock: Black Resistance in a Revolutionary Age* (Princeton, NJ: Princeton University Press, 1991), 84; Quarles, *Negro in the American Revolution*, 118, 148–49.

29. George F. Tyson, "The Carolina Black Corps: Legacy of Revolution (1782–1798)," *Revista/Review Interamericana* 5 (1975–76): 649, 657–58, 660, 663; René Chartrand, "Black Corps in the British West Indies, 1793–1815," *Journal of the Society for Army Historical Research* 76 (1998): 249; Alfred B. Ellis, *The History of the First West India Regiment* (London: Chapman and Hall Ltd., 1885), 56–98.

30. Tyson, "The Carolina Black Corps: Legacy of Revolution (1782–1798)," 652–55.

31. Elsa Goveia, *Slave Society in the British Leeward Islands* (New Haven, CT: Yale University Press, 1965), 145–51; Lowell Ragatz, *The Fall of the Planter Class in the British Caribbean, 1763–1833: A Study in Social and Economic History* (New York: Appleton-Century-Crofts, 1928; reprint ed., New York: Octagon Books, 1971), 25; Tyson, "The Carolina Black Corps," 656.

32. Buckley, *Slaves in Red Coats*, 5, 8–13; Orde to Sydney, April 16, 1786, National Archives, Public Records Office, CO 71/10 (hereafter cited as PRO); Effingham to Grenville, September 12, 1790, PRO, CO 137/88; Roger Norman Buckley, *The British Army in the West Indies: Society and the Military in the Revolutionary Age* (Gainsville: University Press of Florida, 1998), 85–88, 119; John W. Fortescue, *A History of the British Army,* (London: Macmillan and Co., Ltd., 1899–1930), 4(part I):77; Tyson, "The Carolina Black Corps," 662; Chartrand, "Black Corps in the West Indies," 248.

33. Buckley, *Slaves in Red Coats*, 47–50, 53–54; Buckley, *The British Army in the West Indies,* 121–22; Frey, "The British and the Black," 226.

34. Chartrand, "Black Corps in the British West Indies," 248–54; Buckley, *The British Army in the West Indies*, 22–23, 30.

35. Buckley, *The British Army in the West Indies*, 85–87, 270–71; Buckley, *Slaves in Red Coats*, 55–56, 62.

36. Buckley, *Slaves in Red Coats*, 63–65; "Remarks . . . ," enclosed in Hislop to the Duke of York, July 22, 1804, PRO, WO 1/95; Fortescue, *History of the British Army*, 4 (part I):543; Milne to King, November 6, 1798, PRO, CO 318/16.

37. Ellis, *History of the First West India Regiment*, 11–12; Buckley, *Slaves in Red Coats*, 65–81; Castlereagh to Henry Bowyer, December 26, 1805, PRO, CO 318/16; *Tobago Gazette*, December 11, 1807.

38. George E. Buker, *Jacksonville: Riverport-Seaport* (Columbia: University of South Carolina Press, 1992), 6–7; Kenneth R. Andrews, *The Spanish Caribbean: Trade and Plunder, 1530–1630* (New Haven, CT: Yale University Press, 1978), 136; Paul E. Hoffman, *The Spanish Crown and the Defense of the Caribbean, 1535–1585: Precedent, Patrimonialism and Royal Parsimony* (Baton Rouge: Louisiana State University Press, 1980), 40.

39. Buker, *Jacksonville*, 9–10; Edwin L. Williams, Jr., "Negro Slavery in Florida," *Florida Historical Quarterly* 28 (1949): 94; Landers, *Black Society in Spanish Florida*, 23.

40. Peter H. Wood, *Black Majority: Negroes in Colonial South Carolina from 1670 through the Stono Rebellion* (New York: 1974), 95–130.

41. Eugene P. Southall, "Negroes in Florida Prior to the Civil War," *Journal of Negro History* 19 (1934): 77–78; Robert L. Anderson, "The End of an Idyll," *Florida Historical Quarterly* 42 (1963): 35; Williams, "Negro Slavery in Florida," 94; Royal Officials to Charles II, March 3, 1699, in Irene Wright, "Dispatches of Spanish Officials Bearing on the Free Negro Settlement of Gracia Real de Santa Teresa de Mose," *Journal of Negro History* 9 (1924): 151–52; Landers, *Black Society in Spanish Florida*, 25–26; Charles W. Arnade, *The Siege of St. Augustine in 1702* (Gainesville: University of Florida Press, 1959), 35; Buker, *Jacksonville*, 10–12.

42. Wood, *Black Majority*, 127–30, 305; Hatley, *The Dividing Path*, 27–28; Landers, *Black Society in Spanish Florida*, 26–27.

43. Southall, "Negroes in Florida Prior to the Civil War," 78–79; Robert Olwell, *Masters, Slaves, and Subjects: The Culture of Power in the South Carolina Low Country, 1740–1790* (Ithaca, NY: Cornell University Press, 1998), 21–26; Landers, *Black Society in Spanish Florida*, 28–36.

44. Frank L. Owsley, Jr., and Gene A. Smith, *Filibusters and Expansionists: Jeffersonian Manifest Destiny, 1800–1821* (Tuscaloosa: University of Alabama Press, 1997), 25–26; Royal decree in Luís de Las Casas to Governor Zéspedes, July 21, 1790, Letters from the Captain General, 1784–1821, East Florida Papers (microfilm reel 1), U.S. Library of Congress, Manuscript Division, Washington, DC (herafter cited as EFP); Thomas Jefferson to Juan Nepomuceno de Quesada, March 10, 1791, to and from the United States, 1784–1821, EFP (microfilm reel 41).

45. Jane Landers, "Jorge Biassou: Black Chieftain," *Escribano: The St. Augustine Journal of History* 25 (1988): 87–91.

46. Lyle N. McAlister, "William Augustus Bowles and the State of Muskogee," *Florida Historical Quarterly* 40 (1962): 317–28; David H. White, "The Spaniards and William Augustus Bowles in Florida, 1799–1803," *Florida Historical Quarterly* 54 (1975): 145–55; Gilbert C. Din, *War on the Gulf Coast: The Spanish Fight against William Augustus Bowles* (Gainesville: University Press of Florida, 2012), 166–73; Landers, "Jorge Biassou; Black Chieftain," 97–98; Landers, *Black Society in Spanish Florida*, 217–20.

47. Nash, *Red, White and Black*, 184–88; Gary B. Nash, *Forging Freedom: The Formation of Philadelphia's Black Community, 1720–1840* (Cambridge, MA: Harvard University Press, 1988), 11–14; Colin G. Calloway, *The American Revolution in Indian Country: Crisis and Diversity in Native American Communities* (Cambridge, UK: Cambridge University Press, 1995), 2–3.

48. Wright, *African Americans in the Early Republic*, 118–19; Wyatt F. Jeltz, "The Relations of Negroes and Choctaw and Chickasaw Indians," *Journal of Negro History* 33 (1948): 24–25; Porter, "Negroes on the Southern Frontier," 58–59.

49. J. Leitch Wright, Jr., *Creeks and Seminoles: The Destruction and Regeneration of the Muscogulge People* (Lincoln: University of Nebraska Press, 1986), 83–84; Verner W. Crane, *Southern Frontier, 1670–1732* (Durham, NC: Duke University Press, 1928), 185, 287.

50. Chapman J. Milling, *Red Carolinians* (Chapel Hill: University of North Carolina Press, 1940), 153; Porter, "Negroes on the Southern Frontier," 68, 77.

51. Lt. Gov. Bull to Board of Trade, May 8, 1760, PRO, CO 5/377/11; "Extract of a Letter from Frederica in Georgia," *South Carolina Gazette,* August 15, 1743.

52. Olwell, *Masters, Slaves, and Subjects,* 240–42, 278; Wright, *Creeks and Seminoles,* 84–85; Hatley, *The Dividing Path,* 194–203.

53. Wright, *Creeks and Seminoles,* 86–87; Frey, *Water from the Rock,* 226–28; Olwell, *Masters, Slaves, and Subjects,* 278–79; Wright, *African Americans in the Early Republic,* 118–19.

54. Wright, *Creeks and Seminoles,* 87–88; Din, *War on the Gulf Coast,* 211–13.

55. Frey, *Water from the Rock,* 227–32; Edgerton, *Death or Liberty,* 262–63.

56. Milne to King, November 6, 1798, PRO, CO 318/16.

CHAPTER 2: FIGHTING IN THE NORTH
1807–13 AND ON THE SEAS

1. Reginald R. Larrie, *Makin' Free: African-Americans in the Northwest Territory* (Detroit: Blaine Ethridge Books, 1981), 6–7; Clarence Edwin Carter, *Territorial Papers of the United States,* vol. 10, *Michigan Territory, 1805–1820* (Washington, DC: Government Printing Office, 1934–), n252.

2. Carter, *Michigan Territory, 1805–1820,* 10:n252; "Report of Legislative Committee" in William Hull to James Madison, December 22, 1808, Augustus B. Woodward Papers, Burton Historical Collection, Detroit Public Library; Daniel G. Hill, *The Freedom-Seekers: Blacks in Early Canada* (Agincourt, Canada: The Book Society of Canada Limited, 1981), 114; Augustus B. Woodward to the Secretary of War, July 28, 1812, Carter, *Michigan Territory, 1805–1820,* 10: 389–92.

3. Carter, *Michigan Territory, 1805–1820,* 10:n252; "Report of Legislative Committee," in William Hull to James Madison, December 22, 1808, Augustus B. Woodward Papers, Burton Historical Collection, Detroit Public Library; Hill, *The Freedom-Seekers,* 114; Augustus B. Woodward to the Secretary of War, July 28, 1812, Carter, *Michigan Territory, 1805–1820,* 10:389–92; Shirley Wilcox, Mary Lou Little, and Wendy Barry, "Peter Dennison," in *Register of St. John's Church of England at Sandwich, 1802–1827,* Kent and Essex Branch Ontario Genealogical Society, 1990, 43.

4. Reginald Horsman, *The Causes of the War of 1812* (Philadelphia: University of Pennsylvania Press, 1962), 14–16.

5. Horsman, *The Causes of the War of 1812,* 16–17.

6. Hill, *The Freedom-Seekers,* 113–14; Return Jonathan Meigs to Thomas Worthington, January 23 and February 5, 1812, Thomas Worthington Papers, Ohio State Library.

7. Hill, *The Freedom-Seekers,* 113–14; Gerard T. Altoff, *Amongst My Best Men: African-Americans and the War of 1812* (Put-in-Bay, OH: The Perry Group, 1996), 75–76; William Renwick Riddell, "A Negro Slave in Detroit When Detroit Was Canadian," *Michigan History Magazine* 18 (1934): 49.

8. William Hull to Henry Dearborn, June 22, 1807, in *Michigan Historical Collections,* Vol. 40, *Documents Relating to Detroit and Vicinity, 1805–1813* (Lansing: Michigan Historical Commission, 1929), 141; William Kenny to Alexander McKee, September 30, 1795, in Riddell, "A Negro Slave in Detroit when Detroit was Canadian," 49–50; Register of Blacks in Ohio Counties, 1804–1861, Ohio Historical Society Papers; Hill, *The Freedom-Seekers,* 113, n224; Petition for Runaway Slave, October 19, 1807, Alexander David Fraser Papers, Burton Historical Collection, Detroit Public Library; Norman McRae, "Blacks in Detroit, 1736–1833: The Search for Freedom and Community and Its Implications for Education" (Ph.D. diss., University of Michigan, 1982), 105.

9. Fragments of a ledger showing purchases of Detroit and nearby citizens, October 20, 1806, to July 21, 1815, Anonymous MSS L4: 1808–15, Burton Historical Collection, Detroit Public Library; James Askin to Charles Askin, August 18, 1807, John Askin Papers, Burton Historical Collection, Detroit Public Library; Lt. Col. I. Grant to James Green, August 17, 1807, in *Collections and Researches Made by the Michigan Pioneer and Historical Society*, (Lansing, MI: Wynkoop Hallenbeck Crawford Co., 1909), 15:41–43.

10. Petition to President James Madison, in Carter, *Michigan Territory, 1805–1820*, 10:296–99; "Report of Legislative Committee," in William Hull to James Madison, December 22, 1808, Augustus B. Woodward Papers, Burton Historical Collection, Detroit Public Library.

11. Augustus B. Woodward to General Leib, June 14, 1811, Augustus B. Woodward Papers, Burton Historical Collection, Detroit Public Library; Augustus B. Woodward to the Secretary of War, July 28, 1812; Augustus B. Woodward to William Hull, July 23, 1812, both in Carter, *Michigan Territory, 1805–1820*, 10:389–92, 320–24.

12. Any examination of the causes of the War of 1812 has to begin with Horsman's *The Causes of the War of 1812*.

13. William Gray, *Soldiers of the King: The Upper Canadian Militia 1812–1815: A Reference Guide* (Erin, Ontario: Boston Mills Press, 1995), 185–86.

14. Robert S. Quimby, *The United States Army in the War of 1812: An Operational and Command Study* (East Lansing: Michigan State University Press, 1997), 30–39; Augustus B. Woodward to the Secretary of War, July 28, 1812, Carter, *Michigan Territory, 1805–1820*, 10:389–92; Eustis to Hull, June 24, 1812, Cruikshank, *Documents Relating to Detroit*, 37; Diary of John Monteith, 1816, John Monteith Papers, Burton Historical Collection, Detroit Public Library.

15. Diary of Kennedy Deall, July 2 and 26, 1812, MSS A: B366, Filson Club Historical Society, Lexington, Kentucky; Isaac Brock to William Hull, August 15, 1812, William C. H. Wood, ed., *Select British Documents of the Canadian War of 1812*, 3 vols. (New York: Greenwood Press, 1968), 1:461; Quimby, *The U.S. Army in the War of 1812*, 43–46; Altoff, *Amongst My Best Men*, 77–78; Anthony J. Yanik, *The Fall and Recapture of Detroit in the War of 1812: In Defense of William Hull* (Detroit: Wayne State University Press, 2011), 102–3.

16. Quimby, *The U.S. Army in the War of 1812*, 92–101.

17. Material on Joseph Faudril provided by Brian Leigh Dunnigan of the WLCL. It was extracted from the "Fort Wayne Orderbooks, Register of Enlistments," Historical Information Relating to Military Posts and Other Installations, ca. 1700–1900, Records of the Adjutant General's Office, National Archives, RG 94: M661.

18. G. Glenn Clift, ed., "War of 1812 Diary of William B. Northcutt, Part II," *Kentucky Historical Society Register 56* (1958): 257; Muster Roll, December 31, 1812, in *The Battle of the Mississinewa 1812* (Marion, IN: Grant County Historical Society, 1969), 2:45–46; Sgt. Greenberry Keen Diary, December 4, 1812, Sgt. Greenberry Keen MSS, Historical Society of Western Pennsylvania, Pittsburgh.

19. J. C. A. Stagg, *Mr. Madison's War: Politics, Diplomacy, and Warfare in the Early Republic, 1783–1830* (Princeton, NJ: Princeton University Press, 1983), 224–25; Enclosure in Isaac Day to William H. Harrison, January 22, 1813, Letters Received by the Secretary of War, Registered Series, 1801–70, Department of the Army, National Archives, RG 107: M221 (microfilm roll 53); Quimby, *The U.S. Army in the War of 1812*, 132, 136–37; G. Glenn Clift, ed., *Remember the Raisin* (Frankfurt: Kentucky Historical Society, 1961), 125.

20. Stagg, *Mr. Madison's War: Politics, Diplomacy, and Warfare in the Early Republic, 1783–1830*, 224–25; Quimby, *The U.S. Army in the War of 1812*, 132, 136–37; Clift, *Remember the Raisin*, 95; Liani T. Helm, *The Fort Dearborn Massacre*, ed. Nelly Kinzie Gordon (Chicago: Rand McNally and Company, 1912), 98–100; Carl Benn, *The Iroquois in the War of 1812* (Toronto: University of Toronto Press, 1998), 55.

21. Quimby, *The U.S. Army in the War of 1812*, 183–99; Donald R. Hickey, *The War of 1812: A Forgotten Conflict* (Urbana: University of Illinois Press, 1989), 135–36.

22. Benn, *The Iroquois in the War of 1812*, 88–90; Benjamin Lossing, *Pictorial Field Book of the War of 1812* (New York: Harper and Brothers Publishers, 1868), 244; Hill, *The Freedom Seekers*, 114.

23. Benn, *The Iroquois in the War of 1812*, 89–91; Quimby, *The U.S. Army in the War of 1812*, 67–70.

24. Robert Malcomson, *A Very Brilliant Affair: The Battle of Queenston Heights, 1812* (Annapolis, MD: Naval Institute Press, 2003), 273–74; Ernest Green, "Upper Canada's Black Defenders," *Ontario Historical Society Papers and Records* 27 (1931): 367–68, 370; Hill, *The Freedom-Seekers*, 114, 117–18; Elias Darnall, *Journal Containing an Accurate and Interesting Account of the Hardships, Sufferings, Battles, Defeat and Captivity of Those Heroic Kentucky Volunteers and Regulars* (Paris, KY: Joel R. Lyle, 1813), 69; William Gray, *Soldiers of the King: The Upper Canadian Militia 1812–1815; A Reference Guide* (Erin, Ontario: Boston Mills Press, 1995), 180, 185–86; Altoff, *Amongst My Best Men*, 175.

25. Malcomson, *A Very Brilliant Affair*, 186; Green, "Upper Canada's Black Defenders," 368; Hill, *The Freedom-Seekers*, 114–16; Ruth McKenzie, *Laura Secord: The Legend and the Lady* (Toronto: McClelland and Stewart Limited, 1971), 14; William F. Coffin, *1812: The War, and Its Moral: A Canadian Chronicle* (Montreal: John Lovell, 1864), 62.

26. Robert Malcomson, *Lords of the Lake: The Naval War on Lake Ontario, 1812–1814* (Annapolis, MD: Naval Institute Press, 1998), 103–5; Isaac Chauncey to Oliver H. Perry, July 30, 1813, in William S. Dudley, Michael J. Crawford, and Christine F. Hughes, eds., *The Naval War of 1812: A Documentary History* (Washington, DC: Naval Historical Center, 1992), 2:530 (hereafter cited as *Naval War of 1812*); J. Fenimore Cooper, *Ned Meyers; or, A Life Before the Mast* (Annapolis, MD: Naval Institute Press, 1989), 60; Altoff, *Amongst My Best Men*, 43–45.

27. *Niles' Weekly Register*, June 5, 1813, 4:225–26; George Sheppard, *Plunder, Profit, and Paroles: A Social History of the War of 1812 in Upper Canada* (Montreal: McGill–Queen's University Press, 1994), 45; Malcomson, *Lords of the Lake*, 103–10.

28. Malcomson, *Lords of the Lake*, 124–27, 129–30; Captain Fowler to Colonel Baynes, May 29, 1813, in Green, "Upper Canada's Black Defenders," 368–69; letter from an American officer to the editors of the Baltimore *Whig*, May 30, 1813, in Ernest A. Cruikshank, ed., *The Documentary History of the Campaigns on the Niagara Frontier, 1812–1814* (Welland, Ontario: Lundy's Lane Historical Society, 1896–1908), 5:275; Jack L. Summers and Rene Chartrand, *Military Uniforms in Canada, 1655–1970* (Ottawa: National Museum of Man, 1981), 63–65; Altoff, *Amongst My Best Men*, 98.

29. Usher Parsons, April 7, 1813, "A Diary Kept during the Expedition to Lake Erie, under Captain O. H. Perry, 1812–14," Rhode Island Historical Society, Newport; Pierre Berton, *Flames Across the Border: The Canadian-American Tragedy, 1813–1814* (Boston: Little, Brown, 1981), 91–99; Green, "Upper Canada's Black Defenders," 369.

30. Oliver H. Perry to Secretary of the Navy, June 6, 1812, and November 28, 1812, both in *Naval War of 1812* 1:127, 354; Jan M. Copes, "The Perry Family: A Newport Naval Dynasty of the Early Republic," *Newport History* 66 (1994): 63; Isaac Chauncey to Secretary of the Navy, January 21, 1813, *Naval War of 1812*, 2:422; David Curtis Skaggs and Gerard T. Altoff, *A Signal Victory: The Lake Erie Campaign, 1812–1813* (Annapolis, Maryland: Naval Institute Press, 1997).

31. Secretary of the Navy to Isaac Chauncey, April 18, 1813, in *The Naval War of 1812*, 2:433.

32. Isaac Chauncey to Oliver H. Perry, June 3, and Chauncey to the Secretary of the Navy, 8, July 13, 1813, in Chauncey Letterbook, WLCL; Oliver H. Perry to Isaac Chauncey, July 27, 1813, and Chauncey to Perry, July 30, 1813, both in *The Naval War of 1812*, 529–31; Skaggs and Altoff, *A Signal Victory*, 76–78; Altoff, *Amongst My Best Men*, 36–37.

33. Oliver H. Perry to Secretary of the Navy, August 10, 1813, in *The Naval War of 1812*, 2:532–33; William Taylor Affidavit, June 23, 1818, Perry Papers, WLCL; Hambleton Diary, October 12, 1813, MS 983, Maryland Historical Society, Baltimore; Skaggs and Altoff, *A Signal Victory*, 78–79.

34. Oliver H. Perry to Secretary of the Navy, December 27, 1813, *American State Papers, Naval Affairs* (hereafter ASP:NA), 294–97; Alfred Thayer Mahan, *Sea Power in Relation to the War of 1812* (New York: Haskell House, 1969), 2:98–99; Alfred

Thayer Mahan, *The Naval War of 1812* (Annapolis, MD: Naval Institute Press, 1987), 249–56; C. S. Forester, *The Age of Fighting Sail: The Story of the Naval War of 1812* (Garden City, NY: Doubleday and Company, 1956), 182–87.

35. "Samuel Hambleton's Account of the Distribution of Prize Money on Lake Erie" and "List of Killed and Wounded on Board the United States Squadron, under Command of O. H. Perry in the Battle of 10th September 1813," both in *ASP:NA,* 1:566–72, 295–96; "Correspondence Relating to Medalists 1812–14," in Thomas Lynch Montgomery, ed., *Pennsylvania Archives, Sixth Series* (Harrisburg, PA: State Printer, 1907), 9:289; "List of Officers and Men from Newport R.I. under Command of Captain O. H. Perry," Perry Papers, WLCL; *Nashville Globe,* August 29, 1813, and *The Illustrated Buffalo Express,* August 31, 1813, in Charles A. Dickson Papers, The Western Reserve Historical Society, Cleveland, Ohio; Lossing, *Pictorial Field-Book,* 538; Altoff, *Amongst My Best Men,* 40–43; Skaggs and Altoff, *A Signal Victory,* 79.

36. Anonymous and Miscellaneous Manuscripts, Perry Papers, WLCL; Altoff, *Amongst My Best Men,* 40–41.

37. Altoff, *Amongst My Best Men,* 40, 43; Skaggs and Altoff, *A Signal Victory,* 79; The most thorough analysis of the issue is found in Gerard T. Altoff, *Deep Water Sailors and Shallow Water Soldiers: Manning the United States Fleet on Lake Erie* (Put-in-Bay, OH: The Perry Group, 1993); Usher Parsons to George Livermore, October 18, 1862, in "Negroes in the Navy," *Massachusetts Historical Society Proceedings* 6 (1862): 239–40; Seebert J. Goldowsky, *Yankee Surgeon: The Life and Times of Usher Parsons (1788–1868)* (Boston: Francis A. Countway Library of Medicine and Rhode Island Publications Society, 1988), 410–11.

38. Sandy Antal, *A Wampum Denied: Procter's War of 1812* (Ottawa, Ontario: Carleton University Press, 1997), 336–37; Quimby, *The U.S. Army in the War of 1812,* 279–84; Stagg, *Mr. Madison's War,* 330; Hickey, *The War of 1812,* 137–39.

39. Hickey, *The War of 1812,* 139; Stagg, *Mr. Madison's War,* 330–31; Quimby, *The U.S. Army in the War of 1812,* 285–86; Usher Parsons to George Livermore, October 18, 1862, in "Negroes in the Navy," 239–40; Greene, *Black Defenders of America,* 35.

40. Oliver H. Perry to Isaac Chauncey, July 27, 1813, Perry Letterbook, WLCL.

41. Joseph T. Wilson, *The Black Phalanx* (New York: Arno Press and the *New York Times,* 1968), 72–78; Ira Dye, "Seafarers of 1812: A Profile," *Prologue* 5 (Spring 1973): 8; Marcus Rediker, *Between the Devil and the Deep Blue Sea* (Cambridge, UK: Cambridge University Press, 1987), 10–73; Charles R. Foy, "Seeking Freedom in the Atlantic World, 1713–1783," *Early American Studies* 4 (Spring 2006): 50–53.

42. Martha S. Putney, *Black Sailors: Afro-American Merchant Seamen and Whalemen Prior to the Civil War* (Westport, CT: Greenwood Press, 1987), 1, 40–42; W. Jeffrey Bolster, "'To Feel Like a Man': Black Seamen in the Northern States, 1800–1860," *Journal of American History* 76 (March 1980): 1173–74.

43. Leon F. Litwack, *North of Slavery: The Negro in the Free States, 1790–1860* (Chicago: University of Chicago Press, 1961), 32–33; Secretary of the Navy Hamilton to Capt. John Cassin, November 30, 1812, in *The Naval War of 1812,* 1:611–12; Oliver H. Perry to William C. Greene, December 14, 1812, RG 45: NR, Box 353, #12; *Federal Gazette & Commercial Daily Advertiser,* National Archives (Baltimore), March 15, 1813.

44. Wilson, *The Black Phalanx,* 72–78; Dye, "Seafarers of 1812," 8; Jeffrey Bolster, *Black Jacks: African American Seamen in the Age of Sail* (Cambridge, MA: Harvard University Press, 1997), 114; Charles F. Adams, "Wednesday, August 18, 1812, 6:30 P.M.: The Birth of a World Power," *American Historical Review* 18 (April 1913): 519–20; Altoff, *Amongst My Best Men,* 22–23; Putney, *Black Sailors,* 90; Mark Hyman, "Black Participation in the War of 1812," *The Crisis* 85 (December 1978): 356; Dennis D. Nelson, *The Integration of the Negro into the U.S. Navy* (New York: Farrar, Straus and Young, 1951), 2.

45. Kenneth Poolman, *Guns Off Cape Ann* (London: Richard Clay and Company, 1961), 48, 86–125, 145–60; James E. Valle, *Rocks and Shoals, Order and Discipline in the Old Navy, 1800–1861* (Annapolis, MD: Naval Institute Press, 1980), 153; Altoff, *Amongst My Best Men,* 24–26.

46. David S. Cecelski, *The Waterman's Song: Slavery and Freedom in Maritime North Carolina* (Chapel Hill: University of North Carolina Press, 2001), 33–36; D.S. to Thomas Crossley, March 4, 1819, Fredericksburg, VA. Overseers of the Poor, WLCL.

47. Putney, *Black Sailors,* 33–38.

48. Dye, "Seafarers of 1812," 9; Putney, *Black Sailors,* 15–16, 66–70, 79–85, 153–59; See Sheldon H. Harris, *Paul Cuffe, Black America and the African Return* (New York: Simon and Schuster, 1972); Lamont D. Thomas, *Paul Cuffe: Black Entrepreneur and Pan-Africanist* (Urbana: University of Illinois Press, 1986); Henry N. Sherwood, "Paul Cuffe," *Journal of Negro History* 8 (1923): 153–229; and Henry N. Sherwood, "Paul Cuffe and His Contribution to the American Colonization Society," *Proceedings of the Mississippi Valley Historical Society* (1913): 370–402; P. J. Staudenraus, *The African Colonization Movement: 1816–1865* (New York: Octagon Books, 1980), 9–11. Statistics from selected cities during the antebellum period reveal more than 150 black mates and 50 black captains; of this number prior to 1816 there were sixteen mates and nine captains.

49. Bolster, *Black Jacks,* 5. Records relating to protection papers reveal many black seamen during the War of 1812 era. National Archives records of the Bureau of Customs contain seamen's protection certificate applications as well as quarterly abstracts and crew lists. There are also many records available in New Bedford, Massachusetts, and Newport, Rhode Island. Historian Ira Dye conducted a statistical study on the port of Philadelphia for the years 1812–1815 and found that blacks composed 18 percent of the seamen sailing from that city. Although the records were sometimes vague as to the race of a seaman, Martha Putney, using not only National Archives records but also those in New Bedford and Newport, has devised methods to approximate by description the number of black captains and seamen. By using a combination of crew lists and protection papers she was able to estimate with some certainty that a considerable number of blacks did participate in the merchant service and whaling industry, and much to the discredit of many ship owners, they were often paid less for the same work. Putney, *Black Sailors,* 80–5.

50. Claire Pauline Phelan, "In the Vise of Empire: British Impressment of the American Sailor," (Ph.D. diss., Texas Christian University, 2008), 45–46; Bolster, *Black Jacks,* 93; Dye, "Seafarers of 1812," 3–13.

51. Computer-Processed Tabulations of Data from Seamen's Protective Certificate Applications to the Collector of Customs for the Port of Philadelphia 1812–1815, National Archives, RG 36 (microfilm roll M972); Dye, "Seafarers of 1812," 3–13. Although the U.S. Navy recruited blacks in large numbers, it remains difficult to determine the exact or even approximate number of blacks who served during the War of 1812. Navy policy apparently frowned on listing black sailors as *black.* Official documents record them as *colored,* but this designation also included South Sea Islanders as well as those of African descent and others of color throughout the world. Additionally, sailors signed directly onto the ship on which they served, making the crew list the only record of their service. Unfortunately, many crew lists have been lost to history. Others are included in obscure manuscript holdings of a number of different archives and libraries scattered over the world. Harold D. Langley, "The Negro in the Navy and Merchant Service—1798–1860," *Journal of Negro History,* 52 (October 1967): 273–75.

52. Hickey, *The War of 1812,* 90–92.

53. William C. Nell, *The Colored Patriots of the American Revolution, with Sketches of Several Distinguished Colored Persons: To Which Is Added a Brief Survey of the Condition and Prospects of Colored Americans* (Boston: Robert F. Walcutt, 1855), 14; Bolster, "'To Feel Like a Man,'" 1179.

54. Robert J. Allison, *Stephen Decatur: American Naval Hero, 1779–1820* (Amherst: University of Massachusetts Press, 2005), 132–33; Charles F. Grandison to Paul Hamilton, November 7, 1812, in *Naval War of 1812,* 1:596–97; Sarah McCulloh Lemmon, *Frustrated Patriots: North Carolina and the War of 1812* (Chapel Hill: University of North Carolina Press, 1974), 129; Thomas N. Gautier to William Jones, April 28, 1813; in *Naval War of 1812,* 2:65–67; Noah Johnson, *Journals of Two Cruises Aboard the American Privateer Yankee* (New York: Macmillan, 1967), 62–141.

55. *Niles' Weekly Register,* February 26, 1814; *Essex Register* (Salem, MA), February 26, 1813; *Harper's New Monthly Magazine* 29 (June–November 1864): 600; George Coggeshall, *History of the American Privateers and Letters-of-Marque, during Our War with England in the Years 1812, '13, and '14* (New York: 1846), 140–43.

56. Charles F. Grandison to Paul Hamilton, November 7, 1812; in *Naval War of 1812,* 1:596–97; Lemmon, *Frustrated Patriots,* 129; Johnson, *Journals of Two Cruises Aboard the American Privateer Yankee,* 62–141; William Allen to Governor James Barbour, July 10, 1813, Governor's Papers, Virginia State Library, Richmond.

57. Report of the Committee of Ways and Means on the Petition of John Gooding and James Williams, January 5, 1819, House Report 1, 16th Congress, 1st session, *U.S. Congressional Serial Set,* Vol. 40, no. 1; Senate Committee on Naval Affairs, February 4, 1822, Senate Doc. 31, 17th Congress, 1st session, U.S. Congressional Serial Set, Vol. 59, no. 1.

58. Elijah Smith to Unknown, February 9, 1810, Nathaniel Evans Papers, Special Collections, Hill Memorial Library, Louisiana State University, Baton Rouge; Cecelski, *The Waterman's Song,* xvi–xvii.

59. Wesley B. Turner, *British Generals in the War of 1812: High Command in the Canadas* (Montreal: McGill-Queen's University Press, 1999), 152; Altoff, *Amongst My Best Men,* 102.

CHAPTER 3: THE FLORIDA PATRIOT WAR OF 1812

1. Statement of Prince, January 9, 1789, Census Returns, 1784–1814, EFP (microfilm reel 148); Runaway notice included in Alexander Semple to Commander McFernan, December 16, 1786, To and From the United States, 1784–1821, EFP (microfilm reel 41).

2. Petition of Prince, November 12, 1789, Memorials, 1784–1814, EFP (microfilm reel 77); Census Returns, 1784–1814, EFP (microfilm reel 148); Jane Landers, *Black Society in Spanish Florida* (Urbana: University of Illinois Press, 1999), 94.

3. Landers, *Black Society in Spanish Florida,* 97; "Relation of the Free Blacks," July 27, 1807, Miscellaneous papers, 1784–1858, EFP (microfilm reel 174); Memorial of Benjamín Seguí, July 5, 1798, Memorials, 1784–1821, EFP (microfilm reel 79).

4. Landers, *Black Society in Spanish Florida,* 215–16, 268.

5. Jefferson to Washington, April 2, 1791, H. A. Washington, ed., *The Writings of Thomas Jefferson* (Washington, DC: Taylor and Maury, 1853-54), 3:235; Landers, *Black Society in Spanish Florida,* 205.

6. Juan Nepomuceno de Quesada to Luis de Las Casas, December 10, 1792, and April 24, 1794, Cuba 1439, *Archivo General de Indias,* Seville, Spain (hereafter cited as *AGI*); Junta de Guerra, January 14, 1794, Records of Criminal Proceedings: Rebellion of 1795, EFP (microfilm reels 128–29); Juan Nepomuceno de Quesada to Luis de Las Casas, July 23, 1795, Letters to the Captain General, 1784–1821, EFP (microfilm reel 10); Landers, *Black Society in Spanish Florida,* 206–08; James G. Cusick, *The Other War of 1812: The Patriot War and the American Invasion of Spanish East Florida* (Gainesville: University Press of Florida, 2003), 51.

7. Juan Nepomuceno de Quesada to Luis de Las Casas, July 23, 1795, Letters to the Captain General, 1784–1821, EFP (microfilm reel 10); Landers, *Black Society in Spanish Florida,* 206–208; Jane Landers, "Transforming Bondsmen into Vassals: Arming Slaves in Colonial Spanish America," in Christopher Leslie Brown and Philip D. Morgan, eds., *Arming Slaves: From Classical Times to the Modern Age* (New Haven, CT: Yale University Press, 2006), 134.

8. Juan Nepomuceno de Quesada to Luis de Las Casas, October 26, 1795; Letters to the Captain General, 1784–1821, EFP (microfilm reel 10).

9. Landers, "Transforming Bondsmen into Vassals," 129–34; Juan Nepomuceno de Quesada to Luis de Las Casas, March 5, 1796, Cuba 1439, *AGI.*

10. Orders to General Biassou, 1801, Correspondence between the Governor and Subordinates on the St. John and St. Mary's River, EFP (microfilm reel 55); Landers, *Black Society in Spanish Florida,* 215–17; Memorials of Jorge Biassou, November 2 and December 6, 1799, Letters from the Captain General 1784–1821; and Marques de Someruelos to Enrique White, March 15, 1800, and March 28, 1801, all in EFP (microfilm reel 2).

11. Landers, *Black Society in Spanish Florida.*, 217–18; David H. White, "The Spaniards and William Augustus Bowles in Florida, 1799–1803," *Florida Historical Quarterly* 54 (1975): 144–55; cited in Lyle N. McAlister, "The Marine Forces of William Augustus Bowles and His 'State of Muskogee,'" *Florida Historical Quarterly* 32 (July 1953): 3–27, especially 10–11.

12. David Hart White, *Vicente Folch, Governor in Spanish Florida, 1787–1811* (Washington, DC: University Press of America, 1981), 60; Landers, *Black Society in Spanish Florida,* 219–20; Report of Fernando de la Puente, August 19, 1809, to and from Military Commanders and Other Officers, 1784–1821, EFP (microfilm reel 68).

13. Kathryn Trimmer Abbey, *Florida—Land of Change* (Chapel Hill: University of North Carolina Press, 1941), 100; Joseph Burkholder Smith, *The Plot to Steal Florida: James Madison's Phony War* (New York: Arbor House, 1983), 98–100; Cusick, *The Other War of 1812,* 47–49.

14. New York *Evening Post,* April 30, 1810; Herbert Aptheker, *American Negro Slave Revolts* (New York: Columbia University Press, 1943), 244–48; Cusick, *The Other War of 1812,* 47–48; newspaper articles enclosed in Robert Lyman to James Barbour, July 16, 1813, Governor's Papers, Virginia State Library, Richmond.

15. John Forbes to Vicente Folch, April 3, 1809, PC 221, B #16, *AGI;* Buckner Harris to David Mitchell, September 11 and November 8, 1810, Governor's Letterbook, 1809–1814, Georgia Department of Archives and History, Atlanta (hereinafter cited as GDAH); *National Intelligencer and Washington Advertiser,* February 22, 1809.

16. Frank L. Owsley, Jr., and Gene A. Smith, *Filibusters and Expansionists: Jeffersonian Manifest Destiny, 1800–1821* (Tuscaloosa: University of Alabama Press, 1997), 7–15; William C. Davis, *The Rogue Republic: How Would-Be Patriots Waged the Shortest Revolution in American History* (Boston: Houghton Mifflin Harcourt, 2011), passim; James Madison to Thomas Jefferson, October 19, 1810, in Irving Brant, *James Madison: The President, 1809–1812* (New York: The Bobbs-Merrill Company, Inc., 1956), 182–86; Vicente Folch to President Madison, December 2, 1810, Walter Lowrie, et al., eds., *The American State Papers: Foreign Relations* (Washington, DC: Gales and Seaton, 1832), 3:398 (hereafter cited as ASP:FR.); Isaac J. Cox, *The West Florida Controversy, 1798–1813* (Gloucester, MA: Peter Smith, 1967), 471–72.

17. James Monroe to George Mathews, January 26, 1811, and April 4, 1812, EFP, transcript also in Alabama Department of Archives and History, Montgomery; A. H. Phinney, "The First Spanish-American War," *Florida Historical Quarterly* 4 (1926): 116–19; Isaac J. Cox, "Border Missions of General Mathews," *Mississippi Valley Historical Review* 12 (December 1925): 316–18.

18. Kenneth Wiggins Porter, "Negroes and the Seminole Indiana War, 1817–1818," *Journal of Negro History* 36 (July 1951): 253; James Monroe to George Mathews, January 26, 1811, EFP; William Earl Weeks, *John Quincy Adams and American Global Empire* (Lexington: University Press of Kentucky, 1992), 39.

19. Phinney, "The First Spanish-American War," 118–19; Philip Coolidge Brooks, *Diplomacy and the Borderlands: The Adams-Onís Treaty of 1819* (Berkeley: University of California Press, 1939), 32–33.

20. Cox, "Border Missions of General Mathews," 318–19, 323–24; T. Frederick Davis, ed., "United States Troops in Spanish East Florida, 1812–1813," *Florida Historical Quarterly* 9 (1930): 4; Thomas Smith to Secretary of War, March 18, 1812, 5.

21. Cox, "Border Missions of General Mathews," 318–19; Owsley and Smith, *Filibusters and Expansionists,* 68–69; D. C. Corbitt, "The Return of Spanish Rule to the St. Mary's and the St. Johns, 1813–1821," *Florida Historical Quarterly* 20 (1941): 47–49; Davis, "United States Troops in Spanish East Florida," 4.

22. Hugh G. Campbell to Hamilton, March 21, 1812, in *The Naval War of 1812,* 1:87–88; Justo Lopez to Luis Onís, March 19, 1812, enclosure in Onís to James Monroe, April 14, 1812, *Notes from the Spanish Legation,* vol. 3, Record Group 59, M59; Report and Dispatch of Pedro Labradore, Secretary of State, December 31, 1812, to the Deputed Secretaries of the General and Extraordinary Cortes, EFP; G. I. F. Clarke to O'Rilley, March 19, 1812, "The Surrender of Amelia, March 1812," *Florida Historical Quarterly* 4 (1925): 91; Phinney, "The First Spanish-American War," 120–21; Cox, "Border Missions of General Mathews," 329; Cusick, *The Other War of 1812,* 131.

23. Claudio Saunt, *A New Order of Things: Property, Power, and the Transformation of the Creek Indians, 1733–1816* (New York: Cambridge University Press, 1999), 237–38; José de Estrada to Marqués de Someruelos, March 26, 1812, EFP, bnd. 31E3, doc. 101, 4812, reel 12; Sebastián Kindelán to Juan Ruiz de Apodaca, August 13, 1812, EFP, bnd. 31E3, doc. 39, 4931, reel 12.

24. Saunt, *A New Order of Things,* 237–38; Sebastián Kindelán to Juan Ruiz de Apodaca, August 13, 1812, EFP, bnd. 31E3, doc. 39, 4931, reel 12; Tuskegee Tustunugee to Benjamin Hawkins, September 18, 1812, Lockey Collection, P. K. Yonge Library of Florida History, University of Florida, Gainesville.

25. Cusick, *The Other War of 1812,* 142.

26. Cusick, *The Other War of 1812,* 144–54; Thomas Smith to U.S. Adjutant and Inspector, April 26, 1812, in Davis, "United States Troops in Spanish East Florida," 9–10; Kenneth Wiggins Porter, "Negroes and the East Florida Annexation Plot, 1811–1813," *Journal of Negro History* 30 (1945): 10.

27. Cusick, *The Other War of 1812,* 157, 161; Thomas Smith to Secretary of War, April 14, 1812, in Davis, "United States Troops in Spanish East Florida," 7–9.

28. Phinney, "The First Spanish-American War," 120–21; Brooks, *Diplomacy and the Borderlands,* 33; James Madison to Thomas Jefferson, April 24, 1812, in Gallard Hunt, ed., *The Writings of James Madison* (New York: G. P. Putnam's Sons, 1908), 8:187; James Monroe to Gen. George Mathews, April 4, 1812, *Florida Historical Quarterly* 6 (1928): 235–37.

29. Thomas Smith to Governor David Mitchell, May 14, 1812, in Davis, "United States Troops in Spanish East Florida," 12–13; James Monroe to David Mitchell, April 10, 1812, EFP; Report of Pedro Labrador to the Deputy Secretaries of the General and Extraordinary Cortes, December 31, 1812, EFP; Rembert W. Patrick, *Florida Fiasco: Rampant Rebels on the Georgia-Florida Border, 1810–1815* (Athens: University of Georgia Press, 1954), 179–94.

30. Landers, *Black Society in Spanish Florida,* 221–22; Patrick, *Florida Fiasco,* 184–85.

31. Benigno Garzia to David Mitchell, December 12, 1812, in *Niles' Weekly Register,* January 16, 1813, 311–12; Patrick, *Florida Fiasco,* 139–43; Landers, *Black Society in Spanish Florida,* 222; Sebastián Kindelán to Juan Ruiz de Apodaca, September 30, 1813, Cuba 1790, *AGI.*

32. Sebastián Kindelán to Juan Ruiz de Apodaca, September 30, 1813, Cuba 1790, *AGI;* Cusick, *The Other War of 1812,* 186; Patrick, *Florida Fiasco,* 184.

33. Order to Jorge Jacobo, Juan Baustista Witten, and Benjamín Seguí, July 19, 1812, to and from Military Commanders and Other Officers, 1784–1821, EFP (microfilm reel 68); Thomas Flournoy to Thomas Smith, February 2, 1813, in *Clarion,* July 13, 1813.

34. Patrick, *Florida Fiasco,* 184–86; Porter, "Negroes and the East Florida Annexation Plot," 19; J. H. Alexander, "The Ambush of Captain John Williams, U.S.M.C.: Failure of the East Florida Invasion, 1812–1813," *Florida Historical Quarterly* 61 (January 1978): 288–89.

35. Kenneth Wiggins Porter, *The Negro on the American Frontier,* (New York: Arno Pres, 1971), 186–94; David Mitchell to James Monroe, July 17, 1812, quoted in Julius W. Pratt, *Expansionists of 1812* (Gloucester, MA: Peter Smith, 1957), n194–95; David Mitchell to James Monroe, September 19, 1812, *Territorial Papers,* National Archives; Patrick, *Florida Fiasco,* 184.

36. Cusick, *The Other War of 1812,* 187; William Kinnear to his mother and brother, September 11, 1812, in Rembert W. Patrick, ed., "Letters of the Invaders of East Florida, 1812," *Florida Historical Quarterly* (July 1949): 61–63; Thomas Smith to Governor David Mitchell, August 21, 1812, in Davis, "United States Troops in Spanish East Florida, Part II," 110–12.

37. John Williams to Miller, September 6, 1812, in Edwin N. McClellan, "Indian Fights, 1807–1813, Material and Sources of Chapter XIX, Volume I, History of the United States Marine Corps," (1925), 10; John Williams to Wharton, September 15, 1812, *National Intelligencer,* October 20, 1812; Cusick, *The Other War of 1812,* 232–35.

38. John Williams to Wharton, September 15 and October 20, 1812, *National Intelligencer;* Cusick, *The Other War of 1812,* 232–35; Alexander, "The Ambush

of Captain John Williams," 293–94; Porter, "Negroes and the East Florida Annexation Plot," 20–21; Kenneth W. Porter, *The Black Seminoles: The History of a
Freedom-Seeking People* (reprint; Gainesville: University Press of Florida, 1996),
8–9.

39. Sebastián Kindelán to Juan Ruiz de Apodaca, September 13, 1812, Cuba 1789, *AGI;*
Landers, *Black Society in Spanish Florida,* 362, n100; Cusick, *The Other War of
1812,* 235.

40. Landers, *Black Society in Spanish Florida,* 225–28.

41. Daniel Newnan to David Mitchell, November 7 and December 12, 1812, *Niles'
Weekly Register;* Porter, *The Black Seminoles,* 10; Porter, "Negroes and the Seminole
Indian War, 1817–1818," 255–56.

42. Porter, "Negroes and the Seminole Indian War, 1817–1818," 10–11; Porter, "Negroes and the East Florida Annexation Plot," 22–24; Cusick, *The Other War of
1812,* 242–43; Saunt, *A New Order of Things,* 239–40; Pratt, *Expansionists of
1812,* 209.

43. Governor's Message of November 2, 1812, in Minutes of the Executive Department,
October 1, 1812–April 30, 1814, 30, 1812, GDAH; John Campbell to David Camp-
bell, October 17, 1812, Campbell Family Papers, William R. Perkins Library, Duke
University, Durham, NC; Porter, "Negroes and the East Florida Annexation Plot,"
24–25; James H. Campbell to Robert Pogue, November 26, 1812, James Campbell
Papers, MSS CC, Filson Club Historical Society, Louisville, KY; Thomas Flournoy to
Thomas Smith, February 2, 1813, in *Clarion,* July 13, 1813; Patrick, *Florida Fiasco,*
230–36; Cusick, *The Other War of 1812,* 253–57.

44. Confidential Proceedings of the Senate, *Annals of Congress,* 12th Cong., 2nd sess.
(December 1812–January 1813), 127–28; Buckner Harris to David Mitchell, May
24, 1813, and José Hibberson to Charles Harris, November 19, 1814, both in "East
Florida Documents," *Georgia Historical Quarterly* 13 (June 1929): 154–58; Cusick,
The Other War of 1812, 273.

45. Cusick, *The Other War of 1812,* 275–92; José Hibberson to Charles Harris, November 19, 1814, in "East Florida Documents," 156–58.

46. Cusick, *The Other War of 1812,* 283–84; Saunt, *A New Order of Things,* 240–41.

47. Ruíz Apodaca to the Governor of East Florida, December 10, 1813, PC Leg. 1856,
AGI; Ruíz Apodaca to the Minister of War Juan O. Donoju, November 18, 1813,
April 26, 1814, PC Leg. 1856, *AGI;* Jane Landers, "Black Community and Culture
in the Southeastern Borderlands," *Journal of the Early Republic* 18 (Spring 1998):
123.

48. Aptheker, *American Negro Slave Revolts,* 244–48; Charles Ball, *Slavery in the
United States: A Narrative of the Life and Adventures of Charles Ball* (New York:
John S. Taylor, 1837), 471–73; Landers, *Black Society in Spanish Florida,* 247.

CHAPTER 4: TERROR IN THE CHESAPEAKE, 1813–14

1. Ball, *Slavery in the United States,* 11–16.

2. Ball, *Slavery in the United States,* 14–23.

3. John Lehman, *On Seas of Glory: Heroic Men, Great Ships, and Epic Battles of the
American Navy* (New York: Simon and Schuster, 2001), 127–28; Ball, *Slavery in the
United States,* 33–36.

4. Lehman, *On Seas of Glory,* 127–28; Ball, *Slavery in the United States,* 479–80.
Charles Ball's story, written and edited with the help of white lawyer Isaac Fisher,
reportedly omits any beliefs or feelings Ball may have expressed about slavery in the
attempt to bring unbiased attention to the plight of slaves. Although Fisher's admis-
sion of significant editing has led scholars to debate the authenticity of Ball's narrative, it nonetheless found widespread publication before the Civil War and influenced
other fugitive slave narratives.

5. John Borlase Warren to Lord Melville, November 18, 1812, February 25, 1813,
and November 16, 1813, Warren Papers, National Maritime Museum, Greenwich,
England (hereinafter cited as NMM); Bathurst to Prevost, January 12, 1813, PRO,
CO 43/23; Bathurst to Thomas Sydney Beckwith, March 18, 1813, PRO, CO
43/23.

6. James Stirling to Viscount Melville, March 17, 1813, James Stirling Memorandum, The Historic New Orleans Collection, New Orleans, Louisiana (hereinafter cited as THNOC); Henry Hotham Book of Remarks, 1813, Hotham Collection, DDHO 7/99, Brynmor Jones Library, University of Hull, Hull, England; Brian Jenkins, *Henry Goulburn, 1784–1856: A Political Biography* (Montreal: McGill-Queen's University Press, 1996), 79–80; James Pack, *The Man Who Burned the White House: Admiral Sir George Cockburn, 1772–1853* (Emsworth, Hants, England: Mason, 1987), 171; Lord Bathurst to Lords Commissioners of the Admiralty, March 25, 1813, British Public Records Office, Admiralty Office Papers, 1/4223, Kew, England (hereinafter cited as PRO, ADM); Viscount Melville to Admiral Hope, November 13, 1812, Robert Saunders-Dundas Papers, NMM; John Borlase Warren to Lord Melville, November 18, 1812, Warren Papers, NMM.

7. Earl Bathurst to Sydney Beckwith, March 20, 1813, Alexander Foster Inglis Cochrane Papers, National Library of Scotland, Edinburgh (hereafter cited as CP), MS 2326, fos. 3–10; Copy in CP, MS 2326, fo. 233, and *Naval War of 1812,* 2:325–26; Frank A. Cassell, "Slaves of the Chesapeake Bay Area and the War of 1812," *Journal of Negro History* 57 (1972): 145.

8. Christopher T. George, *Terror on the Chesapeake: The War of 1812 on the Bay* (Shippensburg, PA: White Mane Books, 2000), 6–8; Charles Stewart to William Jones, March 17, 1813, in *Naval War of 1812,* 2:315–16; Tommy L. Bogger, *Free Blacks in Norfolk Virginia, 1790–1860: The Darker Side of Freedom* (Charlottesville: University Press of Virginia, 1997), 37.

9. William Preston to John Preston, March 10, 1813, Preston Papers, Virginia Historical Society, Richmond; Lt. James Polkinghorne to John Warren, April 3, 1813, in *Naval War of 1812,* 2:339–40; George, *Terror on the Chesapeake,* 9–10; Wade G. Dudley, *Splintering the Wooden Wall: The British Blockade of the United States, 1812–1815* (Annapolis, MD: Naval Institute Press, 2003), 90–91; *Daily National Intelligencer,* April 6, 1813; *The War* (New York), April 6, 1813; *Columbian Centinel* (Boston), April 10 and 17, 1813.

10. Polkinghorne to Warren, April 3, 1813, in *Naval War of 1812,* 2:339–40; Pack, *The Man Who Burned the White House,* 150–51; *Columbian Centinel* (Boston), April 17 and 21, 1813; Warren to John W. Coker, May 28, 1813, PRO, ADM, 1/503, 278–80; *Daily National Intelligencer,* April 30, 1813; William P. Palmer, ed., *Calendar of Virginia State Papers and Other Manuscripts, 1652–1781, Preserved in the Capitol at Richmond,* 11 vols. (1875–1893; reprint, New York: Kraus, 1968), 10:267, 388; Sally E. Hadden, *Slave Patrols: Law and Violence in Virginia and the Carolinas* (Cambridge, MA: Harvard University Press, 2001), 163; Levin Winder to President James Madison, April 26, 1813, Records of the States of the United States, Maryland, E.2. Reel 3, 1787–1820; *Columbian Centinel* (Boston), April 17, 1813.

11. Cockburn to Warren, May 3, 1813, George Cockburn Papers, Library of Congress, Washington, DC (hereafter cited as Cockburn Papers); Christopher T. George, "Hartford County in the War of 1812," *Hartford County Historical Bulletin* 76 (Spring 1998): 29–37; Keith S. Dent, "The British Navy and the Anglo-American War of 1812 to 1815" (M.A. thesis: University of Leeds, 1949), 200; James Scott, *Recollections of a Naval Life* (London: R. Bentley, 1834), 3:122 ff., 158–60.

12. Cockburn to Warren, May 6, 1813, PRO, ADM, 1/503, 679–85; *Niles' Weekly Register,* May 22, 1813; *Connecticut Mirror,* August 9, 1813.

13. *Daily National Intelligencer,* May 12, 1813; Kendall Addison to Warren, May 14, 1813, in Warren to John Wilson Croker, May 28, 1813, PRO, ADM, 1/503, 278–80; Warren to Lieutenant Colonel Addison, May 16, 1813, PRO, ADM, 1/503, 284.

14. Ball, *Slavery in the United States,* 471–73; Warren to Lieutenant Colonel Addison, May 16, 1813, PRO, ADM, 1/503, 284; Christopher T. George, "Mirage of Freedom: African Americans in the War of 1812," *Maryland Historical Magazine* 91 (Winter 1996): 432–33.

15. Warren to John Wilson Croker, May 28, 1813, PRO, ADM, 1/503; Logbook of *Narcissus,* June 6, 1813, PRO, ADM, 51/2609; Earl Bathurst to Sydney Beckwith, March 1813, PRO, ADM, 1/4224.

16. London *Times,* August 11 and 16, 1813; J. Mackay Hitsman and Alice Sorby, "Independent Foreigners or Canadian Chasseurs," *Military Affairs* 25 (Spring 1961): 12; Geoffrey M. Footner, "The Battle of Craney Island, Virginia, June 22, 1813: A Reassessment," *Journal of the War of 1812* (Spring 2002): 4–9; Lt. Gen. Sir W. Napier, *The Life and Opinions of General Sir Charles Napier, G.C.B.,* 4 vols. (London: John Murray, 1857), 1:213; *Richmond Enquirer,* July 3, 1813.

17. Alistair J. Nichols, "'Desperate Banditti'? The Independent Companies of Foreigners," *Journal of the Society for Army Historical Research* 79 (2001): 282–83; Sir George Cockburn's Journal, 1797–1818, 114, Sir George Cockburn COC/11 NMM; Dent, "The British Navy and the Anglo-American War of 1812 to 1815," 205; "Thursday March 23, 1815," Frontier Wars Papers, Vol. 17, Series U, page 186, Lyman Draper Collection, State Historical Society of Wisconsin, Madison; Napier, *Life and Opinions,* 1:214, 221; George Prevost to Colonel Torrens, August 12, 1813, PRO, WO 1/96; Sta. Crutchfield to James Barbour, June 28, 1813, *The Enquirer* (Richmond), July 3, 1813; Richard Parker to the Editor of the *Richmond Enquirer,* no date but printed July 16, 1813, in Parke Rouse Jr., ed., "The British Invasion of Hampton in 1813," *The Virginia Magazine of History and Biography* 76 (July 1968): 326–27.

18. Warren to John Wilson Croker, May 28, 1813, PRO, ADM, 1/503; *Weekly Messenger* (Boston), July 9, 1813; Letter from Dolley Madison, May 12, 1813, in *Life and Letters of Dolly* [sic] *Madison,* Allen C. Clark, ed. (Washington, DC: Press of W. R. Roberts Co., 1914), 151–52; *Niles' Weekly Register,* May 15 and 22, 1813, January 8, 1814, June 6 and 25, 1814; Pack, *The Man Who Burned the White House,* 155; Frank A. Cassell, "Slaves of the Chesapeake Bay Area and the War of 1812" *Journal of Negro History* 57 (April 1972): 142–154; Geoffrey Jules Marcus, *Age of Nelson; The Royal Navy, 1793–1815* (New York: Viking, 1971), 42; Geoffrey Francis Andrew Best, *Humanity in Warfare: The Modern History of the International Law of Armed Conflicts* (London: Weidenfeld and Nicolson, 1980), 111–12.

19. *The Enquirer* (Richmond), July 30, 1813; *The Independent Chronicle* (Boston), August 2, 1813; Robert Taylor to Gov. James Barbour, July 2, 1813, and James McDowell to Barbour, July 30, 1813, Robert Parker to Barbour, July 6, 1813, Lieutenant Governor to Barbour, September 7, 1813, all in Governor's Papers, Virginia State Library, Richmond; Levin Winder to Gen. Caleb Hawkins, August 27, 1813, and Winder to James Monroe, August 25, 1813, Maryland State Papers Series A, Maryland Hall of Records, Annapolis; Summer 1813 Diary Entry, in Claude G. Bowers, ed., *The Diary of Elbridge Gerry, Jr.* (New York: Brentano's, 1927), 198–99.

20. *The Enquirer* (Richmond), July 30, 1813, October 8, 1813; *Niles' Weekly Register,* September 11, 1813.

21. Kendall Addison to James Barbour, July 19, 1813, Governor's Papers, Virginia State Library, Richmond; Margaret Bayard Smith to Mrs. Kirkpatrick, July 20, 1813, in Gaillard Hunt, ed., *The First Forty Years of Washington Society* (New York: Scribner's Sons, 1906), 89–90; *Boston Gazette,* August 30, 1813; *Daily National Intelligencer,* August 24, 1813; *Niles' Weekly Register,* July 24, 1813; *The Enquirer* (Richmond), July 6, 1813, August 30, 1813; Cassell, "Slaves in the War of 1812," 146–49.

22. *Niles' Weekly Register,* August 14, 1813; Cockburn to Warren, September 26, 1813, George Cockburn Papers, LOC; Oswald Tilghman, and S. A. Harrison, *History of Talbot County Maryland, 1661–1881* (Baltimore: Williams and Wilkins Company, 1915), 172; *Connecticut Mirror,* November 15, 1813; St. George Tucker to Joseph C. Cabell, April 27, 1814, Cabell Family Papers (MSS 38-111), University of Virginia, Charlottesville; William A. Hoge, "The British Are Coming . . . Up the Potomac," *Northern Neck Historical Magazine* 14 (1964): 1271; William M. Marine, *The British Invasion of Maryland, 1812–1815,* edited by Louis Henry Dielman (Baltimore: Society of the War of 1812 in Maryland, 1913), 57; Pack, *The Man Who Burned The White House,* 161–62; George, *Terror on the Chesapeake,* 64.

23. James McDowell to James Barbour, July 30, 1813, John W. Jaynes to Barbour, July 29, 1813, both in Governor's Papers, Virginia State Library, Richmond; *The Enquirer* (Richmond), 5, August 30, 1813; Hoge, "The British Are Coming," 1271; Robert Barrie to Warren, November 13, 1813, PRO, ADM, 1/505; Henry Goulburn to John Barrow, October 1, 1813, CP, MS 2340.

24. Henry Goulburn to John Barrow, October 1, 1813, CP, MS 2340; Robert Barrie to Warren, November 13, 1813, PRO, ADM, 1/505; Napier, *Life and Opinions*, 1: 369–70.

25. Cochrane to Cockburn, April 24 and 28, 1814, and Cochrane to Melville, March 10, 1814, CP; Pack, *The Man Who Burned the White House*, 166–67; Cochrane to Croker, March, 1814, PRO, 1/505, 633; Draft by Cochrane, ca. April 27–28, 1812, CP, MS 2574, fo. 3.

26. Robert Barrie to Warren, November 14, 1813, enclosed in Warren to John Croker, December 29, 1813, PRO, ADM, 1/505; John Croker to Alexander Cochrane, January 21, 1814, PRO, ADM, 2/1379; Goulburn to Crocker, January 19, 1814, copy in CP, MS 2342, fos. 63–66; Goulburn to John Barrow, October 1, 1813, CP, MS 2340.

27. George Cockburn's Journal, 1797–1818, COC/11, 122–23, Sir George Cockburn Papers, Greenwich Maritime Museum; Roger Morriss, *Cockburn and the British Navy in Transition: Admiral Sir George Cockburn, 1772–1853* (Exeter, Devon, UK: University of Exeter Press, 1997), 98; Cochrane to John Warren, March 8, 1814, CP, MS 2326.

28. Cochrane to Melville, March 10, 1814, CP, MS 2345; Cochrane's Observations to Lord Melville Relative to America, 1814, and Cochrane to Robert Saunders Dundas, March 25, 1814, all in the War of 1812 MSS, Lilly Library, Indiana University, Bloomington; Cochrane to George Prevost, March 11, 1814, CP, MS 2549.

29. Cochrane to Cockburn, April 8, 1814, CP, MS 2349; Cochrane's Proclamation, April 2, 1814, PRO, ADM, 1/508, 579; Cochrane to Robert Saunders Dundas, March 25, 1814, War of 1812 MSS, Lilly Library, Indiana University, Bloomington; Marianne Buroff Sheldon, "Black-White Relations in Richmond, Virginia, 1782–1820," *Journal of Southern History* 45 (February 1979): 36; Virginia House Journal, January 8, 11, 17, 26, and 27, 1814, Microfilm Collection of Early State Records, Class A.16 (reel 6, Library of Congress); Cockburn to Cochrane, April 2, 1814, CP, MS 2574.

30. Cockburn to John Warren, April 13, 1814, CP, MS 2333; James Scott, *Recollections of a Naval Life*, 3:118–19.

31. Lt. G. C. D. Lewis Notebook on Field Engineering, Royal Engineers Museum, Chatham, England; Adam Wallace, *The Parson of the Islands: A Biography of the Rev. Joshua Thomas* (1861; reprint, Cambridge, MD: Tidewater Publishers, 1961), 129, 131; Richard Brooks, *The Royal Marines, 1664 to the Present* (Annapolis, MD: Naval Institute Press, 2002), 154; Capt. John Robyns, Royal Marines, Diary, April 5, 1814, 11/13/061, Royal Marines Museum, Swansea; Cockburn to Cochrane, May 9, 1814, CP, MS 2333; George Cockburn's Journal, 1797–1818, COC/11, 123, Sir George Cockburn Papers, Greenwich Maritime Museum.

32. George Cockburn's Journal, 1797–1818, COC/11, 124, Sir George Cockburn Papers, Greenwich Maritime Museum; Cockburn to John Warren, April 13, 1814, CP, MS 2333; Cockburn to Warren, April 27, 1814, George Cockburn Papers, LOC; Scott, *Recollections of a Naval Life*, 3: 118–20; Hoge, "The British Are Coming," 1273; Cockburn to Charles B. H. Ross, April 17, 1814, CP, MS 2333; Enclosure 10 and 11, May 9, 1814, in Cockburn to Cochrane, May 9, 1814, CP, MS 2333.

33. Cockburn to Cochrane, April 29, 1814, and Cochrane to Cockburn, May 26, 1814, both in George Cockburn Papers, LOC; and Cockburn to Cochrane, June 26, 1814, CP, MS 2333.

34. Cockburn to Cochrane, April 29, 1814, and Cochrane to Cockburn, May 18, 26, 1814, all in George Cockburn Papers, LOC; Cockburn to Charles B. H. Ross, April 17, 1814, CP, MS 2333; Cockburn to Cochrane, May 9, 1814, CP, MS 2333; David Milne to Commodore Evans, April 23, 1814, Sir David Milne Papers, MLN/18, Greenwich Maritime Museum; Cochrane to Cockburn, April 8, 1814, CP, MS 2349.

35. Cockburn to Cochrane, April 29, 1814, George Cockburn Papers, LOC; Cockburn to William Hammond, May 19, 1814, PRO, ADM, 1/507; Cochrane to John Wilson Croker, September 2, 1814, CP, MS 2348; Unknown to Cochrane, October 20, 1814, PRO, ADM, 2/1212; George Cockburn Journal, 1797–1818, COC/11, 124, Sir George Cockburn Papers, Greenwich Maritime Museum; Cockburn to Cochrane, May 10, 1814, CP, MS 2574.

36. Cockburn wrote a series of letters to Cochrane between April 2 and June 25, 1814, CP, MS 2574, fos. 99–139; MS 2333, fos. 18–138; Morriss, *Cockburn and the*

British Navy in Transition, 98–99; Brooks, *Royal Marines,* 154; Third Battalion Order Book, RM 7/7/13, October 25, 1814, Royal Marines Museum, Swansea; Scott, *Recollections of a Naval Life,* 3:115, 120–21.

37. Cockburn to Cochrane, May 10, 1814, CP, MS 2574; Cockburn to Robert Barrie, May 26, 1814, Robert Barrie Papers, WCLC; Hoge, "The British Are Coming," 1273–74; Cassell, "Slaves in the War of 1812," 153; Hadden, *Slave Patrols,* 162–63.

38. Capt. John Robyns, Royal Marines, Diary, May 11, 29, and 30, 1814, 11/13/061, Royal Marines Museum, Swansea; Cockburn to Cochrane, June 25, 1814, CP, MS 2574; Robert Barrie to Cockburn, May 29, 1814, PRO, ADM, 1/507; *Niles' Weekly Register,* June 11, 1814, 244.

39. Robert Barrie to Cockburn, June 1, 1814, PRO, ADM, 1/507; *Naval Chronicle,* 32 (July–December 1814): 504; Pack, *The Man Who Burned the White House,* 172–73; George, *Terror on the Chesapeake,* 70–72; Barrie to Cockburn, June 19, 1814, CP, MS 2333; Donald G. Shomette, *Flotilla: Battle for the Patuxent* (Solomons, MD: Calvert Marine Museum Press, 1981), 41, 50–55.

40. George C. Urmston to Barrie, June 1, 1814, included in Barrie to Cockburn, June 5, 1814, all in PRO, ADM, 1/507; Barrie to Cockburn, June 3, 1814, Cockburn Papers, LOC; Pack, *The Man Who Burned the White House,* 172–73; George, *Terror on the Chesapeake,* 170–71.

41. Shomette, *Flotilla,* 66–71; *Daily National Intelligencer,* June 20, 1814; *American and Commercial Daily Advertiser,* June 23, 27, 1814; *The War* (New York), July 5, 1814.

42. Shomette, *Flotilla,* 82–97; Cockburn to P. Foster, June 6, 1814, Cockburn Papers, LOC; Cockburn to Cochrane, June 25, 1814, CP, MS 2574; Brooks, *The Royal Marines,* 154.

43. Cockburn to George Watts, no date (falls between June 22–29, 1814), Cockburn Papers, LOC; Cockburn to Watts, June 30, 1814, CP, MS 2333; Cochrane to Cockburn, July 1, 1814, CP, MS 2346; Hoge, "The British are Coming," 1273–74; Brooks, *The Royal Marines,* 154; "A Personal Narrative of Events by Sea and Land, from the Year 1800 to 1815 Concluding with a Narrative of Some of the Principal Events in the Chesapeake and South Carolina in 1814, and 1815," *Chronicles of St. Mary's* 8 (January 1960): 3.

44. Cochrane to Cockburn, July 1, 1814, CP, MS 2346; Milne to Unknown, April 26, 1814, Edgar Eskine Hume, ed., "Letters Written During the War of 1812 by the British Naval Commander in American Waters (Admiral Sir David Milne)," *William and Mary Quarterly* 2nd Ser. 10 (October 1930): 293.

45. Cochrane to Cockburn, July 1, 1814, CP, MS 2346; Cochrane to Earl Bathurst, July 14, 1814, PRO, WO 1/141; Cochrane to Robert Saunders Dundas Melville, July 17, 1814, War of 1812 MSS, Lilly Library, Indiana University.

46. Cockburn to Joseph Nourse, July 15, 1814, Cockburn Papers, LOC; Cochrane to Cockburn, July 18, 1814, and Cochrane to James M. Hardy, Secret Memorandum, September 4, 1814, both in MAL/103, Sir Pulteney Malcolm Papers, Greenwich Maritime Museum; Clem Hollyday to Urban Hollyday, July 12, 1814, Clem Hollyday Papers, LOC; Cochrane to Commanding Officers of the North American Station, July 18, 1814; CP, MS 2346.

47. Joseph Nourse to Cockburn, July 23, August 4 and 12, 1814, all Cockburn Papers, LOC; Shomette, *Flotilla,* 123.

48. Cockburn to Cochrane, July 17 and 21, 1814; CP, MS 2333; Cockburn to Cochrane, July 19, 1814, PRO, ADM, 1/507; Capt. John Robyns, Royal Marines, Diary, May 11, 29, and 30, 1814, 11/13/061, Royal Marines Museum, Swansea.

49. Scott, *Recollections of a Naval Life,* 3: 129–36.

50. Cockburn to Cochrane, July, 31, August 4, 8, 1814, PRO, ADM, 1/507; Scott, *Recollections of a Naval Life,* 3:131; Captain John Robyns, Royal Marines, Diary, July 26, August 4, 1814, 11/13/061, Royal Marines Museum, Swansea; John Hungerford to James Barbour, August 5, 1814, Governor Papers, Virginia State Library, Richmond; Joshua Barney to William Jones, August 4, 1814, Crawford, *Naval War of 1812,* 3: 184–186; Pack, *The Man Who Burned the White House,* 178.

51. Earl Bathurst to Robert Ross, August 10, 1814, PRO, WO 6/2; Morriss, *Cockburn and the British Navy in Transition,* 100–104; George, *Terror on the Chesapeake,* 81;

Gleig, *A Narrative of the Campaigns of the British Army, at Washington, Baltimore, and New Orleans, under the Generals Ross, Packenham, and Lambert in the Years 1814 and 1815 with Some Account of the Countries Visited* (Philadelphia: M. Carey and Sons, 1821), 148.

52. Lawrence Hartshorne to Cochrane, July 29, 1814, CP, MS 2327; Joseph Nourse to Cockburn, July 23, 1814, Cockburn Papers, LOC; Cockburn to Cochrane, July 31, 1814, PRO, ADM, 1/507.

53. Goulburn to Crocker, January 19, 1814, copy in CP, MS 2342; Melville to Cochrane, August 10, 1814, CP, MS 2574; Melville to Cochrane, August 10, 1814, CP, MS 2374; Melville to Cochrane, August 10, 1814, War of 1812 MSS, Lilly Library, Indiana University; Bathurst to Cochrane, October 26, 1814, CP, MS 2327; Cochrane to Bathurst, July 14, 1814, PRO, WO 1/141.

54. "Recollections of the Expedition to the Chesapeake, and Against New Orleans, in the Years 1814–15," *The United Service Journal and Naval and Military Magazine* (London: Henry Colburn, 1840), 28.

55. Lehman, *On Seas of Glory,* 127–28.

CHAPTER 5: WASHINGTON, BALTIMORE, AND OTHER TARGETS

1. Christopher T. George, "Mirage of Freedom: African Americans in the War of 1812," *Maryland Historical Magazine* 91 (Winter 1996): 446; George, *Terror on the Chesapeake,* 13.

2. *Niles' Weekly Register,* November 14, 1812; George, *Terror on the Chesapeake,* 13.

3. *Niles' Weekly Register,* March 25, 1815; "Another Old Defenders Gone," *The Sun* (Baltimore), January 16, 1861; George, "Mirage of Freedom," 446; Edgar Stanton Maclay, *A History of American Privateers* (New York: D. Appleton and Company, 1899), 279–300.

4. *Niles' Weekly Register,* April 15, 1815; Scott S. Sheads and Anna Von Lunz, "Defenders' Day, 1815–1898: A Brief History," *Maryland Historical Magazine* 93 (Fall 1998): 301; *The Sun* (Baltimore), January 16, 1861.

5. Christopher Phillips, *Freedom's Port: The African American Community of Baltimore, 1790–1860* (Urbana: University of Illinois Press, 1997), 235–38.

6. Cassell, "Slaves in the War of 1812," 152–53; T. H. Dowing to James Barbour, July 23, 1814; Memorial from Caroline County, August 3, 1814; John T. Lomax to Barbour, July 31, 1814; Petition from Citizens of Essex County to Barbour, August 1814, all in Governor Papers, Virginia State Library, Richmond.

7. *Daily National Intelligencer,* August 24, 1814; *Independent Chronicle* (Boston), August 29, 1814.

8. *The Enquirer* (Richmond), August 31, 1814; *Daily National Intelligencer,* August 22, September 10, 1814; Mordecai Booth to Thomas Tingey, August 22, 1814, in *Naval War of 1812,* 3:202–204; Margaret Bayard Smith to Maria Kirkpatrick, August 1814, in Gailard Hunt, *The First Forty Years of Washington Society in the Family Letters of Margaret Bayard Smith* (New York: Ungar Publishing, 1906), 99–101; *Federal Republican,* September 7, 1814; Anthony Pitch, *The Burning of Washington: The British Invasion of 1814* (Annapolis, MD: Naval Institute Press, 1998), 39–50; Samuel Smith to Levin Winder, August 16, 1814, Adjutant General's Papers 4176-6/11/39, Maryland Hall of Records, Annapolis.

9. Joshua Barney to William Jones, August 29, 1814, in *Naval War of 1812,* 3:207–208; Paul A. Jennings, *A Colored Man's Reminiscences of James Madison* (Bladensburg Series, Number 2, Brooklyn, NY: George C. Beadle, 1865), quoted on http://www.jmu.edu/madison/center/main_pages/madison_archives/era/african/life/jennings.htm.

10. Ball, *Slavery in the United States,* 467–68; Pitch, *The Burning of Washington,* 71–73; George, *Terror in the Chesapeake,* 93–94.

11. James M. Varnum to Mary Varnum, August 31,1814, War of 1812 MSS, Lilly Library, Indiana University; Capt. John Robyns, Royal Marines, Diary, August 24, 1814, 11/13/061, Royal Marines Museum, Swansea; Pitch, *The Burning of Washington,* 73–77; 1814 Expedition Diary of Sir Arthur Brooke, August 24, 1814,

D3004/D/2, Ulster American Folk Park, Omagh, Northern Ireland; Henry Fulford, August 26, 1814, in Marine, *British Invasion of Maryland,* 114; Third Battalion Order Book, RM 7/7/13, August 24, 1814, Royal Marines Museum, Swansea.

12. Joshua Barney to William Jones, August 29, 1814, in *Naval War of 1812,* 3:207–208; Ball, *Slavery in the United States,* 362; Pitch, *The Burning of Washington,* 81–85; George, *Terror in the Chesapeake,*100–103; Gleig, *A Narrative of the Campaigns of the British Army,* 67, 127.

13. Louis Arthur Norton, *Joshua Barney: Hero of the Revolution and 1812* (Annapolis, MD: Naval Institute Press, 2000), 184; Diary of Anna Maria Thornton, August 24, 1814, 175, and Dolley Madison to Mary Elizabeth Hazelhurst Latrobe, December 3, 1814, 166, both in Allen C. Clark, ed., *Letters of Dolly Madison* (Washington, DC: Press of W. R. Roberts Co., 1914); Jennings, *A Colored Man's Reminiscences,* 11; Elizabeth Dowling Taylor, *A Slave in the White House: Paul Jennings and the Madisons* (New York: Palgrave Macmillan, 2012), 51–52; George, "Mirage of Freedom," 449, n40.

14. Return of Killed, Wounded, and Missing under Robert Ross on August 24, 1814, PRO, WO 1/141; Cockburn to Cochrane, August 27, 1814, *Naval Chronicle* 32 (July–December 1814), 348; George, *Terror in the Chesapeake,* 105; "Recollections of the Expedition to the Chesapeake, and Against New Orleans," 455; 1814 Expedition Diary of Sir Arthur Brooke, August 24, 1814, D3004/D/2, Ulster American Folk Park, Omagh, Northern Ireland; Cochrane to John Wilson Croker, September 2, 1814, CP, MS 2348; Charles G. Muller, *The Darkest Day: The Washington-Baltimore Campaign During the War of 1812* (Philadelphia: University of Pennsylvania Press, 1963), 136–37.

15. Louis Serurier to Maurice de Talleyrand, August 27, 1814, Foreign Affairs, Political Correspondence, Paris-United States, LOC; Pitch, *The Burning of Washington,* 104–22; George, *Terror in the Chesapeake,* 105–109.

16. Pitch, *The Burning of Washington,* 130–48; George, *Terror in the Chesapeake,* 110–12; 1814 Expedition Diary of Sir Arthur Brooke, 24 August 1814, D3004/D/2, Ulster American Folk Park, Omagh, Northern Ireland; C. H. J. Sinder, *The Glorious "Shannon's" Old Blue Duster and other Faded Flags of Fadeless Fame* (Toronto: McClelland and Stewart, 1923), 65; Cochrane to Richard Hussey, August 1814, War of 1812 MSS, Lilly Library, Indiana University; William Kirke to Charles Kirke, 13 November 1814, DD.MM 43, Notthinghamshire Archives, Nottingham, England; Captain John Robyns, Royal Marines, Diary, August 26, 27, 28, 29, 1814, 11/13/061, Royal Marines Museum, Swansea.

17. Hadden, *Slave Patrols,* 163–65; Margaret Bayard Smith to Jane Kirkpatrick, July 20, 1813, in Hunt, *First Forty Years of Washington Society,* 89–91; Report of General Tobias Stansbury, November 15, 1814, *American State Papers: Military Affairs* (Washington: Gales and Seaton, 1832), 6:562; Charles J. Ingersoll, *Historical Sketch of the Second War between the United States of America, and Great Britain* (Philadelphia: Lea and Blanchard, 1849), 2:207–08.

18. Margaret Bayard Smith to Samuel Harrison Smith, 1815, Hunt, *First Forty Years of Washington Society,* 123; Sam Maynard to Levin Winder, August 28, 1814, Maryland State Papers, Series A, 6636/97/4; Irving Brant, *James Madison* (Indianapolis: Bobbs-Merrill, Co., 1961), 6:306; Margaret Bayard Smith to Maria Kirkpatrick, August 1814, 113, and September 11, 1814, 118–19, both in Hunt, *First Forty Years of Washington Society;* Gleig, *Narrative of the Campaigns,* 144; "Recollections of the Expedition to the Chesapeake, and Against New Orleans," 27.

19. Melville to Cochrane, May 22, 1814, CP, MS 2574; Robert Barrie to Lord Melville, August 19, 1814, Dropmore Papers, British Library; Dudley, *Splintering the Wooden Wall,* 115–19.

20. Phillips, *Freedom's Port,* 109–10, 199; Seth Rockman, *Scraping By: Wage Labor, Slavery, and Survival in Early Baltimore* (Baltimore: Johns Hopkins University Press, 2009), 262; Scott S. Sheads, "A Black Soldier Defends Fort McHenry, 1814," *Military Collector and Historian* 41 (Spring 1989): 20; William D. Hoyt, ed., "Civilian Defense in Baltimore: 1814–1815," *Maryland Historical Magazine* 39 (September 1944): 200–01, 221; *New York Evening Post,* September 5, 1814.

21. Rockman, *Scraping By,* 69–70; Phillips, *Freedom's Port,* 110; Thomas Jefferson to Edward Coles, August 25, 1814, Thomas Jefferson Papers, LOC; "Recollections of the Expedition to the Chesapeake, and Against New Orleans," 28.

22. 1814 Expedition Diary of Sir Arthur Brooke, September 12, 1814, D3004/D/2, Ulster American Folk Park, Omagh, Northern Ireland; Thomas V. Huntsberry and Joanne M. Huntsberry, *Western Maryland, Pennsylvania, Virginia Militia in Defense of Maryland, 1805 to 1815* (Baltimore: Baker and Taylor, 1983), 47, 55, 59; Muller, *The Darkest Day,* 186–87.

23. Arthur Brooke to Earl Bathurst, September 17, 1814, PRO, WO 1/141; 1814 Expedition Diary of Sir Arthur Brooke, September 13, 1814, D3004/D/2, Ulster American Folk Park, Omagh, Northern Ireland; James McCulloch to Samuel Smith, September 14, 1814, Samuel Smith Family Papers, LOC; Capt. John Robyns, Royal Marines, Diary, September 13, 1814, 11/13/061, Royal Marines Museum, Swansea.

24. *The Citizen Soldiers at North Point and Fort McHenry, September 12 & 13, 1814* (Baltimore: Charles C. Saffell, 1889), 11; *American and Commercial Daily Advertiser* (Baltimore), May 21, 1814; Scott S. Sheads, "A Black Soldier Defends Fort McHenry, 1814," *Military Collector and Historian* 41 (Spring 1989), 20–21; Altoff, *Amongst My Best Men,* 125–28.

25. Cochrane to Cockburn, September 13, 1814, War of 1812 MSS, Lilly Library, Indiana University; Capt. John Robyns, Royal Marines, Diary, September 13 and 14, 1814, 11/13/061, Royal Marines Museum, Swansea; George, "Mirage of Freedom," 443–44.

26. September 26, 1814, 3rd Battalion Orderbook, RM 7/7/13, March–December 1814, Royal Marines Museum, Southsea, Hants; Brant, *James Madison,* 6:270.

27. J. L. Moulton, *The Royal Marines* (Eastney, Southsea, Hampshire, UK: The Royal Marines Museum, 1981), 35; Richard Brooks, *The Royal Marines: 1664 to the Present* (London: Constable, 2002), 154; Cochrane to Robert Saunders Dundas, August 31, 1814, War of 1812 MSS, Lilly Library, Indiana University; Cochrane to John Wilson Croker, September 28, 1814, PRO, ADM, 1/507; Unknown to Cochrane, October 20, 1814, PRO, ADM, 2/1212; Joseph W. A. Whitehorne, *The Battle for Baltimore, 1814* (Baltimore: Nautical and Aviation Publishing Company of America, 1996), 196; "Recollections of the Expedition to the Chesapeake, and Against New Orleans," 27–28; Cochrane to Cockburn, December 8, 1814, and Joseph Nourse to Cockburn, August 12, 1814, both in Cockburn Papers, LOC.

28. *Columbian Centinel* (Boston), November 5, 1814; William Lambert to James Barbour, November 4, 1814, and James Bankhead to James Barbour, December 2, 1814, and John H. Cocke to James Barbour, December 4, 1814, and James Monroe to James Barbour, January 4, 1815, all in Executive Papers, Virginia State Library, Richmond; Tilghman and Harrison, *History of Talbot County,* 180; Whitehorne, *The Battle for Baltimore,* 198–200; Robert Barrie to Cockburn, December 7, 1814, PRO, ADM, 1/509.

29. Cockburn to Andrew F. Evans, December 12, 1814, Cockburn Papers, LOC.

30. Cockburn to Cochrane, May 10, 1814, CP, MS 2574; Cassell, "Slaves in the War of 1812," 153; Hadden, *Slave Patrols,* 162–63; Cockburn wrote a series of letters to Cochrane between April 2 and June 25, 1814, CP, MS 2574.

31. Cochrane to John Croker, July 23, 1814, PRO, ADM, 1/506; Shane White, "'We Dwell in Safety and Pursue Our Honest Callings': Free Blacks in New York City, 1783–1810," *Journal of American History* 75 (September 1988): 446–48; David N. Gellum, *Emancipating New York: The Politics of Slavery and Freedom, 1777–1827* (Baton Rouge: Louisiana State University Press, 2006), 199–203.

32. Dixon Ryan Fox, "The Negro Vote in Old New York," *Political Science Quarterly* 32 (June 1917): 255; Gellum, *Emancipating New York,* 201–05; White, "'We Dwell in Safety and Pursue Our Honest Callings,'" 467–68; Robert J. Swan, "John Teasman: African-American Educator and the Emergence of Community in Early Black New York City, 1787–1815," *Journal of the Early Republic* 12 (Fall 1992): 352.

33. Swan, "John Teasman," 352–53; *New York Evening Post,* August 20, 1814; Leslie M. Harris, *In the Shadow of Slavery: African Americans in New York City, 1626–1863* (Chicago: University of Chicago Press, 2003), 93; Leslie M. Alexander, *African*

or American?: Black Identity and Political Activism in New York City, 1784–1861
(Urbana: University of Illinois Press, 2008), 27.

34. *New York Evening Post,* August 13 and 22, September 9, 10, 12, 13, and 17, and
    October 31, 1814; *The Columbian,* April 25 and 26, August 19, and October 24, 26,
    and 29, 1814; R. S. Guernsey, *New York City and Vicinity During the War of 1812*
    (New York: Charles L. Woodward, 1895), 2:210; Swan, "John Teasman," 352–54.
35. Thomas Lefferts to Secretary of War, September 6, 1814, and October 24, 1814,
    Laws of New York, Chapter 18, 38th Session, both in "The Negro in the Military
    Service of the United States, 1639–1886," National Archives and Records Admin-
    istration, Roll 1, M 858; J. C. A. Stagg, "Soldiers in Peace and War: Compara-
    tive Perspectives on the Recruitment of the United States Army," *William and Mary
    Quarterly* 57 (January 2000): 91–92; James Oliver Horton and Lois E. Horton, *In
    Hope of Liberty: Culture, Community, and Protest Among Northern Free Blacks,
    1700–1860* (New York: Oxford University Press, 1997), 183; Leo H. Hirsch, Jr.
    "The Slave in New York" *Journal of Negro History* 16 (October 1931): 394.
36. James Monroe to Samuel Smith, September 19, 1814, Samuel Smith Family Papers,
    LOC; Julie Winch, *A Gentleman of Color: The Life of James Forten* (New York:
    Oxford University Press, 2002), 174; *Poulson's American Daily Advertiser,* August
    26, 27, and 29, 1814.
37. *A Brief Sketch of the Military Operations on the Delaware during the Late War:
    Together with a Copy of the Muster-Rolls of the Several Volunteer-Corps Which
    Composed the Advance Light Brigade, as They Stood at the Close of the Campaign
    on One Thousand Eight Hundred and Fourteen* (Philadelphia: Robert P. M'Culloh,
    1820), 27–28; *Minutes of the Committee of Defense of Philadelphia, 1814–1815*
    (Philadelphia: J. B. Lippincott & Co. for the Historical Society of Pennsylvania,
    1867), 47; William Duane to Thomas Jefferson, August 11, 1814, in *Proceedings of
    the Massachusetts Historical Society* 20 (May 1907): 373–75.
38. *National Era,* July 22, 1847; Richard S. Newman, *Freedom's Prophet: Bishop Rich-
    ard Allen, the AME Church, and the Black Founding Fathers* (New York: New York
    University Press, 2008), 191–93; Gary B. Nash, *Forging Freedom: The Formation
    of Philadelphia's Black Community, 1720–1840* (Cambridge, MA: Harvard Univer-
    sity Press, 1988), 212; *Poulson's American Daily Advertiser,* September 19, 1814;
    Winch, *A Gentleman of Color,* 175; Rebecca Gratz to Benjamin Gratz, September
    1814, David Philipson, ed., *Letters of Rebecca Gratz* (Philadelphia: Jewish Publica-
    tion Society of America, 1929), 8.
39. *Poulson's American Daily Advertiser,* September 3, 1814; *Journal of the Pennsyl-
    vania Senate* (1814–15): 56; Providence *Rhode Island American,* January 6, 1815;
    J. Thomas Scharf and Thompson Westcott, *History of Philadelphia, 1699–1884,*
    3 vols. (Philadelphia: L. H. Everts, 1884), 1: 575; Winch, *A Gentleman of Color,*
    175–76; Nash, *Forging Freedom,* 212–13; Stagg, "Soldiers in Peace and War," 93–
    94, n34; Robert Ewell Greene, *Black Defenders of America, 1775–1973* (Chicago:
    Johnson Publishing Company, Inc., 1974), 29; Newman, *Freedom's Prophet,* 193.
40. Sarah Cary to Henry Cary, September 7, 1814, in Caroline G. Curtis, ed., *The Cary
    Letters* (Cambridge, MA: Riverside Press, 1891), 199; Henry Champion, *Report of
    the Committee on Defence. To the Hon. the General Assembly* (New Haven, CT:
    Hudson & Woodward, Printers, 1813), 4; Samuel Tenney to M. Edward Brown,
    June 15, 1814, Edward Brown Papers, LOC.
41. Sarah Cary to Henry Cary, September 7, 1814, in Caroline G. Curtis, ed., *The Cary
    Letters* (Cambridge, MA: Riverside Press, 1891), 199; Champion, *Report of the
    Committee on Defence,* 4; Samuel Tenney to M. Edward Brown, June 15, 1814,
    Edward Brown Papers, LOC; Cochrane to George Prevost, March 11, 1814, CP, MS
    2549; David G. Fitz-Enz, *The Final Invasion: Plattsburgh, the War of 1812's Most
    Decisive Battle* (New York: Cooper Square Press, 2001), 77; Greene, *Black Defend-
    ers of America,* 30–39; Altoff, *Amongst My Best Men,* 114.
42. Thomas Macdonough to William Jones, April 11, 1814, 3:428, Macdonough to
    Jones, August 27, 1814, 3:541–42, George Izard to Macdonough, August 12, 1814,
    enclosed in Macdonough to Jones, August 16, 1814, 3:540–41, all in *Naval War of
    1812;* Greene, *Black Defenders of America,* 38; Harold D. Langley, "The Negro in
    the Navy and Merchant Marine," *Journal of Negro History* 52 (October 1967): 277.

43. Thomas Macdonough to William Jones, September 11, 1814, in *Naval War of 1812,* 3:607; Hickey, *The War of 1812,* 292–98.

44. Swan, "John Teasman," 352.

CHAPTER 6: WAR ALONG THE SOUTHERN COASTS, 1814

1. Frank Moore, ed., *Anecdotes, Poetry and Incidents of the Civil War: North and South, 1860–1865* (New York: Bible House, 1867), 117–18; Mary R. Bullard, "Ned Simmons, American Slave: The Role of Imagination in Narrative History," *The African Diaspora Archaeology Network Newsletter* (June 2007): 20–21, http://www .diaspora.uiuc.edu/news0607/news0607-7.pdf (accessed June 3, 2011).

2. Mary R. Bullard, *Cumberland Island: A History* (Athens: University of Georgia Press, 2003), 139–40.

3. George Cockburn Papers, LOC, vol. 46, "Fleet Orders, January–April, 1815," 12.

4. Cockburn to Thomas Spalding and Thomas Newall, March 7, 1815, vol. 26: 97 and subsequent unnumbered pages, Cockburn Papers, Library of Congress; Mary R. Bullard, *Black Liberation on Cumberland Island in 1815* (DeLeon Springs, FL: E. O. Painter Printing Company, 1983), 88–90; Bullard, *Cumberland Island,* 121–22.

5. Moore, *Anecdotes, Poetry and Incidents,* 117–18; Bullard, "Ned Simmons, American Slave," 18, 10, 44; http://www.diaspora.uiuc.edu/news0607/news0607-7.pdf (accessed June 3, 2011); Bullard, *Cumberland Island,* 139–40.

6. Cochrane to Melville, March 10, 1814, CP, MS 2345, fos. 1–5; Cochrane's Observations to Lord Melville Relative to America, 1814, and Cochrane to Dundas, July 17, 1814, both in War of 1812 MSS, Lilly Library, Indiana University; Lord Melville to William Domett, July 23, 1814, and Domett to Melville, July 26, 1814, both in Melville Castle Muniments, GD 51/2/523/1-2, National Archives of Scotland, Edinburgh; John Wilson Croker to Alexander Cochrane, August 10, 1814, PRO, WO 1/141, 15–24.

7. G. C. Moore Smith, ed., *The Autobiography of Lieutenant-General Sir Henry Smith,* (London: John Murray, 1901), 200–01; Sarah McCulloh Lemmon, *North Carolina and the War of 1812* (Raleigh: Division of Archives and History, 1974), 39–40; *The New-England Palladium* (Boston), October 5, 1813.

8. R. H. Taylor, "Slave Conspiracies in North Carolina," *The North Carolina Historical Review 5* (January 1928): 23–24; Hadden, *Slave Patrols,* 163–65; Aptheker, *American Negro Slave Revolts,* 244–47; Guion Griffis Johnson, *Ante-bellum North Carolina: A Social History* (Chapel Hill: University of North Carolina Press, 1937), 516–17; William Croom to William Miller, December 26, 1814, Records of the States of the United States, NC E.2b, Reel 8; Sarah McCulloh Lemmon, *Frustrated Patriots: North Carolina and the War of 1812* (Chapel Hill: University of North Carolina Press, 1973), 197–98.

9. Johnson, *Ante-bellum North Carolina,* 600; Act of the General Assembly of North Carolina, November 21, 1814, in "The Negro in the Military Service of the United States, 1639–1886," National Archives, M858, Roll 1, 332; Lemmon, *Frustrated Patriots,* 196.

10. Sir George Cockburn's Journal, 1797–1818, 147, Sir George Cockburn Papers, Greenwich Maritime Museum, London; Cochrane to Robert Saunders Dundas, March 25, 1814, War of 1812 MSS, Lilly Library, Indiana University, Bloomington, Indiana; Bathurst to Robert Ross, August 10, September 28, 1814, PRO, WO 6/2; Morriss, *Cockburn and the British Navy in Transition,* 114, 115; June Hall McCash, *Jekyll Island's Early Years: From Prehistory through Reconstruction* (Athens: University of Georgia Press, 2005), 119–23.

11. Betty Wood, "Some Aspects of Female Resistance to Chattel Slavery in Low Country Georgia, 1763–1815," *The Historical Journal* 30 (September 1987): 620; Thomas Gamble, Jr., *A History of the City Government of Savannah, Ga., from 1790–1901* (Savannah, GA, no publisher: 1901), 103–105; Walter J. Fraser, *Savannah in the Old South* (Athens: University of Georgia Press, 2003), 149–51, 181; Whittington B. Johnson, *Black Savannah, 1788–1864* (Fayetteville: University of Arkansas Press, 1996), 43.

12. Samuel Jenkins to Cochrane, October 26, 1814, CP, MS 2326, and George Cockburn to Robert Barrie, January 14, February 27, 1814, CP, MS 2334, both at the

National Library of Scotland, Edinburgh; Sir George Cockburn's Journal, 1797–1818, Sir George Cockburn COC/11, Greenwich Maritime Museum; Peter Early to David Blackshear, January 19, 1815, and Early to John Floyd, January 19, 1815, both in Georgia Governor's Letterbook, GA E.2, Reel 2, Unit 3; Bullard, *Black Liberation on Cumberland Island*, 47–51; No. 31, January 12, 1815, 3rd Battalion Order Book, Royal Marines Museum, Southsea, UK; Roswell King to Pierce Butler, January 20, 1815, Butler Papers, Historical Society of Pennsylvania, Philadelphia; Robert Barrie to Mrs. George Clayton, January 22, 1815, Robert Barrie Papers, WCLC; *Niles' Weekly Register,* February 4, 1815, VII: 361–64.

13.   John Miller to Thomas Miller, February 12, 1815, in Arsène Lacarrière Latour, *Historical Memoir of the War in West Florida and Louisiana in 1814–15: With an Atlas,* edited by Gene A. Smith (Gainesville: University of Florida Press and Historic New Orleans Collection, 1999), 334–35; Cockburn to Cochrane, February 11, 1815, CP, MS 2334, National Library of Scotland, Edinburgh; Bullard, *Cumberland Island,* 119–20; John Sawyer to General David Blackshear, January 27, 1815, Stephen F. Miller, ed., *Memoir of General David Blackshear* (Philadelphia: J. B. Lippincott and Co, 1858), 455; Zephaniah Kingsley, *A Treatise on the Patriarchal, or Co-Operative System of Society as It Exists in Some Governments, and Colonies in America, and in the United States, under the Name of Slavery, with Its Necessity and Advantages; by an Inhabitant of Florida* (1829), 11.

14.   Malcolm Bell, Jr., *Major Butler's Legacy: Five Generations of a Slaveholding Family* (Athens: University of Georgia Press, 1987), 172.

15.   Roswell King to Pierce Butler, January 20, February 12 and 26, and March 4, 1815, Butler Papers, Historical Society of Pennsylvania, Philadelphia; Bell, *Major Butler's Legacy,* 176–79.

16.   Bell, *Major Butler's Legacy,* 172; John Sawyer to Gen. David Blackshear, January 27, 1815, Miller, *Memoir of General David Blackshear,* 455–56; Pack, *The Man Who Burned the White House,* 210.

17.   Sebastián Kindelán y Oregón to Cockburn, January 31 and February 18, 1815, and Cockburn to Kindelán, February 13 and 22, 1815, PRO, WO 1/144: 31–32, 35–38, 106–107; William S. Coker and Thomas D. Watson, *Indian Traders of the Southeastern Spanish Borderlands: Panton, Leslie & Company and John Forbes & Company, 1783–1847* (Gainesville: University of Florida Press, 1986), 292–93.

18.   Sebastián Kindelán y Oregón to Cockburn, January 31, February 18, 1815, and Cockburn to Kindelán, February 13 and 22 1815, PRO, WO 1/144: 31–32, 35–38, 106–107; John Forbes to Cockburn, February 26, 1815, Cockburn to Forbes, February 26, 1815, PRO, WO 1/144: 45–47; Coker and Watson, *Indian Traders of the Southeastern Spanish Borderlands,* 292–93.

19.   Morriss, *Cockburn and the British Navy in Transition,* 117–18.

20.   Treaty of Ghent, Article I; Cockburn to Cochrane, February 28, 1815, vol. 26: 71–80, Cockburn Papers, Library of Congress; Bullard, *Cumberland Island,* 120–21.

21.   Bullard, *Black Liberation on Cumberland Island,* 85–87; Pack, *The Man Who Burned the White House,* 211–12; Morriss, *Cockburn and the British Navy in Transition,* 119–20.

22.   Cockburn to Thomas Spalding and Thomas Newall, March 7, 1815, vol. 26: 97 and subsequent unnumbered pages, Cockburn Papers, Library of Congress; Bullard, *Black Liberation on Cumberland Island,* 88–90; Bullard, *Cumberland Island,* 121–22.

23.   George Woodbine to Cochrane, July 25, 1814, CP, MS 2328; Cochrane to Chiefs of the Indian Nations, July 1, 1814, PRO, WO 1/143, 157; Cochrane to Lambert, February 3, 1815, PRO, WO 1/143, 23–27; Cochrane to Governor Cameron, July 4, 1814, MS 2549, and Hugh Pigot to Cochrane, June 6, 1814, MS 2326, both CP, National Library of Scotland, Edinburgh; *The War,* July 5, 1814; John Lee Williams, *A View of West Florida, Embracing Its Geography, Topography, & etc.* (Philadelphia: H. S. Tanner and the Author, 1827), 96.

24.   Cochrane to Bathurst, July 14, 1814, PRO, WO 1/141; George Woodbine to Hugh Pigot, May 25 and 28, 1814, and Edward Nicolls to Cochrane, August 12, 1814, CP, MS 2328; Cochrane to Governor Cameron, July 4, 1814, CP, MS 2549, National Library of Scotland; Earl Bathurst to Robert Ross, September 6, 1814, and Earl Bathurst to General E. Pakenham, October 24, 1814, both in PRO, WO 6/2.

25. Edward Nicolls, "Orders for the First Battalion of Royal Colonial Marines," 1814, Lockey Collection, P. K. Young Library, University of Florida, Gainesville (hereafter cited as PKY); Proclamation printed in *London Times,* November 22, 1814.

26. James Innerarity to the Governor of West Florida, March 1815, Greenslade Papers, PKY; Nicolls to Cochrane, Report, Aug. 12 to Nov. 17, 1814, July 27, August 12 and 17, and October 27, 1814, all in CP, MS 2328, National Library of Scotland (hereafter cited as NLS); George Woodbine to Hugh Pigot, May 25 and 28, 1814, both in CP, MS 2328; "Occupation of Pensacola by the British," *Boston Independent Chronicle,* July 7, 1814.

27. Saunt, *A New Order of Things,* 277; Captain Breveford to Cochrane, August 4, 1814, and Nicolls to Commissioners for Victualling, October 1814, both in CP, MS 2328, NLS; Cochrane to Captain Gordon, September 6, 1814, CP, MS 2346, NLS; Frank Lawrence Owsley, Jr., *Struggle for the Gulf Borderlands: The Creek War and the Battle of New Orleans, 1812–1815* (Gainesville: University of Florida Press, 1981), 105–107.

28. "File of Witnesses that may be examined by Commissioners in Pensacola in the Suit of Woodbine-Testimony of Peter Gilchrist," 1815, Cruzat Papers, PKY; Nicolls to Cochrane, October 27, 1814, CP, MS 2328; "Indictment of William Augustus Vesey for Perjury," 1816, Cruzat Papers, PKY; Nathaniel Millett, "Slave Resistance during the Age of Revolution: The Maroon Community at Prospect Bluff, Spanish Florida" (Ph.D. diss., University of Cambridge, 2002), 124–26, n44.

29. Cochrane to Don Mateo Manrique, August 11, 1814, CP, MS 2549, National Library of Scotland; Owsley, *Struggle for the Gulf Borderlands,* 105–107.

30. Captain Breveford to Cochrane, August 4, 1814, CP, MS 2328, NLS; Nicolls to Cochrane, Report, Aug. 12 to Nov. 17, 1814, CP, MS 2328; Owsley, *Struggle for the Gulf Borderlands,* 105–109; John Innerarity to James Innerarity, November 7, 1814, "Letters of John Innerarity," *Florida Historical Quarterly* 9 (1931): 127–30; Vincente de Ordozgoitti to Juan Ruíz Apodaca, September 21, 1814, Archivo General de Indies, Cuba, legajo 1856; James Gordon to Cochrane, November 18, 1814, PRO, ADM 1/505; Frank L. Owsley, Jr., "British and Indian Activities in Spanish West Florida During the War of 1812," *Florida Historical Quarterly* 46 (1967): 119–20.

31. Latour, *Historical Memoir,* 35–41; Percy to Cochrane, September 9, 1814, PRO, ADM, 1/505; Andrew Jackson to Secretary of War, September 17, 1814, in *Baltimore Patriot and Evening Advertiser,* October 17, 1814; William Lawrence to Andrew Jackson, September 15, 1814, in *The Columbian* (New York), October 19, 1814.

32. Robert V. Remini, *Andrew Jackson and the Course of American Empire, 1767–1821* (New York: Harper & Row, 1977), 239–42; Jackson to Willie Blount, November 14, 1814, Harold D. Mosier, *The Papers of Andrew Jackson* (Knoxville: University of Tennessee Press, 1991), 3:185; John Innerarity to James Innerarity, November 7, 1814, "Letters of John Innerarity," *Florida Historical Quarterly* 9 (1931): 127–30; Vincente de Ordozgoitti to Juan Ruíz Apodaca, September 21, 1814, Archivo General de Indies, Cuba, legajo 1856; James Gordon to Cochrane, November 18, 1814, PRO, ADM 1/505; Owsley, "British and Indian Activities," 119–20.

33. Hawkins to John Armstrong, August 16, 1814, 693; Hawkins to Jackson, August 30, 1814, 694, both in C. L. Grant, ed., *Letters, Journals and Writings of Benjamin Hawkins* (Savannah, GA: Beehive Press, 1980); Jackson to W. C. C. Claiborne, August 30, 1814, 3: 125–26; July 21, 1814, 3: 91; Claiborne to Jackson, August 12, 1814, 3: 115–16; all in *Papers of Andrew Jackson;* A. B. Bradford to William W. Worsley, September 20, 1814, Lyman Draper Collection, Kentucky Manuscripts, State Historical Society of Wisconsin, Madison; Caryn Cossé Bell, *Revolution, Romanticism, and the Afro-Creole Protest Tradition in Louisiana, 1718–1868* (Baton Rouge: Louisiana State University Press, 1997), 52; Claiborne to Colonel Alexander Declouet, September 19, 1814, David Rees Papers, Special Collections, Howard-Tilton Memorial Library, Tulane University, New Orleans, Louisiana.

34. Nicolls to Cochrane, August 12, 1814, CP, MS 2328; Cochrane to Hugh Pigot, June 9, 1814, CP, MS 2346; Edward Codrington to Mrs. Edward Codrington, June 7, 1814, Sir Edward Codrington Papers, COD/7/1, National Maritime Museum, Greenwich; Cochrane to Admiralty, October 3, 1814, CP, MS 2348, fos. 86–87.

35. Cochrane to Admiralty, October 3, 1814, CP, MS 2348, fos. 86–87; Cochrane to Nicolls, December 3, 1814, CP, MS 2346, fos. 16–17; see also MS 2349, fos. 214–16, 252–53; Cochrane to Cockburn, January 5, 1815, CP, MS 2349, fo. 234; Owsley, *Struggle for the Gulf Borderlands*, 96–101; Robin Reilly, *The British at the Gates: The New Orleans Campaign in the War of 1812* (New York: G. P. Putnam's Sons, 1974), 161–64; Hickey, *The War of 1812*, 204–205.

36. Remini, *Andrew Jackson*, 251, 57–59; John Spencer Bassett, ed., *Major Howell Tatum's Journal* (Northampton, MA: Department of History, Smith College, October 1921–April 1922), 102–104; Jackson to John Coffee, December 16, 1814, 3: 205–206; Jackson to New Orleans Citizens, December 16, 1814, 3: 206–20, both in *Papers of Andrew Jackson*; Proclamation "To the Men of Color," *National Intelligencer*, January 21, 1815.

37. Jackson to W. C. C. Claiborne, September 21, 1814, *Papers of Andrew Jackson*, 3:144; Proclamation, September 21, 1814, Latour, *Historical Memoir*, 205–206; Proclamation "Colored Troops" printed in *Boston Gazette*, December 5, 1814, and Federalist Boston *Columbian Centinel*, December 7, 1814.

38. Claiborne to Jackson, October 24, 1814, *Official Letter Books of W. C. C. Claiborne, 1801–1816*, Dunbar Rowland, ed. (1917; reprint, New York: AMS, 1972), 6: 289; Claiborne to Jackson, October 17, 1814, *Papers of Andrew Jackson*, 3: 164–65; Marcus Christian, *Negro Soldiers at the Battle of New Orleans* (New Orleans: Battle of New Orleans, 150th Anniversary Committee of Louisiana, 1965), 22.

39. Claiborne to Jackson, November 4, 1814, in Rowland, *Official Letter Books of W. C. C. Claiborne*, 6:308; *Major Howell Tatum's Journal*, 104; Samuel Carter, *Blaze of Glory* (New York: St. Martin's Press, 1971), 85–86; "Resolutions of the Legislature of Louisiana," Latour, *Historical Memoir*, 295; Christian, *Negro Soldiers in the Battle of New Orleans*, 24–44.

40. Roland C. McConnell, *Negro Troops of Antebellum Louisiana: A History of the Battalion of Freemen of Color* (Baton Rouge: Louisiana State University Press, 1968), 67–69; Individual names, occupations, and addresses compiled from Barthelemy Lafon, *Annuaire Louisianais Pour L'Année* (New Orleans: For the Author, 1808); Thomas H. Whitney, *Whitney's New-Orleans Directory, and Louisiana and Mississippi Almanac for the Year 1811* (New Orleans: Printed for the Author, 1810); 3rd Decennial Census Office. "Population Schedules for the 1810 Louisiana Census." NARA microfilm publication M252. National Archives and Records Administration, Washington, DC.

41. Proclamation, September 21, 1814, Latour, *Historical Memoir*, 204; McConnell, *Negro Troops of Antebellum Louisiana*, 70–72; Individual names, occupations, and addresses compiled from Lafon, *Annuaire Louisianais Pour L'Année*; Whitney, *Whitney's New-Orleans Directory, and Louisiana and Mississippi Almanac for the Year 1811*; "Population Schedules for the 1810 Louisiana Census."

42. McConnell, *Negro Troops of Antebellum Louisiana*, 69; Claiborne to General Thomas, December 17, 1814, in Rowland, *Official Letter Books of W. C. C. Claiborne*, 6:323; Adjutant General's Office, December 16, 1814, in *Weekly Recorder* (Chillicothe, Ohio), January 11, 1815; Latour, *Historical Memoir*, n122.

43. David Weller to Samuel Weller, January 6, 1815, MSS A W448 2, Weller Family Papers, Filson Club Historical Society; James H. Dormon, "The Persistent Specter: Slave Rebellion in Territorial Louisiana," *Louisiana History* 18 (Fall 1977): 389–404; Peter Ogden to Nathaniel Evans, January 11, 1811, Nathaniel Evans Papers, Special Collections, Hill Memorial Library, Louisiana State University, Baton Rouge; Daniel Rasmussen, *American Uprising: The Story of America's Largest Slave Revolt* (New York: HarperCollins, 2011), passim; Remini, *Andrew Jackson*, 235–36; James Roberts, *The Narrative of James Roberts, a Soldier Under Gen. Washington in the Revolutionary War, and Under Gen. Jackson at the Battle of New Orleans, in the War of 1812: "A Battle Which Cost Me a Limb, Some Blood, and Almost My Life"* (Chicago: For the Author, 1858), 13, 15–16; Latour, *Historical Memoir*, 149; Proclamation "To the Men of Color," *National Intelligencer*, January 21, 1815; William C. Nell, *The Colored Patriots of the American Revolution, with Sketches of Several Distinguished Colored Persons: To Which Is Added a Brief Survey of the Condition and Prospects of Colored Americans* (Boston, 1855), 295.

44. Bassett, *Major Howell Tatum's Journal,* 119; Resolution of the Legislature of Louisiana, in Latour, *Historical Memoir,* 294, also 49–50, 90, 115–16; Jackson to W. C. C. Claiborne, December 10, 1814, *Papers of Andrew Jackson,* 3:202; U.S. Senate *Proceedings,* January 20, 1819, (Washington, DC: Gales and Seaton, 1819), 62; Roberts, *The Narrative of James Roberts,* 14.

45. Christian, *Negro Soldiers in the Battle of New Orleans,* 33–34; Latour, *Historical Memoir,* 72–74, 83; Jackson to Secretary of War, December 27, 1814, Latour, *Historical Memoir,* 229–30; Remini, *Andrew Jackson,* 263–65.

46. Latour, *Historical Memoir,* 83–84, 90, 105–07; Christian, *Negro Soldiers in the Battle of New Orleans,* 36.

47. Action Report, January 8, 1815, in Latour, *Historical Memoir,* 243; Christian, *Negro Soldiers in the Battle of New Orleans,* 37–39.

48. Gene A. Smith, *A British Eyewitness at the Battle of New Orleans: The Memoir of Royal Navy Admiral Robert Atchison, 1808–1827* (New Orleans: Historic New Orleans Collection, 2004), 61; Gleig, *A Narrative of the Campaigns of the British Army,* 241; C. R. B. Barrett, ed., *The 85th King's Light Infantry* (London: Spottiswoode & Co., Ltd., 1913), 220; Samuel Luce to David Luce, January 19, 1815, MSS C L, Samuel Luce Papers, Filson Club Historical Society, Louisville, Kentucky; Andrew Walker, *Jackson and New Orleans: An Authentic Narrative of the Memorable Achievements of the American Army, Under Andrew Jackson, before New Orleans, in the Winter of 1814, '15* (New York: J. C. Derby, 1856), 337; John Spencer Cooper, *Rough Notes of Seven Campaigns in Portugal, Spain, France, and America During the Years 1809–1815* (Staplehurst, UK: Spellmount Ltd., 1996), 130, 132; Benson E. Hill, *Recollections of an Artillery Officer: Including Scenes and Adventures in Ireland, America, Flanders, and France* (London: R. Bentley, 1836), 353; George Laval Chesterton, *Peace, War, and Adventure: An Autobiographical Memoir of George Laval Chesterton* (London: Longman, Brown, Green, and Longmans, 1853), 205.

49. John Lambert to Earl Bathurst, January 29, 1815, PRO, WO 1, 141; Return of Casualties in the Army under the Command of Maj. Gen. Edward Pakenham, January 8, 1815, PRO, WO, 1, 141; Casualty Return for the 5th West India Regiment, PRO, WO 25/2259; Adam Rothman, *Slave Country: American Expansion and the Origins of the Deep South* (Cambridge, MA: Harvard University Press, 2005), 152.

50. Chesterton, *Peace, War, and Adventure,* 205; Smith, *A British Eyewitness at the Battle of New Orleans,* 61, 64; Journal of A. Emment, Royal Engineers, 50, 4601-57/1; Journal of John Fox Burgoyne, Royal Engineers M68, Entry: January 8, 1815, both in Royal Engineers Museum, Chatham, UK; Alexander Dickson, "Artillery Services in North America in 1814 and 1815," *Journal of the Society for Army Historical Research* 8 (April 1929): 97, 152–54.

51. *New York Spectator,* February 15, 1815; C. R. Forrest, Journal of the Movements of the Army Acting on the Southern Part of the North American Coast, 91, MAL/104, Sir Pulteney Malcolm Papers, Greenwich Maritime Museum, London, UK; Hill, *Recollections of an Artillery Officer,* 2:80, 1:318–19; Edward Codrington to Captain Lockyer, January 24, 1815, and Codrington to Respective Captains, January 22, 1815, both in COD/6/4; Codrington to Captain Detafons, January 22, 1815, COD/6/1, all in the Sir Edward Codrington Papers, Greenwich Maritime Museum.

52. Cochrane to Jackson, February 12, 1815, 260–61; Lambert to Jackson, February 19 and 27, March 18, 1815, 261, 268–69, 290; Jackson to Cochrane, February 20, 1815, 262; Jackson to Lambert, March 7, 1815, 273; Joseph Woodruff to Lambert, March 17, 1815, 270–71, all in Latour, *Historical Memoir;* John K. Mahon, "British Strategy and the Southern Indians: The War of 1812," *Florida Historical Quarterly* 44 (April 1966): 299; Logbook of HMS *Royal Oak,* March 30, 1815, Pulteney Malcolm Papers, WCLC.

53. General Orders, January 21, 1815, Latour, *Historical Memoir,* 339–42.

54. McConnell, *Negro Troops of Antebellum Louisiana,* 91–93; Rothman, *Slave Country,* 154–58; Robert McCausland to Jackson, February 24, 1815, *Papers of Andrew Jackson,* 3:287.

55. Cochrane to Bathurst, July 14, 1814, PRO, WO 1/141; George Woodbine to Hugh Pigot, May 25, 1814; Edward Nicolls to Cochrane, August 12, 1814, CP, MS 2328; Latour, *Historical Memoir,* 136–37, 148–49; Nell, *The Colored Patriots,* 299.

56. Cochrane to Bathurst, July 14, 1814, PRO, WO 1/141; George Woodbine to Hugh Pigot, May 25 and 28, 1814; Edward Nicolls to Cochrane, August 12, 1814, CP, MS 2328; Latour, *Historical Memoir,* 149, 205–06.

CHAPTER 7: DIFFERENT PLACES,
SAME RESULTS, 1815 AND AFTER

1. *The Daily Picayune* (New Orleans), June 21, 1890.
2. *The Daily Picayune* (New Orleans), June 21, 1890; Compiled Military Service Records of Volunteer Union Soldiers Who Served With the United States Colored Troops: 1st U.S. Colored Infantry, 1st South Carolina Volunteers (Colored) Company A, 1st U.S. Colored Infantry (1 Year), National Archives, M1819, roll 19; McConnell, *Negro Troops of Antebellum Louisiana,* 74, 85, 114–15; Christian, *Negro Soldiers in the Battle of New Orleans,* 32; Military Pension File of Jordan B. Noble, National Archives RG 15.
3. McConnell, *Negro Troops of Antebellum Louisiana,* 112; *The Daily Picayune* (New Orleans), January 9, 1851.
4. McConnell, *Negro Troops of Antebellum Louisiana,* 114–15; *Commercial Bulletin* (New Orleans), January 9, 1860, http://www.prcno.org/programs/preservationin print/piparchives/2001%20PIP/February%202001/25.html (accessed June 10, 2011).
5. *The Daily Picayune* (New Orleans), June 21, 1890; Freddie Williams Evans, "Jordan B. Noble: The Drummer of Chalmette," *Preservation in Print* (February 24, 2001): 24–25.
6. City of New Orleans, *A History of the Proceedings in the City of New Orleans, on the Occasion of the Funeral Ceremonies in Honor of James Abram Garfield, Late President of the United States* (New Orleans: A. W. Hyatt, 1881), 87, 192–93; *The Daily Picayune* (New Orleans), June 21, 1890.
7. Gregory Evans Dowd, *A Spirited Resistance: The North American Indian Struggle for Unity, 1745–1815* (Baltimore: Johns Hopkins University Press, 1992), 188; James W. Covington, "The Negro Fort," *Gulf Coast Historical Review* 5 (Spring 1990): 79; Eugene P. Southall, "Negroes in Florida Prior to the Civil War," *Journal of Negro History* 19 (1934): 83; Charles H. Coe, *Red Patriots: The Story of the Seminoles* (1898; reprint ed., Gainesville: University of Florida Press, 1974), 16–17; Duncan Clinch to R. Butler, August 2, 1816, "Operation, Negro Fort," National Archives, RG 45: HJ Box 181, 1816 (hereafter cited as "Operation Negro Fort").
8. Cochrane to Nicolls, December 5, 1814, and Cochrane to Captain Spencer, February 28, 1814, both in CP, MS 2349, NLS; George Fram to Cochrane, February 15, 1815, CP, MS 2330, NLS; J. Leitch Wright, Jr., "A Note on the First Seminole War," *Journal of Southern History* 34 (1968): 569; Southall, "Negroes in Florida Prior to the Civil War," 82–83; Nathaniel Millett, "Defining Freedom in the Atlantic Borderlands of the Revolutionary South," *Early American Studies* 5 (Fall 2007): 381–82, 386–87; Kenneth Wiggins Porter, *The Negro on the American Frontier* (New York: Arno Press, 1971), 216.
9. Deposition of Samuel Jarvis, May 9, 1815, enclosure Gaines to the Secretary of War, Letters of the Secretary of War, National Archives, RG 107. There is no doubt that Jarvis's report is accurate. It is probably not possible to give an exact count of the arms sent to Prospect Bluff by the British or to determine how many had already been distributed to the Indians, but the memorandum cited below as an enclosure from Bathurst to Ross on September 10, 1814, states that three thousand muskets, one thousand carbines, five hundred rifles, and one thousand swords were shipped from England for the attack on New Orleans. Previously some two thousand muskets had been shipped aboard HMS *Orpheus* and landed at Apalachicola by Capt. Hugh Pigot. There were apparently other shipments as well, but the records are not as clear and detailed. Listed below are references that document these arms shipments: Cochrane to Nicolls, December 28, 1814, PRO, ADM, 1/505; Bathurst to Ross, August 10, 1814; and memorandum enclosed in Bathurst to Ross, September 10, 1814, PRO, WO, 6/2; "Expedition against New Orleans," PRO, WO 1/142; Charles Cameron to Cochrane, August 2, 1814, MS 2328, CP, NLS; Hugh Pigot to

Cochrane, June 8, 1814, PRO, ADM, 1/506; *Charleston Courier,* January 23, 1815; Benjamin Hawkins to Peter Early, February 12 and 20, 1815, Telamon Cuyler Collection, Box 76, Folder 25, Documents 21, 22; Junius P. Rodriguez, "Ripe for Revolt: Louisiana and the Tradition of Slave Insurrection, 1803–1865" (Ph.D. diss., Auburn University, 1992), 87–111.

10. Conde de Fernan-Nuñez to Vizconde Castlereagh, December 8, 1815, PRO, FO 72/180; Petition of the Pensacola Citizens to his Excellency the Governor of West Florida, March 1815, CP, MS 2328, NLS; González Manrique to Alexander Cochrane, December 5, 1814, and José Urcerllo to Manrique, January 23, 1815, Forbes Papers, Mobile Public Library; Cochrane to Cockburn, CP, MS 2349, NLS; Cochrane to Manrique, February 10, 1815, Cruzat Papers, Florida Historical Society, University of South Florida, Tampa; Ruíz Apodaca to the Minister of War, May 6, 1815, and June 15, 1815, PC Leg 1856, *AGI;* Count de Frenan Nuñez to Viscount Castlereagh, December 8, 1815, PRO, FO 72/180; Kevin Mulroy, *Freedom on the Border: The Seminole Maroons in Florida, the Indian Territory, Coahuila, and Texas* (Lubbock: Texas Tech University Press, 1993), 13; John Innerarity to James Innerarity, May 10, 1815, Forbes Papers, Mobile Public Library.

11. Hawkins to Jackson, May 5, 1815; Gaines to Jackson, May 14, 1815; Gaines to the Secretary of War, May 22, 1815, all in Letters to the Secretary of War, Registered Series, 1801–70, Department of the Army, NA, RG 107, M221; David S. Heidler and Jeanne T. Heidler, *Old Hickory's War: Andrew Jackson and the Quest for Empire* (Mechanicsburg, PA: Stackpole Books, 1996), 50–53; Mark F. Boyd, "Events at Prospect Bluff on the Apalachicola River 1808–1818," *Florida Historical Quarterly* 14 (1937): 75–76; Porter, *The Negro on the American Frontier,* 217; Southall, "Negroes in Florida," 83; Thomas Freeman to Josiah Meigs, April 12, 1816, in Carter, *Territorial Papers,* 6:677–78; Covington, "The Negro Fort," 81.

12. Heidler and Heidler, *Old Hickory's War,* 64–65; Coker and Watson, *Indian Traders,* 306.

13. Remini, *Andrew Jackson and the Course of American Empire,* 344; Rembert W. Patrick, *Aristocrat in Uniform: General Duncan L. Clinch* (Gainesville: University of Florida Press, 1963), 27–29; Boyd, "Events at Prospect Bluff," 77; Duncan Clinch to R. Butler, August 2, 1816, "Operation, Negro Fort" National Archives, RG 45:HJ Box 181, 1816.

14. Dudley W. Knox, "A Forgotten Fight in Florida," *United States Naval Institute Proceedings* 62 (1936): 510; Covington, "The Negro Fort," 84; Duncan Clinch to R. Butler, August 2, 1816, "Operation, Negro Fort"; James W. Silver, *Edmund Pendleton Gaines, Frontier General* (Baton Rouge: Louisiana State University Press, 1949), 62–63; Boyd, "Events at Prospect Bluff," 78; Porter, *The Negro on the American Frontier,* 218.

15. Duncan Clinch to R. Butler, August 2, 1816, "Operation, Negro Fort"; Knox, "A Forgotten Fight in Florida," 522; Millett, "Defining Freedom in the Atlantic," 390.

16. Millett, "Defining Freedom in the Atlantic," 390–91.

17. Duncan Clinch to R. Butler, August 2, 1816, "Operation, Negro Fort"; Knox, "A Forgotten Fight in Florida," 512–13; Covington, "Negro Fort," 83, 86–87. Covington gives the date of the attack as July 25, whereas Knox and the letter cited above gives the date as July 27, 1816; Dowd, *A Spirited Resistance,* 188.

18. Duncan Clinch to R. Butler, August 2, 1816, "Operation, Negro Fort"; Coker and Watson, *Indian Traders,* 308–309; Boyd, "Events at Prospect Bluff," 81; Mulroy, *Freedom on the Border,* 15; Patrick, *Aristocrat in Uniform,* 33.

19. Daniel Todd Patterson to Secretary of War, August 15, 1816, in *Annals of Congress,* 5th Cong., 2nd Sess., 2:1981–83.

20. Ira Dye, "American Maritime Prisoners of War, 1812–1815," *Ships, Seafaring and Society* (Detroit: Wayne State University Press, 1987), 293–320; Robin F. A. Fabel, "Self-Help in Dartmoor: Black and White Prisoners in the War of 1812," *Journal of the Early Republic* 9 (Summer 1989): 167–90; Reginald Horsman, *The War of 1812* (New York: Alfred A. Knopf, 1972), 54, 162, 176, 248–49, 263–64; Reginald Horsman, "The Paradox of Dartmoor Prison," *American Heritage* 26, No. 2 (February 1975): 13–17, 85; W. Jeffrey Bolster, *Black Jacks,* 113.

21. Bolster, *Black Jacks*, 101–105; George Little, *Life on the Ocean, or Twenty Years at Sea; Being the Personal Adventures of the Author* (Boston: Waite, Pierce, and Company, 1844), 232; Benjamin Waterhouse, *A Journal of a Young Man of Massachusetts* (Boston: Rowe and Hooper, 1816), 175–76; Joseph Bates, *The Autobiography of Elder Joseph Bates; Embracing a Long Life on Shipboard* (Battle Creek, MI: Steam Press of the Seventh Day Adventist Publishing Association, 1868), 72; Basil Thompson, *The Story of Dartmoor Prison* (London: William Heinemann, 1907), 54–55.

22. Charles Andrews, *The Prisoner's Memoirs, or Dartmoor Prison* (New York: Printed for the Author, 1852), 38; Bolster, *Black Jacks*, 101–105; Little, *Life on the Ocean*, 232; Thompson, *The Story of Dartmoor Prison*, 54–55.

23. Little, *Life on the Ocean*, 234; Andrews, *The Prisoner's Memoirs, or Dartmoor Prison*, 38; Benjamin F. Palmer, *The Diary of Benjamin F. Palmer Privateersman While a Prisoner on Board English Warships at Sea, in the Prison at Melville Island and at Dartmoor* (n.p.: Acorn Club, 1914), 38, 141, 161; Bolster, *Black Jacks*, 105–106; Waterhouse, *Journal of a Young Man*, 176.

24. Paul Gilje, *Liberty on the Waterfront: American Maritime Culture in the Age of Revolution* (Philadelphia: University of Pennsylvania Press, 2004), 179; Bolster, *Black Jacks*, 102–103, 107; Nathaniel Pierce, "Journal of Nathaniel Pierce of Newburyport, Kept at Dartmoor Prison, 1814–1815," *Essex Institute Historical Collections* 73 (January 1937): 33–34; Dye, "American Maritime Prisoners of War, 1812–1815," 303–307; Fabel, "Self-Help in Dartmoor," 181–85.

25. Dye, "American Maritime Prisoners of War, 1812–1815," 303–07; Fabel, "Self-Help in Dartmoor," 181–85; Bolster, *Black Jacks*, 108–13, 125; Gilje, *Liberty on the Waterfront*, 179–83.

26. Palmer, *The Diary of Benjamin F. Palmer*, 126–27; Bolster, *Black Jacks*, 114–17; Gilje, *Liberty on the Waterfront*, 138–39.

27. Palmer, *The Diary of Benjamin F. Palmer*, 179–80; Waterhouse, *A Journal of a Young Man of Massachusetts*, 213–15, 218; Gilje, *Liberty on the Waterfront*, 187.

28. Andrews, *The Prisoner's Memoirs*, 95; Thompson, *The Story of Dartmoor Prison*, 177–81.

29. Thompson, *The Story of Dartmoor Prison*, 186–88; Bates, *The Autobiography of Elder Joseph Bates*, 83–84; Bolster, *Black Jacks*, 129–30.

30. Smith, *A British Eyewitness at the Battle of New Orleans*, 117; Dudley, *Splintering the Wooden Wall*, 61.

31. Bermuda Legislative Council to George Horsford, no date, PRO, CO 37/70, fo. 91; Henry Hotham to Commodore Evans, March 8, 1813, Hotham Collection, DDHO 7/31, Brynmor Jones Library, University of Hull; John Noble Harvey to George Horsford, August 14, 1813, CP, MS 2326, NLS; Henry Goulburn to John Barrow, October 1, 1813, CP, MS 2340, NLS.

32. Henry Hotham to Robert Barrie, January 11, 1814, and Henry Hotham to Commodore Evans, February 1 and 4, 1814, all in Hotham Collection, DDHO 7/31, Brynmor Jones Library, University of Hull; Cochrane to John Warren, March 8, 1814, CP, MS 2326; George Horsford to Earl Bathurst, October 5, 1813, PRO, CO 37/70, fo. 98.

33. Henry Hotham Order of April 16 and 24, 1814, Hotham Collection, DDHO 7/32, Henry Hotham to Commodore Evans, April 24 and 28, 1814, DDHO 7/33, all in Hotham Collection, Brynmor Jones Library, University of Hull.

34. Cockburn to Andrew F. Evans, December 12, 1814, Cockburn Papers, LOC; Henry Hotham Order of April 30 and May 29, 1814, Hotham Collection, DDHO 7/33, Hotham Collection, Brynmor Jones Library, University of Hull; Cochrane to Cockburn, May 26, 1814, CP, MS 2549, NLS.

35. James Cockburn to Maj. Gen. H. Torrent, August 23, 1815, PRO, CO 37/73, 42–43.

36. James Cockburn to Earl Bathurst, December 9, 1817, PRO, CO 37/75, 44–45; Smith, *A British Eyewitness at the Battle of New Orleans*, 119.

37. John N. Grant, "Black Immigrants into Nova Scotia, 1776–1815," *Journal of Negro History,* 48 (July 1973): 253–70; Robin W. Winks, *The Blacks in Canada* (Montreal: McGill-Queen's University Press, 1971), 114–41; Harvey Amani Whitfield,

From American Slaves to Nova Scotian Subjects: The Case of the Black Refugees, 1813–1840 (Toronto: Pearson Education Canada Inc., 2005), 8.

38. Lt. Gov. John C. Sherbrooke to Lord Bathurst, April 6, 1815, PRO, CO 217/96, 93–96; Henry Bunbury to John W. Croker, December 14, 1814, PRO, ADM 1/4231; List of American Slaves, Deserters from the Enemy, September 28, 1813, Nova Scotia Archives and Records Management (hereafter cited as NSARM), RG 1, vol. 420, no. 1–8 (microfilm no. 15464); Winks, *The Blacks in Canada*, 115; Whitfield, *From American Slaves to Nova Scotian Subjects*, 36; John N. Grant, *The Immigration and Settlement of the Black Refugees of the War of 1812 in Nova Scotia and New Brunswick* (Hantsport, Nova Scotia: Black Cultural Center for Nova Scotia, 1990), 45–46.

39. *Acadian Recorder* (Nova Scotia), September 3, 1814, NSARM (microfilm no. 5193); Cochrane to Sherbrooke, October 5, 1814, and April 20, 1815, both in CP, MS 2349, NLS; Lavis M. Wilkins to John C. Sherbrooke, April 1, 1815, 97–98, and Cochrane to Sherbrooke, March 25, 1815, 99, both included in Sherbrooke to Bathurst, April 6, 1815, PRO, CO 217/96; Winks, *The Blacks in Canada*, 115–16; Whitfield, *From American Slaves to Nova Scotian Subjects*, 36–37.

40. Sherbrooke to Bathurst, April 6, 1815, PRO, CO 217/96, 93–96; House of Representatives to Sherbrooke, April 1, 1815, *Journal of the House of Assembly*, 1815, 107, NSARM (microfilm no. 3528); Grant, *Immigration and Settlement of the Black Refugees*, 51–52; Iris Shea and Heather Watts, *Deadman's: Melville Island and Its Burial Ground* (Tantallon, Nova Scotia: Glen Margaret Publishing, 2005), 34–35; Bell, *Major Butler's Legacy*, 184–85; Winks, *The Blacks in Canada*, 115–16; Whitfield, *From American Slaves to Nova Scotian Subjects*, 36–37.

41. Sherbrooke to Bathurst, July 20, 1815, 186–87, and Michael Wallace to Sherbrooke, November 17, 1815, 234–34, both in PRO, CO 217/96; Winks, *The Blacks in Canada*, 125.

42. Sherbrooke to Bathurst, April 6, 1815, 93–96; Sherbrooke to Bathurst, May 6, 1815, 131–32; and Sherbrooke to Bathurst, November 21, 1815, 232–33, all in PRO, CO 217/96; Sherbrooke to Bathurst, April 6, 1816, 22–23, and June 5, 1816, 66–67, both in PRO, CO 217/98; Contract between Lewis DeMolitor and Thomas Nicholson Jeffrey, May 1, 1815, NSARM, RG 1, vol. 420, no. 17 (microfilm no. 15464); Shea and Watts, *Deadman's*, 35; Winks, *The Blacks in Canada*, 118–20.

43. Richard Inglis, Returns of Number of Refugees Settled and Provisions Needed, December 30, 1816, PRO, CO 217/98, 158; A List of Blacks Recently Brought from the United States, 1815, NSARM, RG 1, vol. 420, no. 133 (microfilm no. 15464); *Novascotian*, June 27, 1832, NSARM (microfilm no. 8069); Indenture of David Dire, May 18, 1815, NSARM, MG 1, vol. 770A, no. 57; Winks, *The Blacks in Canada*, 121; Whitfield, *From American Slaves to Nova Scotian Subjects*, 38–42.

44. Bathurst to Dalhousie, January 17, 1817, PRO, CO 218/29; Dalhousie to Bathurst, December 29, 1817, PRO, CO 217/98, 155–56; Dalhousie to Bathurst, May 16, 1817, PRO, CO 217/99, 82–83; Winks, *The Blacks in Canada*, 123.

45. Whitfield, *From American Slaves to Nova Scotian Subjects*, 44–46; Sherbrooke to Bathurst, April 20, 1816, PRO, CO 217/98, 54–55; Bathurst to Dalhousie, January 17, 1817, PRO, CO 218/29, cited in Winks, *The Blacks in Canada*, 123.

46. James Kempt to George Harrison, January 20, 1821, PRO, CO 217/40, 211–12; Whitfield, *From American Slaves to Nova Scotian Subjects*, 46.

47. James Kempt to George Harrison, January 20, 1821, PRO, CO 217/40, 211–12; Kempt to Bathurst, October 16, 1823, PRO, CO 217/42, 88; Winks, *The Blacks in Canada*, 123–25; Whitfield, *From American Slaves to Nova Scotian Subjects.*, 46–47.

48. Memorial of Levin Winder, March 13, 1821, NSARM, RG 20, series A, vol. 85 (1821) (microfilm no. 15733); Whitfield, *From American Slaves to Nova Scotian Subjects*, 46–47, 51–52; Winks, *The Blacks in Canada*, 124–25, 128–29; William Moorsom, *Letters from Nova Scotia: Comprising Sketches of a Young Country* (London: Henry Colburn and Richard Bentley, 1830), 126–27; Frederic Cozzens, *Acadia: or A Month with the Blue Noses* (New York: Derby & Jackson, 1859), 64.

49. Winks, *The Blacks in Canada.*, 130–32; Sherbrooke to Bathurst, May 6, 1815, PRO, CO 217/96, 131–32; John N. Grant, "Chesapeake Blacks Who Immigrated to New

Brunswick, 1815," *National Genealogical Society Quarterly* 60 (September 1972): 194–95; Hugo Reid, *Sketches in North America with Some Account of Congress and of the Slavery Question* (London: Longman, Green, Longman and Roberts, 1861), 290; Bell, *Major Butler's Legacy,* 184–85.

50. Smith, *A British Eyewitness at the Battle of New Orleans,* 127; Michael Lewis, *The Navy in Transition, 1814–1864: A Social History* (London: Hodder and Stoughton, 1965), 64–69; Harold E. Raugh, Jr., *The Victorians at War, 1815–1914* (Santa Barbara, CA: ABC-CLIO, 2004), xiv; Roger Norman Buckley, *The British Army in the West Indies: Society and the Military in the Revolutionary Age* (Gainesville: University Press of Florida, 1998), 86.

51. Michael Craton, *Testing the Chains: Resistance to Slavery in the British West Indies* (Ithaca, NY: Cornell University Press, 1982), 259–64, 285; James Leith to Bathurst, April 30, 1816, and "Extract of a Private Letter," April 27, 1816, both in PRO, CO 28/85; George Hibbert to Bathurst, April 1817, PRO, CO 137/145, 39–40.

52. Bathurst to Cochrane, October 26, 1814, PRO, WO 6/2; Cochrane to Cockburn, March 9, 1815, CP, MS 2349, NLS; George Hibbert to Bathurst, April 1817, PRO, CO 137/145, 39–40; Ralph Woodford to Bathurst, June 6, 1815, 51; and August 5, 1815, 139, both in PRO, CO 295/37; K. O. Laurence, "The Settlement of Free Negroes in Trinidad Before Emancipation," *Caribbean Quarterly* 9, 1 & 2 (1963): 26–27.

53. Ralph Woodford to Bathurst, November 30, 1815, PRO, CO 295/37, 229; Woodford to Bathurst, August 28, 1816, PRO, CO 295/40, 104–10; Woodford to Bathurst, February 8, 1816, PRO, CO 295/39, 37–46.

54. Woodford to Bathurst, August 28, 1816, PRO, CO 295/40, 104–10; Woodford to Maj. Andrew Kinsman, August 15, 1816, 159; Kinsman to John Croker, no date, 161; Kinsman to Croker, no date, 163; and Kinsman Address to Colonial Marines, August 20, 1816, 167, all attachments in Andrew Kinsman to John Croker, November 11, 1816, PRO, ADM 1/3319, 155. John McNish Weiss, *The Merikens: Free Black American Settlers in Trinidad, 1815–16* (London: McNish & Weiss, 1995, revised 2002), provides a detailed account of the specific individual refugees who relocated to Trinidad.

55. Woodford to Bathurst, August 28, 1816, PRO, CO, 295/40, 104–10; Kinsman Address to Colonial Marines, August 20, 1816, 167; Kinsman to John Croker, no date, 161; and Kinsman to Croker, no date, 163, all attachments in Andrew Kinsman to John Croker, November 11, 1816, PRO, ADM 1/3319, 155; Laurence, "The Settlement of Free Negroes in Trinidad Before Emancipation," 33; Donald Wood, *Trinidad in Transition: The Years After Slavery* (London: Oxford University Press, 1968), 38.

56. Wood, *Trinidad in Transition,* 38; Laurence, "The Settlement of Free Negroes in Trinidad Before Emancipation," 27–32; Woodford to Bathurst, October 5, 1816, PRO, CO 295/40, 151–58; Woodford to Bathurst, September 26, 1820, PRO, CO 295/51, 3–4; Robert Mitchell to Woodford, April 15, 1823, PRO, CO 295/59.

57. Woodford to Bathurst, December 16, 1820, PRO, CO 295/51; Woodford to Bathurst, April 30, 1823, PRO, CO 295/59, 57; Whitfield, *From American Slaves to Nova Scotian Subjects,* 46; Weiss, *The Merikens,* 14–15.

58. George Arthur to Henry Goulburn, June 12, July 25, August 30, November 1, 1817, and February 25, 1818, all in PRO, CO 123/26; George Henderson, *An Account of the British Settlement of Honduras* (London: C. & R. Baldwin, 1809), 24–25; Craton, *Testing the Chains,* 265.

59. Cochrane to Croker, March 15, 1815, PRO, ADM 1/508, 495–96; Dispatch from Earl Bathurst, February 2, 1815; Statements from James Dunskee, May 15, 1815; and Statements from Andrew Seton, Isaac Baillou, and Charles Rae, May 16, 1815, all attached to William Wylly to Charles Cameron, May 5, 1815, CP, MS 2333, NLS; John Croker to Cochrane, November 28, 1814, PRO, ADM 2/1381, 211; James Burns to Henry Goulburn, February 3, 1815, PRO, CO 23/63; Charles Cameron to Bathurst, May 9, 1815, including attachments, PRO, CO 23/63; Deposition of Nathan Newbold, Richard Wood, and Joseph Stowe Shaw, July 5, 1816; and Deposition of Joseph Newbold, July 4, 1816, all in Cochrane to Bathurst, July 7, 1816, PRO, CO 37/74, 42–52.

60. Cochrane to Cockburn, March 9, 1815, CP, MS 2349, NLS; Cochrane to Bathurst, December 31, 1814, PRO, WO 1/141, 88–89; Cochrane to John Wilson Croker, February 26, 1815, CP, MS 2348, NLS; Cochrane to Croker, March 15, 1815, PRO, ADM 1/508, 495–96.

61. Jenkins, *Henry Goulburn,* 128–29.

62. Joseph C. Tregle, Jr., "Andrew Jackson and the Continuing Battle of New Orleans," *Journal of the Early Republic* 1 (Winter 1984): 373–74; Kimberly Hanger, *Bounded Lives, Bounded Places: Free Black Society in Colonial New Orleans, 1769–1803* (Durham, NC: Duke University Press, 1997), 166–68.

63. McConnell, *Negro Troops of Antebellum Louisiana,* 96–97, 108–109; Hanger, *Bounded Lives, Bounded Places,* 167–68; *Acts Passed at the First Session of the Second Legislature of the State of Louisiana, 1814–15,* 84–90, (a separate volume was published for each session of the legislature with all of the following sources being published in New Orleans); *Acts Passed at the First Session of the Fourth Legislature of the State of Louisiana, 1819,* 8–10; *Acts Passed at the First Session of the Sixth Legislature of the State of Louisiana, 1823,* 70.

64. *Acts Passed at the Extra Session of the Tenth Legislature of the State of Louisiana, 1831,* 9–10; *Acts Passed at the First Session of the Twelfth Legislature of the State of Louisiana, 1835,* 229; *Acts Passed at the Second Session of the Twelfth Legislature of the State of Louisiana, 1836,* 192; *Acts Passed at the Second Session of the First Legislature of the State of Louisiana, 1847,* 84, 99; *Acts Passed at the Third Legislature of the State of Louisiana, 1850,* 223; *Acts Passed at the First Session of the Seventeenth Legislature of the State of Louisiana, 1845,* 59; McConnell, *Negro Troops of Antebellum Louisiana,* 110.

65. Henry C. Harmon, *A Manual of Pension, Bounty, and Bounty Land Laws of the United States of America* (Washington, DC: W. H. & O. H. Morrison, 1867), 54–57, 60–63; McConnell, *Negro Troops of Antebellum Louisiana,* 110–11.

66. *Acts Passed at the Extra Session of the Tenth Legislature of the State of Louisiana, 1831,* 9–10; *Acts Passed at the First Session of the Twelfth Legislature of the State of Louisiana, 1835,* 229; *Acts Passed at the Second Session of the Twelfth Legislature of the State of Louisiana, 1836,* 192; *Acts Passed at the Second Session of the First Legislature of the State of Louisiana, 1847,* 84, 99; *Acts Passed at the Third Legislature of the State of Louisiana, 1850,* 223.

67. Lawrence Delbert Cress, *Citizens in Arms: The Army and Militia in American Society to the War of 1812* (Chapel Hill: University of North Carolina Press, 1982), 173–77; C. Edward Skeen, *Citizen Soldiers in the War of 1812* (Lexington: University Press of Kentucky, 1999), 179–82; *Acts Passed at the Second Session of the Eleventh Legislature of the State of Louisiana, 1833–34,* 143–67; McConnell, *Negro Troops of Antebellum Louisiana,* 104–105.

68. Donald E. Everett, "Emigres and Militiamen: Free Persons of Color in New Orleans, 1803–1815," *Journal of Negro History* 38 (October 1953): 398, 400–401; *The Daily Picayune* (New Orleans), January 9, 1851.

69. George A. Levesque, "Interpreting Early Black Ideology: A Reappraisal of Historical Consensus," *Journal of the Early Republic* 1 (Fall 1981): 274–75.

70. George Arthur to Henry Goulburn, November 1, 1817, PRO, CO 123/26.

EPILOGUE

1. Stuart L. Butler, "Slave Flight in the Northern Neck During the War of 1812," *Northern Neck of Virginia Historical Magazine* 57 (2007): 6842; Harold E. Berquist, Jr. "Henry Middleton and the Arbitrament of the Anglo-American Slave Controversy by Tsar Alexander I," *The South Carolina Historical Magazine* 82 (January 1981): 20–31.

2. *ASP:FR,* 5:808; "Estimates of the Value of Slaves, 1815," *The American Historical Review* 19 (July 1914): 812–38 provides the responses from the individual states regarding the value of slaves in 1815; William Renwick Riddell, "Slavery in the Maritime Provinces," *The Journal of Negro History* 5 (July 1920): 375. Commissioner Henry Clay suggested that the British had taken away 3,601 slaves, but the United States would accept payment for 1,650.

3. *ASP:FR*, 5:808; "Seizure of Slaves Admitted; Schedule and Value of Slaves; Grand Denial of Illegality; Claimant Persists," *Louisiana Historical Quarterly* 1 (1918): 330–32; Cochrane to Sherbrooke, March 25, 1815, PRO, CO 217/96; T. N. Jeffrey to Maj. Gen. G. S. Smith, August 5, 1816, PRO, CO 217/98; John McNish Weiss, *The Merikens: Free Black American Settlers in Trinidad, 1815–16* (London: McNish & Weiss, 1995, revised 2002), offers details regarding individual refugees who relocated to Trinidad; List of Slaves Carried Away by the British During Their Retreat After the Battle of New Orleans, January 1815, THNOC, MSS 199 Slave Evaluation Report; *Documents Furnished by the British Government Under the Third Article of the Convention of St. Petersburg, of 30 June–12 July 1822; and Bayly's List of Slaves and Public and Private Property Remaining on Tangier Island, on Board H.B.M. Ships of War, After the Ratification of the Treaty of Ghent* (Washington, DC: Gales and Seaton, 1827), 1–112.
4. Cassell, "Slaves of the Chesapeake Bay Area and the War of 1812," *Journal of Negro History* 57 (1972): 154–55; Historical Statistics of the United States (Washington, DC: U.S. Department of Commerce, 1970); Harvey Wish, "American Slave Insurrections Before 1861," *The Journal of Negro History* 22 (July 1937): 312.
5. Frey, *Water from the Rock*, 327–29; Ira Berlin, *Slaves Without Masters: The Free Negro in the Antebellum South* (New York: New Press, 1992), 92–99; Nash, *Forging Freedom*, 143–44; Charles M. Christian, *Black Saga: The African American Experience* (Boston: Houghton Mifflin Company, 1995), 82, 88.
6. White, "We Dwell in Safety," 468–69; Phillips, *Freedom's Port*, 108–12; Nash, *Forging Freedom*, 212–13; Swan, "John Teasman," 352.
7. *National Intelligencer*, April 30, 1813; Cassell, "Slaves of the Chesapeake Bay," 154–55.
8. Rothman, *Slave Country*, 220–23.
9. Robin Blackburn, *The Overthrow of Colonial Slavery, 1776–1848* (London: Verso, 1988), 288–90.

INDEX